LOAFING THROUGH
THE PACIFIC

Igorot woman in market-place, Baguio, Philippine Islands

LOAFING THROUGH THE PACIFIC

BY
SETH K. HUMPHREY

ILLUSTRATIONS FROM PHOTOGRAPHS

GARDEN CITY   NEW YORK
DOUBLEDAY, PAGE & COMPANY
1927

CONTENTS

CHAPTER   PAGE

I. THE HAWAIIAN ISLANDS 1

II. AMERICAN SAMOA 26

III. BRITISH SAMOA 38

IV. THE KINGDOM OF TONGA 74

V. THE FIJI ISLANDS 114

VI. NEW ZEALAND 148

VII. AUSTRALIA 169

VIII. THE PHILIPPINE ISLANDS 189

IX. HONG KONG 228

X. CANTON 241

XI. PEKING 256

XII. KOREA 273

XIII. JAPAN 284

LIST OF ILLUSTRATIONS

Igorot woman in market-place, Baguio . *Frontispiece*

FACING PAGE

Tongan house in Nukualofa 76
Tongans in the country, Tongatabu 76
The Tongan Queen's Palace, Nukualofa 77
Tongan house, showing mat-woven sides . . . 100
Tonga's great Trilithon, "Hoamonga" 100
Scene on the Rewa River, Viti Levu 101
Fijian house, Lautoka 101
Maori mixed-blood girl and Maori wood carving . 180
Igorot women road-workers, Baguio 181
Pines Hotel, Baguio 181
Igorot women, weaving 220
Caribou—Philippines 220
Chinese women pulling cart, Hong Kong . . . 221
Chinese woman carrier 221
My rickisha man, Peking 260
Pailou, and ornate palace building, "Coal Hill,"
Peking 260
Funeral bier, Peking 261
Peking wedding—bride's chair 261
Sawing lumber, Peking 276
Peking, street sprinkling 276
Koreans 277
Street scene, Seoul, Korea 277
Daibutsu, in Kobe, Japan 292
Steamer, Lake Biwa, and Boarding School girls . 293
Japanese young ladies at Temple of Ishiyama . . 293

INTRODUCTION

THIS is a tale mostly of browsing around among peoples. Fifteen months of it—with eighty-one days and nights out for time spent on board all sorts of vessels, getting to places.

The journey was done without a schedule, and no preconceived notions to be humoured were taken along under the guise of a fixed purpose. My aim, while wandering through the tropics, was not so much to "improve each shining hour" as to let the shining hours improve me.

Only a few times was I dragged around with parties, seeing things instead of humans. Once, in New Zealand —luckily, or I would not have visited the Glowworm Cave, one of the unique sights in the world. And again in Peking: there, with a stentorian guide, we had a three days' gorge of temples. After that I did without temples for some time.

Four months, first, in Hawaii. Civilized and correct is Hawaii compared with some other places along my way, yet in her sensuous charm there is at least a prosaic foretaste of the South Seas.

The South Sea Islands—the isles of the incorrigible romancer! Their monthly boat gives the wanderer a few hours in each port while it is shifting freight, or a sentence of thirty days. Most travellers stick by the ship—but why not take the thirty days?

In Samoa, for instance, with its upstanding Polynesians, who still "live native" in spite of their adopted religion. And in Tonga, the Friendly Islands—the only native kingdom left in the Pacific; a kingdom without a hotel, but with a twenty-three-year-old native queen, and a brave showing of independence under the quietly steering hand of Great Britain. A high spot in the journey, even if I did have a chronic difference with my Tongan chambermaid as to how many days a towel ought to serve without a recess at the laundry.

Another month in the Fiji Islands. None too long a time for observing the "topheavy human triangle" there, and the world's ex-champion cannibals.

All through the South Pacific, a kaleidoscopic variety of experiences. Lazy peoples? Delightfully so. They enjoy themselves instead of things. We might be learning from them how to be happy though civilized.

To New Zealand and Australia, then a whole winter in the Philippine Islands, where the natural humidity is aggravated by the vapourings of oratorical mixed-blood politicians. I found refuge from them among the little Igorots in the mountains.

In Hong Kong and Canton: for places at sea level, the chilliest in the tropics. China, overrun with bandits and generals, not too graciously endured four weeks of me without exacting ransom.

Across the old Hermit Kingdom, Korea; afterward to Japan for the final weeks, in cherry-blossom time. In this wide circuit of the Pacific are the oldest and the newest of existing civilizations. Where else is life in such fascinating variety?

S. K. H.

LOAFING THROUGH
THE PACIFIC

LOAFING THROUGH THE PACIFIC

CHAPTER I

THE HAWAIIAN ISLANDS

WANDERLUST has the name of being a sort of black sheep among the less disreputable of human emotions. Yet it is —take this from one who has it regularly —nothing worse than an urgent symptom of man's universal desire for change.

The cosmic itch is for something else, or the same thing elsewhere. The multitudes who live on a daily dead-level must have their plays, novels, and movies peppered full of episodes. Blood and crime in the newspapers feed the soul starvation of the timid. It is the factory girl who most avidly reads the society columns; and pampered women of wealth have been known to get a mitigating kick of joy from the prospect of a major operation. And so on, through dreams of earthly bliss to the final hope of heaven—all are first cousins of the wanderlust.

Travel most elegantly gratifies this pervasive longing. Novel experiences, fresh outlooks—and new friendships, such as one makes rather intimately among fellow travellers. Adventure in the old sense, as when much of the

1

earth was unexplored, is fast disappearing. They now hunt lions in Central Africa by motor car, and their friends in New York get the daily kill over the radio. Safety-razor blades and the American flashlight have penetrated to the back side of everywhere—and it is rather annoying to have one's perilous trip into a savage country fetch up against a Singer sewing machine. A South Sea island without a Ford isn't an island—it's an atoll, too narrow for a jitney to perch on.

Yet on a journey such as mine, a complete circling of the Pacific, there is the never-ending fascination of peoples living to-day ages apart—happily barbarous, half civilized, and a thousand years overdone. I coursed lightly through all the stages of man's existence since he took to wearing a clout.

The story of it begins with Hawaii; getting to Honolulu figures as a necessary prelude, to be done in sketchy haste, like the starting of a play with congested facts put across by the butler and maid as the curtain rises.

I made, for a seasoned traveller, a clumsy start. The quiet Monday and Tuesday in New Orleans, planned as a break in the overland trip, turned out to be the two big days of the Mardi Gras. I had no room engaged, and somewhere down in Georgia—after our train had collected eighteen Pullmans—I observed the fact aloud. At once, every gentleman in the smoking compartment warned me earnestly to make reservations for the Mardi Gras at least two months in advance.

Did you ever notice the peculiar, gloating quality of postmortem advice? Luckily, just then our distended train pulled itself in two, and I was spared further penetrating observations.

In New Orleans, with visions of spending two nights in somebody's guest room in the suburbs, I began my quest by falling into line at one of the largest hotels.

"Have you a room?" I asked the clerk, half an hour later.

With the aid of his finger the harassed man studied a big chart.

"Any room with hot and cold water will do," I remarked ingratiatingly, "if it is light and airy and quiet and not far from the bathroom." This was no time to be selfish.

The clerk raised his eyes long enough to bestow a withering look, then bent over his list.

"Room four fifty-six," he finally droned. "Single bed. Four dollars. There are six other beds in the room," he added casually.

I swallowed with effort. "Is—uh—is the ward full?"

"We call a room like that a dormitory," he replied haughtily. "Yes, it's full."

Dormitory. A bell boy led me away. But the other inmates proved to be harmless.

On glaringly posted advice of the police, every cautious man does the Mardi Gras with a strangle-hold on his watch and money; but a more good-natured, accommodating, and decently behaved crowd of revellers I never saw. Next to the sheer joy of seeing so many young people having a whale of a time, the great gaudy carnival and the playful spirit running all through it were the features of two as human days as do not often fall to the lot of the ordinary. I would like to tell about it—but unless my story gets on toward Honolulu I shall have to go back and change the heading of this chapter.

On to southern California, the most heard-of spot in the

country outside of Florida.   A week there—a hectic week, but I got away without eating a real-estate lunch or buying a lot.

Town lots?   In some places the landscape is as full of stakes as a three-ring circus.   Funny things happen when a perfectly good winter playground gets to thinking of itself as the big end of the United States.   They're awfully reckless here with their valuable real estate—just giving away fortunes, according to the prospectuses.

Los Angeles is a great city, most of which is under a high state of cultivation.   I had seen the place thirty years before, when it was beautiful and contented; since then, it has spread into the surrounding country like an epidemic.   Nothing but a lack of people keeps Los Angeles from being the largest city in America.

However, those who own it seem to love it, even if they are willing to sell it rather than disappoint you.   It is an astonishing city—I'll agree to that.   I might have a yearning for Los Angeles, sometime.   If I do, I'll go to Hoboken.

*   *   *

On a clear, hot second of March our steamer was leisurely gliding, with the exaggerated caution of large vessels on such occasions, into her berth at Honolulu.   Seven days out from Los Angeles we had sighted the jagged outlines of Oahu; then Diamond Head, a majestic old crater made over by the United States into a fortress.   From a mile offshore we saw Waikiki, Honolulu's famous bathing beach; and Honolulu itself, half buried in foliage, against a background of volcanic peaks.   Now, our vision was being narrowed to the usual homely trappings of a seaport.

A band made up of Hawaiians—the municipal band of

Honolulu—had begun its welcoming strains while we were well out in the harbour. As the great ship poked her nose alongside the dock, the music shifted to Hawaii's tuneful greeting, "Aloha." Its bursts of melody kept us more than good-natured while the carpeted landing stage trundled up to the ship's side and offered safe conduct to the soil of Hawaii.

The unique thing in this welcome was a pretty custom picked up from the Islands' gentle natives. Long, circular wreaths of flowers hung from the arms of the Americans assembled on the pier; these were Hawaiian *leis* (layees), with which to adorn the necks of expected friends as they step ashore. Once this was the Hawaiian's own token of welcome to adventurous white men who landed on his islands; now, he makes and sells the friendly gesture, like a common peddler, to their descendants, the owners of his country. Who says we're not the noblest of the world's races?

At the pier's entrance I signalled the Chinese driver of an open car. His banker's eye gave me the over-and-back.

"Dolla," said he, holding up an unclean digit.

"Flifty," said I, threatening to cut my forefinger in two.

"Al-lite." Off we went; first through China, then swung into Japan, almost ran down seven other nationalities, and finally pulled up in the United States at an excellent hotel.

For one who has only a few hours in a city, a whirl about it in a motor affords the quickest possible view of the greatest number of objects in a given time. The chauffeur will announce more or less intelligibly what this building is, and who's under that monument, and where the Mayor lives, and the best place to buy post cards. But the traveller who is blessed with sufficient time and has had any experience spares himself the tragedy of having the first bloom of interest knocked off everything in town by the dull hackings of a taxi-driver. He begins by seeing the life of the place, and does the "objects of interest" incidentally, if at all.

"Waikiki"—this was the sign on the trolley car that came along a few minutes after I was baggage-free and down on the street. A car to Waikiki Beach; none better for a start at seeing Honolulu.

An odd thing to say about a trolley system, perhaps, but the air of friendliness about Honolulu seems to extend to her street cars. They open from floor to roof on both sides, as befits the climate of eternal summer. Little cross-seats for two, with an aisle in the middle, discourage crowding. No rat-trap appliances open to receive you, and clap shut to reduce your chances of suing the company for damages. Instead, a placard up forward gives kindly but obscure advice about getting off at the right, in the interest of Safety First. You tender a dime for your fare, wondering whether you will get back a penny or two, or nothing; the conductor gives back a nickel. You ask three separate questions; the conductor answers them as if nobody ever did ask questions, and he was glad to have somebody notice him. It all fits in with the sturdy efforts of the bands, and "Aloha," and the pretty custom of the *leis*.

As many as forty people were on this car. It is one thing to read about Hawaii's population, and quite another to experience it.

First in numbers were the Japanese—a full one half

of the lot. Young girls with jet-black unbraided hair down their backs, gathered at the neck by a long silver clasp; a few men—like the girls, in European costume; and older women, whose full Oriental dress gave emphasis to the numerical predominance of Japanese.

Next in evidence were the brown skins and placid, open countenances of the Hawaiians, all neatly and inconspicuously dressed in the usual summer togs of Americans. We in the States are accustomed to associate brown skins with the mulatto; in the Hawaiian there is a striking absence of Negro characteristics. Not only in their straight hair, but in every feature, they deny all relationship to the Negro. Like the American Indians, they are a race of mysterious origin. Probably the surest thing we know about both races is that neither harks back even remotely to Africa.

In this conglomerate of mortals on the car were Chinese women in native baggy frocks and long pantalettes. A few swarthy, coarse-featured men had to be explained by the conductor—it was in answer to one of those three questions: "Portigees, from the Azores. Brought here like all the rest of 'em to work on the plantations—and same's all the rest of 'em, they don't."

Any Americans? Just six, out of the forty. And this happens to be about the proportion of Americans in Honolulu's eighty-odd thousand. Fifteen to the hundred.

If this car had had on board a Korean or two, a brace of Filipinos, and a kinky-haired black man from Porto Rico, it would have been fairly representative of Hawaii's population. Hawaii's population is one of the two Great American Puzzles in the Pacific. The other is the Philippines.

We rumbled along toward Waikiki, past many blocks

of one-story abodes whose architecture is charitably covered, or at least relieved, by tropical growth in great variety. This is mostly borrowed finery. Honolulu searches the world for everything from humans to vegetables that may help to make her rich and beautiful.

Waikiki Beach would have escaped me had it not been for the third and last question put to the conductor.

"It's behind all them buildings along the shore. Go through the hotel here, and you can't miss it."

Through the great Moana Hotel I went, and gazed upon the famous Waikiki Beach. That is, upon as much of it as spreads out before the Moana Hotel and a few hundred feet off to the left. To see any more of it, one must plant himself successively in front of every hotel, cottage, club, boathouse and such along the shore. Each has built into the sandy frontage, or back from it, or walled it, or ignored it, as fancy pleased, until there is nothing resembling the consecutive stretch of seashore usually called a beach.

But Waikiki has surf riding, the one exclusive feature which gives it fame all over the world. The huge swells which roll majestically shoreward without breaking are due to the odd contour of the bottom. A coral reef several hundred yards out rises to within a few feet of the surface; and from this reef to shore the depth is practically uniform—about waist high.

So when a swell of the right proportions happens along, it piles up above the reef like a smooth wall three or four feet high; and because the water from there in is neither shallow enough to topple it over nor deep enough to let it flatten down, it rolls along as a wall until it peters out near shore.

This is the surf rider's motive power. Those who have the luck to start their surf boards at the right instant, and the skill to balance themselves on their little craft at the crest of the roller, experience a minute or two of ecstatic joy, a thrill exquisite, unique, among the pleasure stunts of man.

The adjectives are not my own. They are gathered from those who have managed to turn the trick of it. Others, thrown headlong to the bottom at the critical moment, with the surf board driving unpleasantly into the small of the back, express themselves differently.

* * *

Fixing upon a place to live in Honolulu should be done only after consulting the trade wind. You want this to blow directly into your windows. Almost continuously the northeast trade comes bowling over the mountain ridges back inland; spilling against them from heavy black clouds part of its gathered moisture before it reaches the city, on the south shore of the island. At times these spillings overreach, and sprinkle the city itself with sudden curiously driving, spraylike showers, while the sun shines out of the cloudless southerly skies.

This is Honolulu's famous "liquid sunshine"; not so much of it in summer, but in March and April often many times a day these gusts of moisture sweep down into the city. Liquid sunshine—an odd name for rain? But the sun obligingly picks the drops off you almost as they fall, and unless the dash is a heavy one—in which case you stop for a minute in a doorway, or under a friendly *lanai* (veranda)—you go along and pay no attention to it at all. Even the weather treats you kindly in Honolulu.

I set out to find quarters invitingly open to the tropical life saver, the trade wind. Room hunting is a prosaic business in one's home town, but in a place as full of novelty as Honolulu it is a revealing pastime.

In Honolulu, quite as in any large American town, the stately mansions of yesterday are as likely as not the glorified boarding houses of to-day. If the relic happens to be a large one with pretentious grounds, it may become, under the magic touch of a landlady, a residential hotel.

The type is familiar: most of the first floor is thriftily annexed to the dining room, while ingenious partitionings upstairs make two bedrooms show where only one appeared before. But these Honolulu landladies conjure up rooms in a manner impossible outside the tropics. In several places I was shown about among low, shed-like structures tucked away here and there in the back yard: little buildings such as one associates with coal, or wood, or storage of some sort. These were living rooms, incredible as it may seem to people not actually reduced to their last dollar; but one is supposed to become reconciled to the proximity of the chicken house through the honour of eating his meals in the music room of a departed First Family.

Housing in this town seems to be a lightly taken, breezy affair, anyhow. With no heating plant, chimneys, stairs, or warmth of structure to be considered, and plastering almost unknown, home building is down to its simplest terms. Broad matched boards nailed upright over the scantiest of frameworks, and a composition roof laid on nearly flat, constitute the shell of Honolulu's bungalows. Board partitions cut the house up into rooms.

So a large majority of Honoluluans live back of one-inch

boards. Boards serve well enough to foil the roving eye, but every sound above a whisper carries all over the place. If the bungalow is located in the middle of a good-sized lot, the household has only its own noises to contend with; but when set in double rows along narrow courts leading off the streets, one sickly baby or an ailing phonograph can be the despair of the neighbourhood.

Yet bird-house existence in a climate always warm but rarely hot has decided points of merit. It contributes to the general air of light living which pervades the town. Things are not so infernally consequential in Honolulu.

Cheerfully dodging liquid sunshine through the flower-laden streets—even the trees bloom generously in Honolulu—I kept up my search for a cool apartment. The Corfu—we will call it that—seemed a good prospect. It was a mile out, on the Waikiki car line.

Those very obliging conductors—this one would be glad to show me where to get off. No trouble at all. And when I figured that we must have gone way beyond the place, I spoke to him.

He snapped his fingers as a mark of chagrin. But he handed me a transfer; take the car there at the crossing— it was going back directly past the Corfu's door. The conductor would let me off at the right spot—just mention the Corfu. "Awful sorry!"

I confided myself to conductor number two. The thought of helping me seemed actually to give him pleasure. In the course of time, familiar landmarks of the town began to pass. We were back in the city. I spoke to conductor number two.

He snapped his fingers in self-reproach. But here was a transfer, back on the Waikiki line. "Just ask the con-

ductor to let you off at Punahou, then walk through a
block. Too bad!"

"Punahou." Something tangible to go on. Once
more I was outward-bound on the Waikiki line, this time
watching the street signs. This riding back and forth
couldn't go on indefinitely, even on free passes. I let
myself off at the right corner without the aid of conductor
number three.

Yet it was done so pleasantly that it seemed like a joke.
The psychic complacency of the town was already affect-
ing me. In Boston or New York, I would have thought
up a stinging letter to the president of the road.

At last, quarters in a stately mansion, up one flight clear
of the shrubbery, and the precious trade wind sweeping
down a green valley after its cleansing spill over the
mountain-tops; beautiful wide *lanais*, and grounds loaded
with the imported fancies of a departed millionaire. Here
the proposed week or two lengthened into four months.

* * *

The visitor to this island, Oahu, usually does the motor
trip "around the island" rather early among the things
done. His friends advise it; and some tourist agent is
sure to have spotted him as a stranger in the land.

Up the Nuuanu Valley the motor glides, over a good
road, past many of Honolulu's older estates, and between
two picturesque ranges of jagged lava peaks. On either
side, near at hand, their sawlike edges may be cutting into
the deep blue of the sky, but always farther up toward the
main range they lose their sharp outline in the black rain-
clouds piled up against them by the northeast trades.
One rarely gets through the Pali—the break in the moun-

tains—to the lowlands beyond without meeting the almost perpetual spill in the form of drifting showers.

The Pali cuts through the big lava wall only a little more than halfway down to sea level; it is a sheer drop of a thousand feet to the strip of country between the mountains and sea. From this high outlook, one gazes off at a picture of unexampled colouring. Fields of pineapples silver-green on a deep brown soil; sugar cane in great patches, seeming in the distance like rank-grown grass; here and there over the landscape hillocks of lava rock break up through the subdued acres and revel in the many colours of their original verdure; dominating all is the blue Pacific, urged on by the incessant trades through three thousand unobstructed miles and dashing in immense crested rollers against the coral reefs far out from shore.

There are scenes grander, and differently inspiring; but nature must have been in a rare fantastic mood when she struck off the Pali.

The wind at the Pali! Through that little break in the mountain range it whistles at the rate of sixty miles an hour; yet everybody gets out to see the view.

From a group to windward of us a cap came whizzing by; then—merciful heavens!—a front piece of feminine hair sped past like a seven-tailed comet.

"A false alarm!" shouted one of our party, and dashed gallantly after it. Back he came, waving aloft both forelock and cap.

"Who belongs to these?" he roared against the hurricane. He found an owner for the cap—but not for the sad-looking curls. At the sound of our unrefined joy, a stately dame hastened into her car; a moment later her Hawaiian chauffeur approached us, grinned, winked, uttered, "Me

fix, aw-right," and hurried back with the disordered relic.
He deserved a raise in pay for saving the lady's dignity.

I had hoped to find off in the island some sign of native
life less manhandled than that in Honolulu. Natives
are plentiful, but the grass house is no more. They live
in nondescript board huts, for the most part, and leave
the work of the island to the imported races. In the rice
fields, deftly transplanting the green shoots one at a time,
were Chinese. The great sugar mill was manned mostly
by Japanese, superintended by white men. Filipinos
were almost the only workers in the cane and pineapple
fields. A motley crew, made up of all the nationalities
in Hawaii—including a few natives—were road building,
with somewhat more than the usual lassitude of construction gangs.

Sugar and pineapples have made the island of Oahu
one of the most valuable bits of land in all of Uncle Sam's
domain. The native Hawaiian in the country districts
gives no sign of resentment over the prosperity which
others have got from his land, but he will not work for
the white man if he can avoid it.

Why should he? Never in his history has he worked
at anything where results were beyond his understanding.
He has his little plot of taro, papaya, and the like; on his
ground and at fishing he will work as hard as anyone, because he knows what he is doing and he is doing it for himself. Clothes? In the rush seasons of the different crops
he may condescend to earn good wages for a few days in
the year—and the few dollars settle the problem of his
clothes. Why should he work for the white man while
his old natural way of living is still open to him?

So he sits by and watches the Chinese and the Japanese

and the Filipinos and Koreans work the great machinery of the white man's civilization, and if he wonders what it is all about, he keeps his wondering to himself. Of the whole lot he is the only one who lives placidly, undriven, contented. Every detail of his life is directly under his own hand. He knows nothing of indirect living through wages, and a wisdom that came to the race before education was invented tells him to pass it by.

* * *

One must get back into Honolulu to see the natives doing white man's work. Most of the police officers and firemen are Hawaiians, as well as a great many of the street-car men, chauffeurs, and general utility men.

Naturally fond of oratory, the Hawaiians take to politics like ducks to water; the intrigues of a dozen grades of chieftainship have been supplanted by as many shades of political deviltry. A session of the legislature may be as entertaining as a comic opera. The Hawaiian vote of Oahu has to be reckoned with; and it is—judiciously. So the whites manage to control the Islands' politics. It's a great sport, this matter of Hawaiian politics.

Hawaiians who take to the white man's ways, either politically or otherwise, almost invariably show an admixture of white blood, just as Negroes do in the States who attain to any success, in white pursuits. After generations of contact with unrestrained white men, the strictly pure-blooded Hawaiian, without at least some distant infusion of white, is somewhat of a rarity. The Polynesian can no more be studied in the Hawaiian Islands.

The Hawaiians of Honolulu, even if as a race they are shading off into white, maintain their own language with a commendable pride. The young children of to-day are taught to speak it fluently. They also have their own various social organizations. Except for a very few of princely blood, and a few more with special aspirations, neither the full-blooded nor mixed Hawaiians mingle socially to any extent with white people. The separation seems to be mutually agreeable. The sentiment for racial purity, instinctive with every race on earth, is basically as unyielding in Hawaii as in any other land, in spite of an almost disastrous political equality.

*   *   *

Everyone in Honolulu for a Sunday should attend a Hawaiian church service. Their principal church is a big stone edifice, in its appointments pretty much like any other Protestant church; the service differs in having usually no set sermon and a very considerable singing. In between songs, speeches are in order.

Everything is in the Hawaiian language; and if some distinguished white visitor is asked to address the meeting, his talk is always interpreted into Hawaiian—although it is doubtful whether there is a single person in the audience who has not understood every word of the English version. It is the Hawaiian way of holding to the past in the midst of an imposed civilization.

There is an indefinable note of pathos in the services; it comes out more clearly in the singing. Even the songs which are set to familiar gospel hymns are sung with a pronounced Hawaiian cadence—a strain of wistfulness that is subtly emphasized in the final note of each line by a curious tapering-off in volume, as if the singers had suddenly thought of something.

These gentle, unassertive Hawaiians, gathered by themselves, cling to their own tongue and colour its songs with reminiscence of other days. One gets the impression that those other days must have been in many ways happier for them. They are poor, while some of the descendants of the very missionaries who brought them to this religion are among the richest people in Hawaii —not through any wrong-dealing, but because the missionaries understood future values and accumulated land, while the natives understood nothing and let their country go for trifles. Yet, poor as they are, there is in their attitude no note of bitterness: simply a puzzled wistfulness, as if they do not understand just what has happened to them. And, upon my soul, I don't believe they do.

*   *   *

Toward the end of my stay, I joined an excursion on the fine steamer *Haleakala* around the island of Molokai, the home of the lepers. Merely to go out, encircle it, and return fills a day. We were not to land at the leper settlement, but a stop was to be made offshore for a view of it.

After a two-hour run—uncomfortable enough for those who never can make out what inter-island seas are up to with their racing tides and cross currents—we got under the southwest lee of Molokai. The leper settlement over on the windward side makes the whole island unpopular as a place of residence. With good soil and an excellent climate, it is treeless, dreary, and almost uninhabited. A charitable attempt is now being made to settle some of the dispossessed Hawaiians of the sugar country on these lands. It is an inexpensive return on the part of the

Honolulu millionaires to the poor devils whose fathers made their fathers rich, but it is better than nothing.

On the leper colony side of Molokai the shore line rises in a series of great crags and cliffs to a height of nearly five thousand feet. We steamed along the northeast shore close up under immense vertical walls, with the trade wind and a heavy sea driving against us. The scene is in vivid contrast to the drab placidity of Molokai's sheltered side; it was hard to believe that we were looking at the same island.

Halfway down this windward shore, an almost level promontory of several hundred acres juts out from the perpendicular wall. Beyond, the sea again lashes itself against the sheer cliffs as far as the eye can see. On this patch of land is the leper settlement.

With its back up against the unbroken wall, the limitless sea in front, and not a landing for a boat for an impossible distance on either side, no more isolated spot could have been made to order. The three hundred lepers are safely on that promontory until death chooses to relieve them.

At a short distance offshore we dropped anchor and lowered a boat that was to take in a few supplies and one or two attendants who had been away on leave. Meantime, as many of the colony as were able to come out had seated themselves on the rocks along the shore and began to sing. With the wind against them and the sea dashing noisily between us, their voices could hardly carry to the steamer; but the swelling cadences which now and then got through to us were those of Hawaii's beautiful fong of welcome, "Aloha."

Sitting there inertly on the vessel seemed a poor sort

of response to this greeting, so we took up a collection for their "luxury fund"—a fund for supplying them with little things that are not on their simple fare. If ever there was a psychological moment for taking up a collection, this was one.

The new cure for leprosy offers bright promise in the fight against this most damnably slow and merciless disease. The sight of Molokai's band of exiles makes one fervently hope that the promise may come true.

* * *

Nobody but those with the stingiest of itineraries would miss a trip to the island of Hawaii for a look down into the seething acres of hot lava in Halemaumau, the always active crater of Kilauea. In daytime the sight is impressive beyond description; but to peer over the crater's edge on a pitch-dark night at the huge, writhing, coiling snakes of red gives a picture of what hell is supposed to be like. It almost induces the timid to make New Year resolutions on the spot.

Then to the neighbouring island, Maui, and up by motor and horseback—a trip only for the rugged—to Haleakala, the largest extinct crater in the world. If one cannot qualify for an altitude of eleven thousand feet and some rough work on horseback and afoot, it is better to see Haleakala in an illustrated lecture.

Kauai, "the Garden Island," is not so much visited as it would be if its beauties were better known. Scenically, Kauai is the gem of the Hawaiian Islands. A motor ride along the northeast coast to Hanalei Bay delights the eye; Waimea Cañon, on the opposite side of the island, is a miniature Grand Cañon of the Colorado, rich in colouring and majestic in its proportions; and Olokele Cañon, a few miles from Waimea—I shall never forget Olokele, for other reasons than its incomparable scenery. A tortuous, narrow road notched out of the mountainside leads through a panorama of dizzy, green-covered heights and depths, while misty rain drifts lazily off the peaks and a new rainbow forms at every shift of the moisture.

If you "do" Olokele—they pronounce it "Ole Kelly," and that combination in itself spells trouble—go in a small car; a Ford, or any car that can take the incredibly short curves without its offside front wheel flirting over the edge at the tree-tops a thousand feet below.

Never have I been more apprehensively interested in a human being than in that native son of Kauai who drove our car. His nonchalant way of running us to the brink of eternity compelled both admiration and alarm. When finally remonstrated with, he laid the blame on the size of the car, and casually informed us that it had always been considered unsafe to run a seven-seater into Olokele. It seemed nothing to him that he was responsible for the seven-seater.

Since there was absolutely no chance to turn around in the entire two miles of the road, his information was worse than useless. Then it occurred to me that not a sign of a turnout had we seen.

"Young man," I asked, "suppose we should meet another car?"

"Gate was shut. I open gate."

The gate had been shut, I remembered, at the place where we entered this midair trail. But this sign of a free road was not convincing.

"And what if someone should come in while we are on our way out?" I asked.

"I lef' gate open. Nobody mus' come in, gate lef' open," he explained confidently.

"But suppose a driver happens along who doesn't understand the open-gate rule and comes in. How could we pass?"

The boy shook his head. "No pass. Him come in gate lef' open, him back up."

The idea of backing up for a mile or two on Olokele trail was too taxing to pursue. I resigned myself to watching the scenery, the boy, and the offside front wheel.

* * *

For visitors to the Hawaiian Islands, the fascinating human interest is in the native population. Those who live here, and have the destinies of the Islands to look after, find in the medley of imported races a human interest decidedly more formidable than fascinating.

The racial situation "stumps" the oldest inhabitant. Only Congressmen who come here and stop over one boat know what should be done about it.

The same passion for quick expansion which loaded us in America with undesirable stocks has brought this predicament upon the Hawaiian Islands. The agricultural interests wanted cheap labour, regardless of its fitness for citizenship in an intelligent democracy. It is the old story of exploiting the present with no vision of the future.

They say it was a question of labour. As a matter of the full truth, it was, and still is, a question of *cheap* labour. There's a difference. They are now looking for something cheaper than the little brown men off the by-ways of Manila and Cebu.

The early planters soon discovered that the native would not work in the fields. He had his own better way of making a living. White labourers, even if they could be induced to work in the heat, would want a white man's living wage; and since sugar cane and other tropical products were nowhere else raised on the basis of a white man's living wage, the planters of Hawaii had to get labour at a level with that of their competitors.

So cheap labour was imported; at first, mostly from Japan.

When children in numbers began to come to these labourers, the good people of Hawaii remarked, "Ah, these are our future citizens. We must educate them up to their responsibilities."

So they educated them. Gave them a smattering of knowledge and a veneer of our own ideals spread over an age-old background of orientalism. Educated them away from any desire to work at manual labour, out of the fields and into—what?

Into a state of general incompetency: into the city, as servants, lawn-tenders; into minor clerkships, from which, at half the wages, they displaced white men and women; into every occupation where they could do their bit toward bringing the life of the Islands down to yellow standards.

But the planters must have cheap labour. One after another, the backward peoples of the earth were drawn upon: Chinese, Portuguese from the Azores, Porto Ricans, Koreans—each in turn educated out of the fields and into the pool rooms, the streets, and the odd jobs of Honolulu.

Now it is the Filipinos who are doing most of the plantation work, while their children, like those before them, are being educated out of the fields and into town.

Honolulu is a beautiful city to live in. It will continue to be a beautiful city to live in so long as American standards can be maintained for the Americans who live there. But the fact now staring Hawaii in the face is that within ten years, or fifteen at most, the Japanese will be in a decided majority over the whole collection of races in the Islands—whites included.

This is coming mostly from the excessive fecundity of the Japanese. Of course, their children are taught in the schools all the principles of good citizenship—in the forenoon. In the afternoon they go to their own Japanese schools and are taught in the Japanese language—what?

Nobody seems to know, but it is not difficult to guess. We regarded their parents, rightly enough, as unfit for political equality; is it likely that they are surrendering their children to our ideals? In their resentment, it is far more likely that they are doing everything to turn their children's present opportunity to the benefit of Japan. These children are to be the future dominant citizens of Hawaii unless something is done about it.

Talk is plentiful, but, just before leaving, I got the first and only sensible clue to a solution. It was from a quiet man of affairs, long in the Islands, who admitted at the start that he had not the slightest idea what would be done; but——

"Are we not overlooking something?" he asked. "The United States Government is spending millions in fortifying this island of Oahu. As a naval base, Pearl Harbour, one of the best landlocked harbours in the world, is the

key to all operations in the Pacific. Look about you,"
he continued. "Already, Oahu bristles with forts way
beyond any need for the defense of Honolulu. Millions
more will be poured in until this island is what our government intends it shall become—an impregnable fortress."

He stopped for a moment, and regarded me quizzically.

"Is the United States Government apt to let Hawaiian
politics drift over to any foreign influence? In spite of
local politics, will Honolulu ever be dominated for more
than a day by any but Americans, and *bona fide* Americans
at that?"

I had to admit the reasonableness of his view.

"As sure as sunrise," he remarked quietly, "the question will eventually be settled in Washington. Perhaps
in some unusual way—but why ask how? It will be
settled our way."

*   *   *

It is midsummer—the first of July. For a month the
sun at noon has been directly overhead, or a bit to the
north of the zenith. One's shadow is a dark spot encircl-
ing the feet.

But with the warming of the sun the northeast trade
blows more faithfully than ever, night and day, tempering
the heat of midday and cooling the air delightfully soon
after the sun goes down. In the shade it is never above
ninety, and rarely that. Except for those who cannot
keep in the shade during the few hours around noon,
Honolulu's climate is as friendly in June as it is in March.

My stay in Hawaii has come to an end. In the South
Sea Islands, twenty-five hundred miles south, it is mid-
winter—hot, of course, but south of the Equator, July,
August, and September make up the dry season, and the

nights are as likely as not to be slightly cooler than during the other months of the year.

July in the Samoan Islands, August among the Tongans —the only independent native kingdom left in the Pacific—and September with the Fijians; this is my itinerary for the three months.

Now, off to Samoa.

CHAPTER II

IN PAGO-PAGO, American Samoa, is laid the scene of the play, "Rain"—the play that had a long run in New York City.

The play overworks the precipitation. The rain lets up at times, and once in a while the sun comes out; but the heavens surely are kept busy watering Pago's tremendous verdure. I remarked this to a scraggly chap who looked as if he needed hanging out to dry.

"Huh!" he snorted, "didn't ye see the sun this mornin'? What more d'ye want? *And*," he added convincingly, "in the dry season there are days when it doesn't rain at all."

The thought was compelling. "How many clear days make a drought?" I inquired anxiously; but the fellow moved on.

Good-bye to Hawaii had been said with *leis* a week before in Honolulu. Then seven days of steaming almost due south, on a sea stirred only by the welcome trades, brought us to Pago-Pago—or Pango-Pango, as it is always pronounced and often spelled. Distance fairly looms out of these calm waters. A week between Los Angeles and Honolulu is something taken for granted—Hawaii is looked upon as a long way out in the Pacific; but a week of moderately fast sailing between islands begins to impress one with the immensity of the Pacific.

We celebrated the glorious Fourth of July on board with decorations, more than the usual deck games, and a big dinner—the last of my big dinners for several months. On a fine afternoon two days later, the crossing of the Line brought out ancient remarks about "feeling the bump," and the like. The usual expectation of heat on the Equator was not realized; we slipped from latitude north to latitude south with the thermometer at 81 and a cool breeze blowing across the decks.

Altogether, a pleasant journey in an uncrowded boat —Sydney bound, so the days were enlivened by mirthful, kindly Australians. Their perfectly good English delivered in a wretched modification of London cockney was always a puzzle to the few Americans aboard.

By the time we were off American Samoa the sun was crossing the heavens well to the north of us, and its shadows crept around against the clock. The Southern Cross, in Honolulu down on the horizon even at its best, showed high over the ship's bow.

Unfamiliar heavens, shadows going wrong, as well as strange lands—is it this combination that makes ecstatic liars of so many writers who go to the South Sea Islands?

Pango-Pango is one of the best sheltered harbours in the Pacific, and admitted to be the most beautiful. A channel with a convenient crook in it leads into what was once a huge oval crater; now, deep in the water; its walls rise hundreds of feet on all sides except at the break toward the sea.

Because it is a good harbour, I suppose, the United States has occupied it since 1875 as a naval base. Of what earthly use it is to us, no one outside of a uniform is able to conjecture. Merchantmen are not permitted to coal here unless actually in distress, and then only to the extent of enough fuel to carry them to the nearest coaling port; and the island (Tutuila) hasn't enough trade to pay for the brass about the place in the shape of buttons and the like. Probably the soundest excuse for our fifty-odd years of costly vigil is the one universal among the Great and Little Powers now capping almost every island in the Pacific: "To keep the other fellows from getting it."

But the taxpaying American, entering this harbour on a sunshiny morning, forgets all this puzzlement and hangs the expense; it is one of the most charming bits of landscape in his whole United States. The almost sheer walls of towering volcanic rock, grand in themselves, are made beautiful by their heavy covering of tropical verdure—rich, dark, and lapping over the jagged tops like enormous green draperies hung between the rival blues of sky and water. Clusters of the lighter coconut palm, waving their graceful branches over the riotous carpeting, touch up the picture exquisitely; and the primitive Samoan village, tucked in among the trees along the upper end of the harbour, gives a finishing enchantment to the prospect.

* * *

The trim landing, the government warehouses, the great wireless towers, the snug houses for the officers and commodious barracks for the men—these merely stared us in the face as we pulled up to the dock. At the head of our gangway a placard informed us of the time of sailing— 1 P.M. Four hours ashore for the through passengers, which meant nearly everybody; not more than a half dozen of us were to stop over.

Through the white man's town the crowd of sightseers

flowed toward the native village, a mile distant along the narrow highway skirting the cliffs. A sticky walk; the climate, unlike Honolulu's, is really tropical. We are in latitude 14 instead of 22.

It is a climate that favours extreme idleness and a lack of clothes. Perhaps this accounts in a way for the primitiveness of Samoan life.

The Hawaiian, in a desultory way, has given himself over to civilization; the Samoan lets civilization spread itself all about him, and calmly ignores it. All over the place he stalks—big, brown, powerful, erect—decked only in the native single-piece waistcloth, the *lava-lava*. And so do his women dress at home, when none but their own people are about. As our band of inquisitive "foreigners" came nosing along, waists were pulled on, or any stray piece of cloth thrown over bare shoulders—a sop to the funny notions of the white man.

After a long sojourn among the Americanized Hawaiians, the naturalness of these similar people was rather startling. They simply don't take to the white man's ways. The grass house (*hale*) had vanished from the Hawaiian Islands a generation ago. Here it is the universal native habitation, its name changed only by a single letter to *fale*. Built, too, as pictured of old—a great oval, bulging roof of grass and palm branches, supported on stout posts over a floor made of smooth pebbles. The eaves of the roof clear the floor by about five feet, so that one has to stoop to enter.

The *fale* is built open on all sides; but mats about four feet broad, hung up under the eaves all round, can quickly be dropped to afford shelter against rain, wind, or sun coming from any direction. The native *fale* appeals for its airiness and general sufficiency as a shelter in the tropics.

In their *fales* whole families were sitting on mats as we passed by—or reclining on mats with other mats rolled up for pillows, and still more mats about, evidently to cover themselves with at night. Furniture consists chiefly of mats; civilization is represented by a kerosene lamp. Chairs are superfluous—all hands squat with their feet snugly pulled up into their laps.

*   *   *

Most of us had an objective; a notice on the pier had informed us that in a big chief's *fale*, at ten o'clock, the great native dance, the *siva-siva*, would be given by the best dancers in the island.

The *siva-siva!* There was an air of delightful apprehension about our jolly shipload; but not many knew that startling exhibitions given by native women are special affairs got up for those who want to see them. Ceremonial dances among the unspoiled Polynesians are mostly done by men, as this one was to be. Interestingly disappointing, perhaps, for some of the crowd, but nearer to a Samoan dance than tourists ordinarily see.

On we walked through the collection of *fales* scattered at random under the coconut trees, to the chief's great house in the centre of the village.

"Come in, ladee! Come in, gelleman!" No lack of cordiality about these Samoans. Dignified courtliness in a *lava-lava*, after the first ten seconds of getting used to it, is quite as effective as from the depths of a high collar and dress suit. In we soon were, on a mat-covered floor and under a great roof—a network of bows and crossbows artistically bent and made fast at a thousand over-lappings with sinnet, a strong cord twisted from the husk of the coconut. Not a nail is used in the whole structure.

"Sit down, ladee—sit down, gelleman!" came the cheerful but chairless invitation. Over nearly one half of the floor the waiting dancers sat cross-legged; opposite them the guests squatted on the mats in more or less unhappy imitation. After the little matter of a dollar apiece had been attended to, the dance began.

Thirty-five or forty stalwart men—it seems superfluous to say "stalwart" of these Samoan men, because no other kind is in evidence about the place—rose from the mats at their end of the *fale* and for an hour and a half, with few rests, put their shining bodies and superb limbs through series after series of complicated, rhythmic motions.

No two of the dances were at all alike, and the number of different figures and facings about, swingings of arms and legs and posturings of body, was no less than incredible. If in all their elaborations of movement a single man of them failed to do exactly the figure that every other man was doing, I did not catch him at it. To memorize such a multitude of separate acts and never forget their sequence seemed to me so impossible that I looked for some sort of coaching from the side-lines. None was apparent. But possibly the key to the performance was in the harmonious chant which flowed on incessantly and kept perfect time with their evolutions.

These songs, rolling musically from some forty swaying, dancing men, added immensely to the effect. More than that, they revealed rather amusingly one result of the long missionary endeavour among the Samoans. In the barbaric, unmetered strain of some wild native song would suddenly appear the unmistakable relics of a gentle Moody and Sankey hymn—and over the faces of Christian ladies in the audience would creep involuntary smiles at this reminder from the old home town.

Some of us men, too, smiled behind the backs of the gentle ladies at their quick adaptation to situations which anywhere else would have made them gasp; huge brown men dressed only in loincloths, with Chesterfieldian politeness offering them water in coconut shells, or solicitously easing their positions with extra mats. Be it said to the credit of the ladies that they accepted the manly attentions with a courtesy that matched the sure kindliness of these Samoans.

*   *   *

It was a charming first glimpse of one of Uncle Sam's most novel possessions. What an ideal place, this gem of ours set in the tropics, for weary, nervous Americans to rest in the serenity of nature at its loveliest, and take lessons in placid living from the Samoans! Comfortable steamers run through from San Francisco by way of Honolulu every month, and the return boat passes three weeks later. Pango forms a natural link, too, in a delightful stopping-over route through the Samoas, the Tongas, and the Fijis; it averages cooler than most other ports in its latitude, and is outside the hurricane belt. An ideal place for a winter resort.

Yet Americans do not come here—or, if they do, they get over to British Samoa, eighty miles away, by the little boat which connects with the steamer.

Why to British Samoa, when Pango-Pango is far more beautiful, cooler, and supposed to be good American territory?

For the reason, quite obvious to anyone who attempts to stop over, that civilians are not wanted by the naval authorities. Probably it is a question of discipline among the men. Several hundred marines at one end of the harbour and a village of careless Samoans at the other must make a situation fit to keep somebody awake nights.

Anyhow, the regulations are such as to encourage civilians to stay away from Pango-Pango. What an unusual experience for an American who is still in America! On landing, he surrenders his passport and fills in a written quiz as if he were entering a foreign country, and when ready to leave, he must get his passport viséd and pay for the service, although he has not been off American soil.

But the big surprise comes when he is asked to deposit one hundred dollars in cash, to guarantee his good behaviour and the price of a ticket to the nearest port. I was not required to do this because I was to leave next day on the little sailboat bound for Apia, British Samoa; otherwise, my two thousand dollars in convertible paper, and a face not so bad, as faces go, except for the usual wear and tear, would not have saved me from putting up the deposit like any potential beachcomber. As it was, I had two unharassed days of browsing around among the Pango-Pango Samoans; and the young navy officers about the place were courtesy itself in little matters, which helped to make my stay agreeable.

But I did feel sorry for an old American school teacher who had to stick it out in Pango until the return boat three weeks later. He could not afford to go over to Apia for the short stay. This man had been teaching for forty-odd years, most of the time in government schools on Indian reservations, in the Philippines, and later in Hawaii. Now he wanted to have three weeks of rest in this beauty spot of his country before going back to his work among the Hawaiians.

The old man had hardly got away from the initial quiz before he was sent for by the naval authorities and ordered to put up the one hundred dollars. He returned much depressed.

"I didn't mind depositing the money," he explained to me wearily. "No doubt it is as safe there as in my pocket. But to *have* to!"

"Didn't your long service with the government count for anything?" I asked.

He shook his grizzled head. "Nothing counts, down there. I had to come across just like any other suspect." He was beyond the age when one indulges in futile resentment; his tired gaze went out across the waters of the harbour before he spoke again:

"I suppose it's all right—but—as an American citizen— I feel humiliated," he said quietly.

An espionage that goes against the Yankee grain, a naval governor whose rule is absolute, unfettered. Well, it's a tight little kingdom, this Pango-Pango on American soil. Somehow the air of it now and then made me shiver in the heat.

*   *   *

In knocking about that first afternoon, I fell in with an old inter-island sea captain, whose stocky-built, weather-worn sailing vessel rode at anchor halfway out across the harbour. He gave me my first tales at first hand about

the South Seas—tales not quite so romantic as those
doctored up for the story books; just a bit uglier and more
sordid. Tales of Bully Hayes, the notorious South Sea
robber of a generation ago; how he would cruise off to
some Tongan or Fijian island, bargain for a trader's
copra, get it all snugly aboard, then give the trader his
choice between signing a receipt in full or being thrown
overboard to the sharks. Mixed in with the lot was one
story which showed Bully's sense of humour:

On a fine afternoon Bully Hayes paddled out in a little
boat to meet a British cruiser, which was approaching
on one side of an island while his own vessel lay hidden
at anchor on the other.

"Bully Hayes?" said Bully, when the war vessel's captain had informed him of the particular pirate he was
looking for. "Why, only this morning that damned
rascal"—here Bully began to shed tears—"that dirty
robber loaded all my copra into his vessel and sailed
away with it."

"Which way?" the captain shouted. Bully's quiver-
ing hand pointed nor'-nor'east.

Off sped the cruiser, back went Bully—and soon he was
sailing cheerily sou'-sou'west.

Thus my sea captain beguiled away half the afternoon,
as we sat on the trunk of a fallen palm in the Samoan village. Children in their birthday suits splashed joyfully
in a near-by fresh-water pool; seated about it were buxom,
lava-clad women, weaving mats and chatting disregard-
fully; at a hint from the captain, a boy shinned up a tree
and got us young coconuts in the prime of their milk—a
cool, refreshing drink; two young girls, playfully tending a
fire over stones which were to cook the evening meal,

cast mischievous glances at us, evidently to see how many times they could catch me looking at them; in an open *fale* a large group of men squatted motionless, listening to their chief's fervid oratory; great hanging fronds of the coconut palms, stirred by the trade wind, seemed lazily to be fanning a touch of coolness into the lazier atmosphere.

The South Seas. Civilization was half a mile and a thousand years away.

But inevitably, as the day idled into its last half hour, I had to go back to Pango's Astoria.

As a bit of civilization, that hotel was a false alarm. Its owner was a half-caste; if it were not the worst thing to be said of any honest man, I would say that he meant well. The cook, a savage imported from a distant island, may have been great in his day at preparing human flesh, but his conversion to ordinary cooking was a mistake. Of the eleven pounds which I lost somewhere in the South Seas, at least two were sacrificed to that cook.

The *valet de chambre*, waiter, bell boy, dishwasher, and assistant cook was a cross between a misguided native and something washed ashore from the fo'c's'le of a Norwegian whaler. So varied were his duties that everything about the place might be said to bear the charm of his personality. To get him to function as bell hop, one leaned over the piazza rail and shouted at the cook shanty.

On my bed were a coverlet and one sheet, both stopping short of the edge of the mattress. I wished at the time that the sheet were wider; not that I cared especially for a drapery effect, but if the sheet had hung down a little I would not have had to see the mattress.

That bed! And the *tout ensemble!* In New Zealand,

two ladies who had stopped here told me they had spent the night out in the back yard under the coconut trees. But men are hardier.

However, having the worst of the journey befall me at the start made all subsequent discomforts a pleasure. I forgot it in the fascinations of another day among the Samoans before taking the dinky little sailboat for Apia.

Farewell, Pango-Pango, U. S. A.   Yours is the prettiest spot, and the oddest welcome, of any white man's foothold in the Mid-Pacific!

CHAPTER III

THE pleasure of a trip across from Pango-Pango to Apia depends on one's fondness for sailing in a twenty-eight-ton sloop, on a sea chopped up by inter-island cross currents and a persistent trade wind. We started at five o'clock in the afternoon, and by aid of the "kicker"—otherwise, the gasoline engine—managed to arrive in the harbour of Apia at seven next morning.

Six first-class passengers in the one little cabin with five berths meant that the latest comer had the floor to himself. But a few life preservers laid out for a mattress made the big half-caste elected for the place so comfortable that he was trumpeting steadily when I dropped off to sleep. Up forward under a huge tarpaulin drawn above the hatch was a mass of native men, women, and children, going "deck passage."

Everybody else aboard seemed to be enjoying this trip as if it were their final one across the Styx. It takes a sense of humour and unimpeachable "sea legs" to get anything more than mileage out of sailing on this little packet from Pango; yet reminiscent of past yachting days along the New England coast was the soft *flap, flap* of the water against the boat's planking after we had dispensed with the engine and were gliding over the seas with

38

the wind on our port quarter. There is a particular "feel" about a sailboat—a jaunty stiffness under the push of her sails, even when she is lifting over the swells in a way most distracting to landsmen. But I had this "feel" to myself. The others viewed all sensation with repugnance.

And the one poor white lady aboard! The very idea of a night in a ship's cabin with five men, only one of whom in the nature of things could possibly be her husband, was a matter of the gravest concern. The thing wasn't done back in Iowa. But after the first heave of the mountainous seas off the harbour's entrance, nothing mattered to the one poor white lady aboard.

* * *

The morning sun, striking at a favourable slant across Apia, did its best to give us a good impression of a tropical scene rather ordinary, when compared with the superlative effects in Pango-Pango. But it is tropical, and it is different—just as every place in any part of the world has something different to interest the traveller who doesn't let the commonplace in a scene dominate his view of it. To get the most out of this first sight of Apia, one should let the nondescript buildings which fringe the shore line merely impress the eye as bits of colour dabbed into the picture between the great blue crescent of the harbour and the variegated greens of the mountains rising in the background; otherwise, Apia might suffer from the first-off notion that it is a desperately inartistic little town.

Taken in this way, it is a pretty view. Those rugged hills—which one of their serene tops has the distinction of holding all that is mortal of the immortal Robert Louis Stevenson? I scanned the different mountain-sides for signs of a habitation which might have been his "Vailima," but heavy unbroken tropical foliage was all I could make out. Yet its roof and gable can be seen from the harbour if one knows where to look for it—nestled at the side of the abrupt peak on which his body rests.

On the street along the shore line the life of far-famed Samoa was astir; and there again, as in Pango-Pango, were the natives—big, brown, erect, striding along in their *lava-lavas* with the freedom and grace peculiar to the habitually untrammelled. White people, too, dressed in white from helmets to soles—New Zealanders, here to govern the Islands under their mandate.

"A moment, please," said the thermometer man—and there was the usual minute of enforced silence.

"Nothing but personal effects?" politely asked the customs official, not mentioning keys to luggage. These covered the port formalities; then big Samoans packed the luggage off to the hotel.

The hotel was like some people—too absolutely done to pattern to pin a remark on, for or against. The hooks on the wall outside the dining-room door; the ladies' parlour up one flight, with its decrepit piano; the bedroom furnishings, gathered from different epochs, yet years away from being either new or antique—I might have been putting up for the night at Somebody's Junction, U. S. A.

All very comfortable—but here's the charm of it: you know that a ten-minute stroll will take you back through centuries to a beautiful South Sea island, where fascinating people live for a living and wonder why we work.

There is a daily routine in the white life of Apia which covers about all its doings in the month-long interval between the comings of the boat.

Arriving at the hotel fully clothed, I missed the great first event of the Apian day—tea and toast in bed; but a hearty meat breakfast was waiting.

The sun had seemed a bit warm on the walk of a few hundred feet from the landing to the hotel. After breakfast it was warmer. By nine o'clock—the beginning of the official day, although the natives had been taking advantage of the comparative coolness for two hours—all hands were mildly interested in locating that tropical life saver, the breeze.

Before ten I was out on the street with my camera, looking for snapshots; but the life of the place had mostly vanished. It had taken to cover. Under the shade of magnificent trees which insufficiently line this one street along the shore were natives, some of them resting behind little piles of taro root, which they were ready to sell at two shillings a pile; others were merely resting. The occasional Europeans abroad were either in automobiles, or in natty little two-wheelers drawn by small ponies. (In the Pacific, all whites are called Europeans, whether they are from Europe, New Zealand, Australia, or born in the Islands.)

When people came out of a shop or office, they usually hastened into another. I seemed to be the only one who persisted in the sunshine. I patrolled Apia's blazing asphalt street, dripping, but interested. Luckily, I had taken my umbrella. Perhaps it saved my life, or at least my reputation among those who were apprehensively regarding me from under shelter.

Back at the hotel, I searched out a window which faintly indicated a movement of air; and while I was studying upon an amended diet—one of a lightness suited to this climate—eleven-o'clock tea was announced. Tea, with hot griddle cakes and short biscuits, buttered.

Feed number three in the daily routine. But one can refuse eleven-o'clock tea without giving offence.

At twelve o'clock everything in town shuts up for two hours, including the one bank and the post office. After a heavy meat luncheon comes the siesta; then the business men attend once more to their affairs, until afternoon tea. Tea, with bread and butter, and generous wedges of freshly made cake. Nourishment the fifth.

A stranger who declines this repast is suspected, but not socially lost.

After tea, work becomes more or less desultory until quitting time, which is between five and six, depending on the kind of work and somebody's disposition. Then, with the relieving coolness, life on the street becomes more animated. Natives come out in considerable numbers. Both men and women are dressed in the *lava-lava;* in the case of the women it is supplemented by a waist, or a gaily coloured piece of cloth thrown over the shoulders.

We generally think of muscle as developed by work; but these Samoan men work little. Scintillating muscles of limbs, chest, and back are built up by working none of them excessively, and all of them moderately—which is just what Samoans do in every one of their free, graceful movements. Rather too bad to shatter a pleasant South Sea fiction, but it might as well be admitted first as last that the men and young girls have a monopoly of the fine figures. Most of the women go straight from youth to corpulency.

Here and there among the strollers are young girls who look like Samoans yet dress as Europeans and wear shoes and stockings. The initiated understand; shoes and stockings on brown legs are a fairly reliable sign of the half-caste.

The half-caste! Racially in a sort of No Man's Land, she flits both ways across the colour line with a freedom undared by either her Samoan or white half sisters—and to the jealous torment of both! We shall come to the half-caste later.

Europeans, both awheel and afoot, make of this a social hour, preceding the simple entertainments of the evening. Chinese—the island's indentured labourers—appear here and there, but Chinese are more in evidence at night, when their work for the day is over. There are Solomon Islanders, too—another brand of imported labour—short, erect, coal black, and kinky haired—sure-enough copies of Africa's blackest, down to their carefree, sunny dispositions.

Among the lot of them, Europeans included, Samoans appear to be far and away the healthiest, happiest, and most fitting to the environment. There is a sufficiency about their broad, open countenances, their strong, generously moulded features, their ample bodies and sturdy limbs, which is lacking in the others. Nature has set their lips at a half smile, and they are ready at the slightest provocation to complete the gesture.

Next in this daily routine is dinner—at seven o'clock, or earlier, as it happens. Of the six food partakings during the day, dinner is the New Zealander's heartiest. It's a meal for a Minnesota Swede in midwinter. Supper, which comes just before bedtime when it comes at all, consists usually of some little tid-bit like a piece of ham.

But the climate and the cemetery are making an impression on these exotics from the Southland of beef and butter. Many of them now omit supper. They brave hunger from dinner-time at night until morning tea and toast in bed.

* * *

A man whose soul is not so dead that it is unresponsive to exhibitions of feminine charm goes down to the beach —as soon after arrival as he can do so without exciting suspicion—to watch the bathing Samoan sirens fetchingly disport themselves in the blue, limpid water—and all that sort of thing, as depicted by the incorrigible romancers of the South Seas.

Alas! there is no beach. Along the two-mile crescent of shore between the points which make Apia's harbour, not a stretch of passable bathing sand is to be found.

The Samoans do almost no bathing in the sea. Now and then one may find two or three corpulent women, swathed from head to foot in a single garment, comfortably splashing up and down in it after the heat of the day.

Samoans bathe in fresh-water pools, and generally to the accompaniment of unromantic soap. The prettily coloured sheetlike wrap which is the women's almost universal garment when at home—tucked in on itself at the waist if none but natives are about, or up under the arms in the presence of Europeans—serves also as a bathing costume. It lends itself to manipulation under water. Samoan damsels can manage a complete bath in the pool without once breaking the onlooker's expectancy.

In covering for the bath to the same extent as she covers for the home, the Samoan girl shows a consistency which her white sister does not. Her unvarying habit of dress leads a mere man to appreciate better the elasticity of the white bathing girl's notion of modesty.

The Samoan girl's costume has at least the virtue of its little-changing scantiness. But it is a covering of the person quite sufficient for its torrid climate, even when she ignores the teaching of the missionaries and follows the Samoan way of tucking it in at the waist.

These pools along the streams are patronized quite like the old swimming holes at home—by the young boys, and sometimes, along the banks, by little girls. The older people usually make a two-minute utilitarian dash of it, and go on their way. On occasions when boys are not monopolizing the pool, young girls under twenty, who are everlastingly washing clothes along the streams, will take advantage of the clear way and have a good swim on their own account. Their easy glidings and turnings under the water and above it are beautiful to see, even if in a pool ten feet deep at its deepest they cannot show off the marvellous aquatic feats pictured by the story-tellers.

The coming of Europeans at these times sends the girls up to their necks in water—silent, defensive, observing. But they need only to be convinced that the visitors have no designs beyond wishing to see them swim about and dive for coins—and, perhaps, to take a few snapshots. Sixpences are an inducement, of course, but confidence invariably has to precede the sixpences.

In taking pictures of natives I always try to get them in the native costume. Photographs of artificial shifts which some busybody thinks they ought to be wearing are not photographs of natives. Natural poses can usually be managed if one shows his honesty of purpose by keeping within the limits of the native sense of propriety. They have their view of what constitutes clothing and hold to it.

The conventionalities of clothing here are merely adjusted to the climate. They are rigid as far as they go. In the tropics, custom, a piece of cloth, and a decent intention are the clothes of perfect modesty.

The best authorities on life in the tropics assert that clothes have had a fearful part in decimating native peoples. In some parts of Papua (New Guinea), selling shirts to natives is a misdemeanour. One of the most uncomfortable sights I saw in Samoa was that of a group of Samoan girls dressed in the enveloping costume of nuns. For a people adapted through generations of bare bodies to Samoa's steamy heat, this starched, black imprisonment is nothing short of slow murder. They cannot, like their white sisters, rush off to some temperate climate when enervated beyond endurance.

*   *   *

One of the most striking things about native life in Samoa is that it is so absolutely native, in spite of the universal missionary influence. Adopting the white man's religion has not led the Samoans to adopt his civilization. They stick to a mode of life as thoroughly suited to the tropics as the European's is unsuited.

In Apia, the oval, grass-covered tops of *fales* are alongside the corrugated iron roofs of a misplaced, sweaty culture, and natives live the serene life of their fathers within a stone's throw of the white man's Main Street. But to see the Samoan in his most natural state one must go to the villages.

I spent many forenoons in the villages; forenoons, because they are not quite so torrid as the afternoons. The *fales* are built like those of American Samoa; an intricate oval framework upon stout five-foot posts set about six feet apart all the way around a raised pebble floor, and covered with a thick roof of long grasses and the full-length fronds of the coconut palm. Native mat curtains drawn up under the eaves are ready to be dropped as a protection against sun, rain, or wind from any quarter; but in this, the dry season, most of the *fales* stand open all around night and day. Very few villages are without friendly trees to shield them from the afternoon sun. The villages are pretty, uncrowded, and clean. Grounds clear of rubbish and trim-cut grass are demanded of every village by the authorities in Apia.

Samoans in their homes are generally cordial—and if they are not cordial they are courteous. So invariably courteous that it is almost as difficult to make out whether you are welcome there as it is in the homes of cultured Bostonians.

They greet you pleasantly with their *"T'Alofa"* (pronounced "Talofa"), meaning literally, "To you a gift." Softly as they always speak it, the word shows its close relationship to the "Aloha" of the Hawaiians. But a gift from a Samoan should never be accepted without paying for it. A gift invariably implies a trade.

Many have a smattering of English, and most of them a few words—gathered mostly from the missionaries, although nearly all of the preaching and teaching is done by natives in the Samoan language. They like to use such words as they know, and invite you in; but if you have a cautious regard for the numerous infections which they carry—chiefly trifling skin infections, and now and then eye troubles more serious—you politely decline, and look the place over from the outside, covering the scrutiny with expressions of interest and admiration. You try to be as courteous as they are.

A *fale* with a chair or bed in it is not strictly Samoan, but without a kerosene lamp the home expresses poverty. They sit, eat, and sleep on the mat-covered pebble floor, and cook in a little shelter near by. The cook stove is a bed of stones which have been heated by burning a slow fire over them—a tedious process. The only common furnishings besides the lamp are a few boxes filled with their simple belongings.

Perhaps you get them out in front of the *fale* and take a picture of the family group. The family group reminds you forcibly that the physical attractiveness of Samoans is with the men and the young people. As a rule, the men retain their magnificent physiques until they are well along in years, while the women, married at fifteen, are middle-aged at twenty-five.

Yet with the vanishing of their physical comeliness they lose none of that complacency toward life which keeps a face anywhere in the world young and good to look at. They don't take on that harried look which so many civilized women have—probably because they have so little to harry them. No worrying to make ends meet, because in their communistic way of living ends always meet. No failures worth mentioning, because there is nothing to strive for.

They fill the day with living. It's the simple life,

simplified. We would find it deadly dull—we who are used to living in a whirl of man-made contrivances. We enjoy *things* instead of ourselves. We're all but lost in paraphernalia.

These children of nature give one a different slant on what we call civilization. Nowhere else in the world, I suppose, is human life so perfectly adapted to its environment, so little dependent upon artifice, as on these tropical islands. In this harmony between nature and man there is a psychic contentment which we know nothing about. It is this that lends perennial enchantment to the South Sea islands.

And we are continually butting in on these people with attempts to *civilize* them! Better for us to be getting pointers from them on how to be happy though civilized.

The sensuous charm—the play of the senses undisturbed —is in every detail of Samoan life. Why stress its one relation to their women? To be sure, Samoan women *are* beautiful—when they are young. Straight-backed, full breasted, ample, shapely—the direct opposite of the animated barrel-stave type pictured in the fashion cuts and affected by flappers. They may not be so delicately feminine, but they are more distinctly females.

This last remark indicates, too, the type of white man who would be most attracted by Samoan girls. But he might as well stay at home. The aim of the Samoan girl, like that of girls elsewhere, is marriage. She knows well enough that marriage is not coming to her from any white man; and she is quite as wary of adventurers as are her white sisters.

When her day comes, the Samoan girl marries a husky brown man who lets her do most of the work and raise all the babies; but he builds a *fale* and grows some taro and gathers breadfruit and somehow gets a pig. So life goes cheerily on in the neat little village under the coconut palms.

*   *   *

The coconut is the natives' tree of life. They build their villages in its groves, and parts of their *fales* from its trunk and branches. The meat of the nut is food for natives, pigs, dogs—and the hens live off the coconut crumbs which these three scatter about. Baskets and some of their coarser mats are made of its long, tough leaves. From the strong fibres of the husk they make a cord—sinnet—of any size up to small rope. Sinnet lashes in place every stick of their *fales,* tethers the pig, and ties up all things that have to be tied. The coconut shell, cut in halves or with merely the top sliced off, is their universal container. They make copra from the meat of the nut, and get the white man's money for it. When the nut has begun to sprout—sending a green shoot out from one of its eyes—its milk turns to a sort of cheese; rather palatable, after one gets accustomed to the insipid taste, and a welcome addition to the Samoan's diet. The lower branches of the coconut trees are constantly dying and falling to the ground; this is the natives' abundant source of dry fuel, to be had for the gathering.

The kindest tree in the world is the coconut, and always in the shade of it is a lazy people.

Watch a group of Samoans making copra. One takes the coconuts as they come from the groves, jabs them violently down upon a sharp stake set in the ground, and strips off the husk; others—women, perhaps—split the nut in halves with a few gentle taps of a heavy knife; the rest of them cleave the meat out from the half shells, and cut it up into strips ready for drying in the sun.

And as they leisurely go through the various motions, chattering sociably, they nibble at the delicious white meat, drink the milk of the fresh coconuts, and eat the cheese of the sprouted ones. Work? In its way it is like the old-fashioned husking bee, minus the little excitement of the red ears—and quite as much like work.

Making copra in their own groves is as near as most of the natives approach to labouring for Europeans. Like the Hawaiians, some of them will do certain kinds of work in the town, but none will labour on the great coconut plantations, where the splitting and cleaving is done in huge sheds under an overseer's eye, and the meat is dried in kilns fired by the discarded coconut husks. It's all too complicated for the native—too much like work.

And why in the name of reason should men and women bred in nature's lap work under the eye of a white man until the pointers on a shiny little tin box have gone round just so many times?

Absurd! So they don't.

* * *

How is it that the Samoans, having no use for our civilization, take so enthusiastically to our religion?

"Enthusiastically" is the right word. On this island —Upolu—the London Missionary Society alone has one hundred and six native churches, and fifty-eight on Savaii, the only other important island in the group. The Methodists, Catholics, Adventists, and Mormons are also well represented by converts. This, in a native population of a little more than thirty thousand.

Of course, the natives do not pick their way through theological distinctions; first in the field and best equipped, the L. M. S. has the most converts. But the Samoans are about all in, somewhere. They accept our religion as cheerfully as they let the rest of our culture go by.

It is difficult to believe that this enthusiasm is due wholly to religious zeal. What else is back of it?

When white men first came to these islands, the Samoans had an elaborate system of control. It was a system which required chiefs and sub-chiefs galore, as well as men who played upon the natives' interest in the supernatural.

Palavers and harangues gave opportunity to the chiefs' innate love of orating, and to the primitives' innate love of listening to oratory. This bred rivalries, politics, everlasting talk; and wars which raise the emotions of all to a single pitch. We don't have to go to the South Sea islands to get the setting.

Life for the Samoans in those days was not the flat, passive, dreamy existence that it is to-day. It had the "kick" of independence in it. The white man's assumption of control reduced the whole system of chieftainship to a mere formality, and with that system went about all that was vitalizing in Samoan life.

This gave the missionaries their day. Their call for natives to preach the Gospel to the people was the cleverest move they ever made. Again, the natives had a chance for leadership, oratory.

Of course, enthusiam for the new religion rose. The old zest for chieftainship found expression in the new zeal for the ministry. Meetings as often as they wished to hold them satisfied the popular longing for palavers.

The teachings of Christianity met their superstitious inclinations in a better way than their discredited magic men ever had. Intense rivalries between the sects, and sometimes hearty rows within the churches—neither of these peculiar to Samoans—offered mimic warfare, with miniature stimulations of the old fighting instinct.

Did ever a single institution fill so many aching voids? The Samoans have a much higher percentage of churchgoers than any of the communities back home which are sending money out here to convert them. They *enjoy* going to church!

One gets a variety of opinions as to whether so many churches are necessary. Some of the worldly say that the expense of supporting all these ministers keeps the natives more steadily at copra-making—and copra stimulates trade. Others think that copra-making and trade should be stimulated in some less expensive way.

The traders—well, the traders! Many a torrid hour I have spent with them in some friendly shade, swapping conversation. If he is not quizzed, the average trader will pour out all his troubles since the day of his landing in the islands, and along with them a considerable volume of South Sea islands history.

The traders, almost to a man, place a light estimate on the good achieved by the missionaries. They go into particulars, more or less convincing; but in all their critical talks I have never heard a trader reflect on the motives or character of a white missionary. This makes it easier to believe their tales about designing native preachers.

Most traders dwell on the paucity of results as shown in the characters of the natives. They assert that the Samoans are less honest now than before they were converted wholesale; and they charge this specifically to the old missionary exhortation, "Give up all your heathenish ways—become like white men!"

The natives did just this, say the traders—lost their sense of obligation to their own code, and took to imitating the tricky ways of the sort of white men they knew best.

In passing judgment on a trader's opinion of missionary work, one has to allow anywhere up to one hundred per cent. for prejudice. Fierce competition has reduced trading to an almost honest business; but in the early days, when nothing but the missionary stood between defenseless natives and rapacious traders—not necessarily the traders here now—there developed a class enmity between the two which persists even after the occasion for it has vanished.

Weighing all the evidence along with one's own observations, the mildest answer seems to be that the multiplication of churches has not been attended by a corresponding moral upheaval in the lives of the Samoans. One can hardly justify the present proportions of the church in Samoa without allowing generously for its value as the great Samoan pastime.

But why not allow generously for this aspect of the church here? Nobody who looks into their past history would deny the Samoans this gratification of their inherited longings. They gave up much of their country to the whites, and lost many of their old incentives. Too much culture kills natives—and the Samoans have shown a joyous will to live by resisting it. As a race they are physically magnificent; in disposition happy, courteous, likable—and childlike. *Laissez faire.*

Robert Louis Stevenson loved the Samoans. From all the local evidence, everybody on Upolu, regardless of race, colour, or previous dislike of each other, loved Robert Louis Stevenson.

A few are still here who knew Stevenson during his four years in Samoa, from 1890 to 1894. In a white population so shifting as that on a tropical island, the presence of even a few after thirty-odd years is remarkable. Grizzled traders who may be doling out grievances against the state of trade, the copra market, the government—especially the government, since New Zealand has been trying her hand at it—soften at the mention of Stevenson's name and declare that Stevenson was a regular fellow. And they may add that he was an odd duck.

Stevenson got himself two or three degrees removed from the heat of Apia by building his "Vailima" two miles back in the hills, in a space as open to the southeast trade wind as any could be on this wrong side of the island. Against the earnest advice of friends he had a fireplace built into the house—but luckily, it wouldn't draw; otherwise, the Stevenson family might have been sacrificed to the pleasures of an open fire.

"Vailima" now is the official residence of the governor. A few of us were invited there to tea one afternoon. The house looks out northward over Apia, into the limitless blue expanse of the Pacific. Ample grounds, almost clear of trees, give freedom to the light and air. Coconut groves surround the place at a respectful distance, and at the left of the house rises the abrupt peak where the body of Stevenson rests.

The building was extensively added to by a rich German who bought the property from the estate, but Stevenson's home is easily distinguishable from the newer part, and little changed. With our gracious hostess, the governor's wife, we saw the intimate places—Stevenson's rooms, the second-story veranda where he did much of his writing, the fireplace; then down the broad stairway into the dining room—an immense dining room for a house of its size; lingering for a moment on the lower few steps at the turn, where Stevenson sank down in the apoplectic stroke which stilled his genius forever.

In this great dining room Stevenson held court with the Samoans, and played enthusiastic host to his visiting white friends. He was a generous entertainer, especially of officers from the war vessels which in those troublous days were almost constantly in the harbour. No other islands in the Pacific have been the cause of so much wrangling among the Powers. The liberality and frequency of his dinners, according to his friends still in Samoa, trimmed his large income from his writings down close to the vanishing point; to such limits that, shortly before he died, he was contemplating a move to some more secluded location. It was to be a running away from his own hospitality—a difficult feat for a free-handed man like Stevenson.

But one can easily imagine that closest to his heart were the councils held in this room with the chiefs and headmen, and with all the Samoans who came up the hill to lay their troubles before the surest white friend they ever had. Their troubles with the Powers, and especially their differences among themselves, kept Stevenson's emotional nature at a disturbing pitch. His intense and sometimes partisan interest in their affairs led him now and then, some friends think, almost to the limits of indiscretion. It is doubtful whether inspiring hope in a just but hopeless cause always serves the ultimate good.

His devotion to the Samoans probably shortened his life. The very fact that he did not die of the lingering disease which sent him to the South Seas, but of another which often comes from mental strain, justifies the belief that Robert Lewis Balfour Stevenson gave his life to the people he loved so unselfishly.

* * *

Those troublous years in Samoa. It is a sordid history, that of the three Great Powers jealously striving here for advantage. Take a walk out along Mulinuu Point—the left arm of Apia's crescent beach—and you will come upon three monuments, one after the other. One was erected by the British, another by the Germans, and the third by the United States—all to the memory of their respective marines who lost their lives in conflicts with the natives.

It seems odd that officers of an American warship should have thought it necessary to fire shells into Samoans—but they did, in 1899; so it must have been necessary. The American marines killed were in a force sent ashore at that time to destroy native villages.

I like to think of that monument as a tribute, not only to the Amèrican boys who lost their lives in the service, but also to the Samoans who had the emotional courage to fight for their homes against odds absolutely hopeless. No shaft perpetuates the names of those Samoans.

* * *

If you want to see Samoans dallying with culture, go to the movie show in Apia.

All films wandering about in the South Seas have to linger in each place for the monthly boat; consequently, all films in the South Sea islands are such as other parts of the world are emphatically through with. In one "Current Events" reel that I saw were scenes from the visit of the Prince of Wales to India, some years ago; in the course of time they may get around to the San Francisco earthquake. One aged film broke so often that the story of it was lost in the intervals of repair—but these intervals were enlivened by two dog-fights in the aisle.

Europeans have a special place set off for them on the floor. The line drawn instinctively by race, call it colour line or not, is drawn in Samoa as in every part of the world where unlike races meet. The Samoans were ranged in tiers rising in great semicircles back of us.

Of course, most of the natives missed the conversational features; perhaps that is one reason why they came in so vociferously for such parts of the action as they could understand. Every discomfiture of the villain brought solid howls of delight. Knockdowns and rough handling sent them off into shrieks of laughter.

They were most interesting to watch in the scenes unfamiliar to them. In a film which pictured among other things a skiing contest, the sliding on white ground puzzled them into a dead silence; but whenever one of the performers spilled into the usual grotesque postures, they laughed heartily. Harold Lloyd, the funniest man in pictures, was too subtle for them except when doing his best to break his neck. Another film showed two comedians riding on brake beams and in box cars; they were comic enough, but rails, trains, and swift motion were beyond the natives. Not until one of the actors was thrown over a thousand-foot cliff did they really enjoy it.

* * *

The human interest in Samoa centres in Samoans, but it radiates to the other varieties of humans in the islands. There are the indentured labourers—Chinese, Solomon Islanders; the whites, in their various relations to each other and to the rest of the lot; and the half-castes—the White-Samoan half-castes—in a class by themselves.

I got my first inkling of the New Zealanders' difficulties with Chinese coolies from a lady at the Vailima tea party. She was the wife of a copra plantation manager. Naturally, my conversation with her turned to plantation affairs. She was soon on the subject of the stubborn Chinese coolie.

"The whole trouble is that the law forbids the beating of coolies," she explained. "Threats, arrests, fines will not make them work if they decide not to work. The only persuasion a coolie understands is physical force. As it is, they have no respect for us. Our overseers cannot beat them," she added ruefully.

The suggestion of the right to beat was novel enough to set me on a tour of inquiry. Coolies are brought from China under a three-year indenture, which provides for their transportation both ways and a shilling a day while in Samoa. On arrival, the coolie's labour is sold to a planter, and that planter has the right to resell it, or trade it for the labour of another coolie. The coolies, of course, have no voice in the matter.

It may seem at first glance that a contract which so ties up a man's liberty should not carry with it the right to beat him. But the very fact of his complete dependence gives the ill-disposed coolie an advantage. He cannot be discharged and he must be fed, and his fare back to China is paid.

Then what happens if he refuses to work?

He can be fined or imprisoned by a magistrate in town —a troublesome and expensive procedure for the planter, but suppose he undertakes it. A fine discloses no money, and jail is a holiday for a coolie who refuses to work. As the lady said, there is no way to compel a stubborn coolie to do his task. Most coolies, it seems, work out their terms faithfully, but the few who do not are maddening.

I had the situation put up to me in a picturesque way by an overseer on one of the plantations. His cockney is beyond transcribing, but this is the gist of his woeful tale:

"Well, say 'ere's a Chow lays down on me." (I had heard Chinamen called about everything except "Chow." "Chow," in these parts, is food.) " 'E's just plain ugly —so mething's gone wrong, 'e's sore and quits work.

"Now, one good sting of my riding whip across 'is thin pants would make a 'appy worker of 'im again. But can I 'and it to 'im? *Naow!* Just talk—that's all *I* can do. And he just sets. I get on me 'oss, and ride off, and give the blooming Chow a chance to come out of 'is fit." The overseer mopped his brow, and began again.

"And 'ere's another kind. I come on a Chow setting down. 'Wot the 'ell,' says I, and a few other things. 'E don't move, but says 'e wants to be transferred to So-and-so's plantation—says 'e's got friends over there.

"Say, right off I know *'is* trouble—'e's in wrong with 'is friends *'ere*. Gambling, likely, and owes the other

Chows; or 'e got the bad end of a fight. 'E's out to seek pastures new, that Chow is.

"Well, s'pose I tell 'im we bought 'is time and 'ere 'e stays. Does 'e get up and go to work? *Naow!* 'E sets, peaceful. Oh, these bloomin' Chows are a patient lot—they win out by waiting.

"Next day it's the same Chow, setting down, same story. I see 'e's made up 'is mind to set it out with me. Now, two good cracks on that lazy back of 'is would make 'im forget those friends over there—but can I 'it 'im?

"*Naow!* I go to the overseer of that other plantation, and if 'e 'as a Chow to trade, we swap. And my Chow knows 'e's done me."

The harried man gazed dourly off into space, while I condoled with him as best I could. But he was not through.

"You can bet it's a rotten job, overseeing Chows. But the most exasperating kind is the Chow that sets down, calm as a coconut, and don't make no complaint at all. I know wot 'e wants, and I'd like to kill 'im—but I can't even knock 'is blooming 'at off." The very thought of his restricted privileges made the overseer's voice quiver.

"'E wants to be arrested for refusing to work. 'E 'asn't seen Apia since 'e landed, and a few days in jail there looks good to 'im. So 'e sets, and says nothing, knowing that a Chow that sets and has no kick makes an overseer maddest of all. It's their way of breaking into jail.

"Do I take him to the magistrate? *Naow*—not at first. So 'e sets, 'oping I'll give 'im the trip to town, and I rides off, 'oping 'e'll forget it."

Pausing for a moment, he glanced at me sheepishly.

"Well, after a few days of it, I give in. The Chow gets 'is outing in jail, and comes back contented—till next time.

"But if I could *only* break 'is yellow 'ead for 'im——"
With a prodigious sigh, the overseer mounted his horse and rode away.

So here are the two horns of the dilemma:

First, without the right to back authority by force, an indentured Chinese coolie disposed to loaf cannot be made to work. And a few such demoralize the many well intentioned.

Second, never in history has the right been given one set of men to beat another set of men that it did not end in the brutalizing of the one and abuse of the other.

The problem looks difficult, but the New Zealanders have solved it—by doing away altogether with the indenture system. The day for the release of indenture labour was to come shortly after my departure from Samoa. All were to be free—free to earn their living at wages or go back to China.

But here's a sequel: many of the coolies do not want to be released. They are mostly those who stand a good chance of being discharged at their first moment of freedom. They see the day coming when they will have to work, starve, or go back to China.

It's an ill wind that blows nobody good. The overseer's happy hour will come with the right to fire his special tormentors out into the cold, cold world.

*   *   *

Apart from all the races is a creation made up of Samoan, white, and a high flavouring of mystery—the half-caste.

Nothing said about half-castes is intended to apply to those of mixed white and Samoan blood who have white connections of acknowledged responsibility. Their destinies are looked after by their families. Little, too, need be said about male half-castes. They either take up with the Samoan life, go to sea, or tinker about at white men's jobs. Here and there one attains marked success in business.

The interesting half-caste is the young woman who either does not know her white relatives or is not acknowledged by them. Her social anchorage, such as it is, is with half-castes or Samoans.

She is a woman without a race. Samoans are sensitively alert to the difference in the half-caste, especially in the half-caste woman. She feels awkwardly the Samoan in her blood, quite as they feel awkwardly the white in one who is part Samoan. The constraint is mutual.

She stands midway, looking at Samoans, looking at Europeans. And unless the white strain in her is flaccid beyond the ordinary, she turns her face toward the Europeans. Being a woman, her interest gravitates to the men. Hence the half-caste girl's unpopularity with white women.

Racially confused as she is, in body and in mind, she looks to the race that brought her into this predicament. Some white man gave her the characteristics which alienate her from Samoans and impel her toward Europeans. Now, some white man can take her out of this racial wilderness in which she has been wandering alone and give her standing in the community.

There's no denying that the heart of the half-caste beats for a white husband. Some, especially the more attractive ones, make a life's ambition of this desire. A few achieve it.

Nature favours the half-caste girl. Quite as likely as not she has inherited the supple beauty of the Samoan, touched here and there by the finer mouldings of the white. Full-figured, light of skin, not at all unwilling that white men should be aware of her, she strives to make herself attractive—dangerously so, think her perspiring washed-out white sisters, as they apprehensively watch her strolling on Apia's Fifth Avenue, decked out in white shoes and stockings and a pretty European dress.

In earlier times, the full-blooded Samoan woman may have figured as a social disturber. She does not now— not in this day of the half-caste.

Apia's climate is against white women. So, to my Yankee way of thinking, is their habit of eating in Apia's climate six times a day. Between the two, even those who were born to be physically attractive don't often make the goal in Apia.

The colour line favours the half-caste. In the public schools of Apia, white and half-caste children are educated together; the Samoans are in separate buildings, with their own teachers. This half-admitted equality, together with her smattering of knowledge, enables the half-caste to get employment with Europeans when she leaves school; perhaps in a store or office. European clothes, acquaintance with white men, familiarity with white ways—these come with her employment. If the white women draw a colour line of their own against the half-caste girl—especially if she is good to look at—well, it is natural that they should. The half-caste girl is not particularly interested in white women.

At one of the dances given in Apia while I was there, this attitude of the women was illustrated. Some of the men invited half-caste girls; because they did, not a white woman would go. So the dance—a wholly respectable affair—was attended only by white men and half-caste women.

Of course, it cannot be denied that the half-caste's Samoan blood is a fearful handicap to her one great ambition. The basic instinct of race is not to mix bloods. No white man in his senses would consider a half-caste girl seriously. But in the presence of alluring feminine beauty a man does not always retain his senses, nor consider seriously. His infatuation may blind him to the fearful complications involved in taking her back to his home in the colonies. He doesn't even see the impossibility of anything better than a patched-up adjustment with his white friends in Samoa, if he elects to stay. And he may be too selfish to think of the blighting handicap which he is putting upon his children.

Any fair man's heart goes out to the half-caste girl. She was taken a mean advantage of before she was born. Yet marrying her to a white man does not square the wrong—it only perpetuates it.

* * *

One day, in a native village not far from Apia, I came upon a group of little children playing—naked, as most little children are in the villages. At my approach they ran for their tiny *lava-lavas*, lined up in front of me, and carefully put them on. I suppose they had been told to put on their *lava-lavas* before Europeans.

In the group I noticed a little girl of six or seven—blonde

haired, blue eyed, and with as fair a skin as many a white child, after allowing for her coat of tan. I thought she must be a white girl, but inquiry afterward proved that she was a half-caste.

The sight of a half-caste, especially a half-caste child, always starts my imagination on a speculative ramble. I do not think of the Samoan; I think of the white individual who is bound for life to a Samoan.

So with this little girl; a white life not only interwoven with that of a Samoan, but, for the time at least, held completely to the Samoan environment. Apparently she did not know a word of English. She chattered, played, dressed, and probably ate with her fingers and slept on a mat like any Samoan.

As many times as I have seen half-castes living with natives, both here and on other South Sea islands, speaking their language and displaying all their attributes, I never escape that first shock of astonishment at seeing a white individual who has been struck off in the mould of another race and holds to the shape of it. Doesn't he *know* that somewhere about him is a *white* man? Or if he has had glimpses of this other personality, has he, for the sake of peace in the native environment, suppressed or ignored it whenever he felt its presence?

I can faintly comprehend the racial perplexity of the half-caste who has risen to an appreciation of both the races mixed in his one person; but the half-caste who stays submerged—carrying his white personality about with him like the passive ghost of his other self—no human being is more weird, uncanny.

Of course, this little girl was too young to understand; but I fell at once to speculating. How early will she begin to know that she is partly white? And what impression on her mixed mentality will the knowledge make? Or, suppose she never does come to an active realization, as has been the fate of many a half-caste—what then?

It is not so very difficult to look a little way ahead into this girl's future. If someone happens to notice her in time, she will probably be taken in and educated with white and half-caste children. Mingled with whites, she will come to a sense of what she is, and before her will be the problems of the half-caste girl who has to fight her unique battle alone.

But unless she is taken away before she is fifteen, the chances are that she will marry a Samoan, and live as a Samoan, knowing of her white inheritance, yet never awakening to it. And then, with the generations, will be born quarter-whites, and eighth-bloods, and sixteenths—until the half-white of this little girl will have dissolved into the lives of a thousand persons—Samoans, each unwittingly bearing a tiny reminder of some white man's careless hour.

* * *

July has come to an end, and with it, my stay in Samoa. The monthly steamer, in at daybreak, is to take me to the Friendly Islands, five hundred miles south. She lies at anchor inside the coral reefs, waiting for the port doctor to come out and give her a clean bill of health. Then she can pull down the yellow flag of quarantine at her crosstree, and her passengers—the few who are to stop over and the many who are not—will come ashore in the flotilla of rowboats hovering about the vessel. The crew is already limbering up the hoisting engines for the prosaic business of unloading cargo into lighters. The passengers on this monthly steamer—the *Tofua*—are mostly New Zealand tourists, making the round trip from Auckland through this part of the South Sea islands. More than a hundred of them this time, the local agent of the company says; and they will "do" Samoa in the businesslike tourist fashion during the two days of the vessel's stay in port.

They will not see Samoan life as it really is; they will see it under the impulse of its monthly kick at the coming of the boat. Already, at eight o'clock in the morning, native women are arriving in squads from the villages, bearing the "souvenirs" which they have been making for weeks, in anticipation of the tourist shillings. At every point of vantage—a point of vantage in Apia is a shady spot—they squat along the street and spread out their wares: necklaces, made of various coloured beans and seeds; baskets, woven of pretty grasses or plaited from reeds—serviceable mostly, and attractive; models of native boats, spears, and even *fales*—all with a very newish look; and a few spreads of tappa cloth—the fibrous cloth beaten out in strips from a kind of mulberry bark, and united into good-sized pieces with a gum of their own gathering.

For a whole month they have awaited Steamer Day, and the tourists, and the shower of shillings; now they laugh and chatter—their voices soft and low, as always—in pleased expectancy.

All the automobiles on the island which ever did condescend to take passengers for hire are assembled under the trees. Over fair to middling roads the tourists will be driven to coconut plantations, the Falls, out to the points of the crescent, and back into the native villages. Coming so far for a single ride in Samoa, they will not mind the expense. The native drivers cannot forget that their harvest comes but once a month; besides, automobiles cost in Samoa more than twice as much as in the States, and gasoline is a dollar a gallon.

The stores have had their post-card supplies replenished for Steamer Day—photographs mostly, printed here. These, and any other things about the place which might catch a tourist's eye, are well displayed; and the pretty half-caste clerks, in their daintiest dresses, await the landing of the little boats—smilingly thinking their own thoughts at the coming of so many white visitors.

The hotel, too, has had a busy time of it, preparing to take care of a hundred or so extra for luncheon. Overseers and managers have come in from the plantations, frankly making a holiday of it if no better excuse is at hand.

Merchants and business men await the monthly mail with eagerness, and clerks and typewriters are ready to make quick work of answering it. Any letters not answered by to-morrow noon will remain unanswered for another month. This, together with their incoming freight and outgoing freight, and business with men from the boat who must leave on the boat, make it a hectic time for the business men of Apia.

So the whole town is agog at the coming of the boat. Even the sagging, humid atmosphere seems to get a feeble boost out of the excitement of Steamer Day.

Everybody watches the doctor's boat, tied up at the vessel's gangway. Now it pulls off—chugs across the harbour toward the customs dock—but the yellow flag on the vessel does not come down. The doctor's boat ties up in its accustomed place—and the ominous little saffron square still flutters at the ship's crosstree.

Then we get the news. The yellow flag is not to come down. There is influenza aboard; nothing more than two or three mild cases, almost well. But the word "influenza" is a terror to the natives. In the fearful visitation of 1918, more than eight thousand Samoans —one quarter of the entire population—died of it.

So no chances can be taken. The thirteen passengers due to get off here will be put into rowboats and paddled directly across to the quarantine station—a small building out on the tip of the point and a mile from town. There they will be held for a week, nicely cared for at their own expense, with nothing to do but think and get to hate each other.

The hundred-odd tourists may sit on the sizzling deck and look across the glare at the spot which they came out principally to see—or they can go below. But they can't go anywhere else. Rather tough, to lose the best thing on their twenty-day tour, but somebody sneezed while the doctor was aboard.

The lightering of freight went on, and the mail came ashore, so the business men had plenty to do; but for everybody else, Steamer Day was a flash-in-the-pan.

Then the elaborate preparation had to unwind itself. The native women gathered up their wares as the prospect of pin money vanished, gazed wistfully at the steamer, and trudged in silence back to their villages. Planters took to their horses or motors and rode off into the country. Few more than the regulars were on hand for the hotel's luncheon. The shops had less customers than usual, and the pretty clerks sadly put the tourist stuff back into storage.

The holiday aspect faded away. Apia read its mail and settled down to another month of somnolescence.

* * *

Quarantine in the South Sea islands is something for every traveller to reckon with. The number of contagious tropical diseases, and the difficulty in controlling them if they get a fair start, leads to a fear that makes quarantine extremely rigid, and sometimes unreasonable. Every island watches every other, and lays restrictions against it at the first prospect of contagion. So likely are travellers to be put off at some quarantine station— at the vessel's expense if the unhappy ones have no money —that some steamers require a deposit from passengers to protect the steamship company against this happening.

Plant infections inspire almost as much fear in the islanders as diseases of humans. The tropics, with never a frost to kill, fairly seethe with microscopic life—and enough of it is dangerous to either man, beasts, or plants. There is never a time when a South Sea island is not quarantined against somebody or something, and is not itself quarantined against.

With all the battling against plant infections, one wonders how it happens that any growing thing has survived the ages in these parts; but through the ages there was comparative isolation. Civilized travel is a spreader of troublous bugs.

Just now, the rhinoceros beetle, a killer of coconut trees, has set the other islands against Samoa. A commercial traveller who unpacks his samples first in Samoa cannot unpack them in the Tongan (Friendly) Islands. On account of this unworthy beetle, all personal luggage has to be fumigated before it can leave Apia, otherwise the passenger cannot land in Tonga, Fiji, and goodness knows where else.

There was no objection to my getting aboard this quarantined steamer; but I had to take the risk of being refused a landing at Nukualofa, the Tongan capital. A vessel held up in quarantine in one port has a lessened chance of clear entry into the next port, even if all are well and nobody sneezes.

Of course, I wanted to see the Tongans—the only people left in the South Seas with an independent kingdom. Luckily, I happened upon a man who had once spent an enforced holiday in the Tongan quarantine station. He said it was on a little island out among the coral reefs and not so bad as it might be; so with a fair prospect of spending a week there out of my short month in the Friendly Islands, I committed my luggage to the fumigator.

The Samoan owners of the rowboats which transfer passengers to vessels have hit upon a novel means of enticing patronage. On the backboard of each boat is painted some common European name—the commoner the better—such as "Charlie," "Tommy," "Freddie," in the hope that the Charleses, Thomases, and Freds among the passengers will ride in no other than a boat named after them. Each husky native takes for the time the ridiculous name of his boat.

So at the landing there were Charlie, Tommy, Freddie, and several more, fixing me with their big dark eyes and hopefully repeating the names; but in vain. My name is Seth.

While I hesitated, a brown giant with a Sandow chest towered over me, waved a corrugated arm as big as a leg at his boat, and whispered ingratiatingly, "Me Willie. You know me."

I pinned my faith on Willie.

The ship was crowded. For a packed-in lot who had just gone through two whole days at anchor in a tropical harbour, they showed an astonishing reserve of good humour. A costume ball had been arranged for the evening, and many were already dressed for it—dinner was only a half hour away. They welcomed the little group of new arrivals with a cordiality which I was beginning to discover is typical of New Zealanders. One of them stepped out and made us a little speech of welcome, saying that they themselves had already become well acquainted (don't see how they could have helped it), and urged us to make ourselves at home.

It was after dark when the ship heaved anchor and steamed away from Samoa. The last we saw of the island, after its black outline had faded from view, was a huge bonfire, built on the shore at the quarantine station by the thirteen "castaways"—their farewell to friends on the vessel.

Good-bye, gentle Samoans! May Progress with its crimes and heartaches keep its ugly hand off you; and may you never know the subtle ferocity which we call Ambition!

CHAPTER IV

THE KINGDOM OF TONGA

THE Tongans have an old belief that when the world had been made ready for habitation, the Creator first made the Tongan, then the pig, and then the white man.

The Tongan's deference to the pig bears out his faith in this order of creation. His hogship is received in all except the best families. At the Queen's palace he is supposed to have the run of the grounds up to the back door—but on occasions I have seen the imperial swine in the front yard, rooting at the royal shrubbery.

Under Great Britain's protection, the Tongans have the only native kingdom in the Pacific, but they are not quite sure how to spell its name. So they spell it "Tonga" on the royal money and "Toga" on the postage stamps. The same trick in pronunciation which twists our "Pago" into "Pango" makes their "Toga" sound like "Tonga." By spelling it both ways they are dead right part of the time, which is doing well for a Tongan.

There is not another nation like it outside of comic opera. They do not have even the comic opera's army of two soldiers and a general. There is no army. There is no Tongan navy. Not a fort or a gun defends the place. Yet with the other nations of the earth the Kingdom of Tonga declared war on Germany. I believe it was the next day that Hindenburg told the German people to prepare for still greater sacrifices.

The Kingdom of Tonga is odd among the nations in other respects. It has no taxes of any sort. No annual struggle here with your conscience and an income-tax sheet, even if you are of the species created subsequent to the pig. Tonga has no public debt; instead, a surplus of eighty thousand pounds sterling is in the royal treasury.

Whence comes the revenue?

From the world's only complete system of ground rents. There is no freehold in the kingdom. Everybody who occupies land pays rent to the government. Not a foot of real estate can be bought or sold in the Friendly Islands.

It is somewhat after the Socialist's ideal—and the results are as might be expected. On this island's wide stretches of level, rich soil there is not a plough.

But I ought to arrive in Tonga before telling about it.

The great, flat coral island of Tongatabu (SacredTonga) came into sight on the morning of the fourth day out from Samoa. Back of the network of half-submerged coral reefs which make a harbour the red roofs and neat white buildings of Nukualofa, capital of the Tongas, showed prettily against an unbroken, level stretch of coconut palms.

After the volcanic ruggedness of our beautiful but socially exclusive Pango-Pango, and the picturesque ranges of British Samoa, Tongatabu looks flat beyond the literal sense of the word. It was the Tongans in the prospect, and the little kingdom, that made Tongatabu seem particularly inviting.

At Vavau, the first of the Tongan ports on the way down from Samoa, the amiable port doctor had settled the quarantine matter in our favour—settled it for the whole kingdom, so there was to be no week on Nukualofa's little island for the isolated. In Nukualofa, so they told us, we were to be searched for rhinoceros beetles. Copra-making is the only industry in Tonga. One pair of healthy beetles might wreck the kingdom.

A crowd was on the pier to meet the boat. Mostly Tongans, naturally; there are less than six hundred Europeans in the whole Friendly Island group, against about twenty-four thousand natives.

At first sight, the Tongans seemed like modified Samoans. Many heads of frizzy hair, running almost to kinkiness, suggested the infusion of another race. Their large, dark eyes evinced the same lively interest in us as newly arrived Europeans, but with a subtle change in attitude. Expressed offhand, the difference between the Samoan and the Tongan gaze is that one is a welcome and the other a scrutiny.

But among themselves there was the same carefree laughter, disarming enough when coupled with a willingness to assist with the luggage for the expected sixpence or two. Dinky little flat cars on a miniature railroad, with a horse for tractive power, soon transferred our effects up the long causeway to the shore.

At the custom house I showed my fumigation certificate and denied all acquaintance with beetles. I also had to declare that in my luggage there were no articles of Samoan make—souvenirs and the like. One article with the Samoan touch would have "queered" the lot; my effects, if admitted at all, would have had to be thoroughly hand-picked and refumigated.

In a kingdom that is without a hotel, the alternative is

Tongan house in Nukualofa

Tongans in the country, Tongatabu

The Tongan Queen's Palace, Nukualofa

the kingdom's one and only boarding house. Here I settled for a month.

A room with one door opening on a veranda, and another back into the house; no windows—not even the usual swinging shutters which give ventilation when the doors are closed. Strict privacy, then, meant an airtight compartment. In my Nukualofa home, I was no stickler for strict privacy.

A shower bath—the only sign of waterworks about the place—with a pump which the bather worked with one hand while he did the best he could with the other. The lack of coördination reminded me of the old trick of trying to pat the head and rub the chest at the same time. My bathing hand had an awkward way of keeping stroke with the pumper.

A portly Tongan woman as chambermaid, who did her work to the accompaniment of an enormous cigarette. Daily she hung out the towels to dry in the sun, until necessity would drive me to ask for clean ones. We differed slightly as to how many days a towel ought to serve without a recess at the laundry; but as she differed in Tongan and I in English, there was no decision.

A table as well supplied as circumstances permitted took care of the inner man; around it, all the detached white persons in Nukualofa—New Zealanders, Australians, and a Britisher or two—made an agreeable company. For a month I was to live in a growing appreciation of the courtesy and kindliness of these men and women from the South.

* * *

The grateful coolness of the air encourages one to get about. Apia's high humidity is absent, and the temperature is a few degrees lower. With an umbrella to keep off the hot sun, walking is a comfortable pastime on almost any winter day in Tongatabu.

This, the first week in August, is midwinter. So was July midwinter in Apia; but Apia is only one thousand land miles south of the Equator, while Nukualofa is fifteen hundred—almost exactly the same distance south as Honolulu is north. That extra five hundred miles away from the Line gives Nukualofa less heat, a more stable trade wind, the vertical sun only at one time in the year —and, because of that, an appreciable change of seasons. With every one of Honolulu's far-famed climatic advantages, and a rich island back of her, Nukualofa holds the promise of a future in the South Pacific. At present it is a town of a few squares, sufficient to take care of the island's copra trade and house the people interested in the government and the various religious organizations. Religious enterprise is almost as much in evidence as in Apia, but the only signs of trade are a few small stores and the buildings of two South Sea corporations which do business in every island port. The little European section of Nukualofa is well painted, neat, and as lively as a Maine village on a hot Sunday afternoon.

As befits the capital of a native kingdom, a large part of the population is native. The word "kingdom" accounts for a striking difference between the non-participating Samoans who live in Apia and the participating Tongans in Nukualofa. The Samoans tuck themselves in back of the Europeans as outsiders; the Tongans, whether their abodes are frame cottages or the native grass house, front on the streets as citizens.

This is the Tongans' country. They know it, they feel

it, and they show it in their bearing. Not that they are overbearing—the Nukualofan Tongans merely give a distinct impression that they are standing on their own ground. Many besides half-castes wear European clothes in Nukualofa.

The Tongans make a display of their independence mostly because they lack a sense of humour. The British Consul exercises a fatherly care over native affairs under the advice of the British High Commissioner in Fiji, who is appointed by the King. Further to assist in this altruistic work, the Chief Justice, Auditor General, Minister of Public Works, and Treasurer are Britishers, as are also the Post and Customs officials. These constitute the British "Protectorate." A native parliament furnishes the political fireworks and satisfies the native yearning for oratory.

So carefully protected, the Independent Kingdom of Tonga can play around at the end of the British leash to its heart's content, until Great Britain gets ready to twitch in the line.

In the absence of an American representative, I called on the British Consul—a man whose many years in government service in Fiji had brought him promotion to Tonga as Silent Dictator. The title is adequate if not verbally consistent. Friendly colonials put me up at their little club, where evening hours which otherwise might have been dull were spent with English periodicals —and the one American weekly whose advertising bulk takes it at less than cost to every corner of the world. In that far-off club I almost learned how to trace predigested reading matter through banks of pepsinized foods and deflated coffees.

The twenty-three-year-old Queen of the Tongans I did not see—she was in retirement during my stay in Nukualofa; but the steadiest patron of the club was the Prince Consort, Tugi. Supply an *n* as usual, and pronounce it *Toongee*.

Tugi, a full-blooded young chief of high degree from one of the outlying islands, was an agreeable sort of chap to know, even if he did share the uncertainty of most colonials regarding everything American. He differed from some of them by not exposing it. About the only American subject on which he would venture with me over our too-warm beer was prohibition. I think he laid my enthusiasm for prohibition to the warmth of the beer. The Prince was also Premier of the Kingdom, and a devoted but indifferent billiard player.

*   *   *

Native life of the sort that a traveller wishes to see is rarely in the towns. After the first day of looking about Nukualofa I struck off into the country, along the inevitable shore road. The street along the shore here is not a promenade—Nukualofa is not given to promenading—but it leads both ways to native villages.

Under an almost continuous spread of great coconut trees—trees that make even this dead-level island beautiful—I strolled past the royal chapel, the palace of the Queen, the unpretentious one-story British consulate, and got away from the white man's town. On the one side, glistening through the foliage, was the intense blue of the Pacific; on the other, set into cleared spaces in the almost impenetrable bush, were native *fales*. Within a half mile these occasional habitations developed into a good-sized village.

A young Tongan girl who talked "missionally" English informed me that I was in Kolomotua. Kolomotua is typical of most native Tongan villages. The oval, grass-roofed native houses are scattered about irregularly, but with plenty of ground room, under tall coconut palms. Through persuasion of the authorities, the Tongans keep the grass trimmed down and the grounds free from rubbish. Tongan and Samoan villages are as neat and cleanly as any thriving village in our own United States; in their exquisite settings they are infinitely more picturesque. If one could keep his mind off the limitations of a native house, he might be able to work up an honest longing to spend the rest of his years in it; but a single day spent on its absolute bareness, and a night on the mats over a pebbly floor to shatter his dreams, would send him to the utilitarian prosiness of a civilized dwelling.

The Tongan *fale* differs from that of the Samoan in being permanently inclosed. This is a concession to the chilly nights of the winter season. If the inclosing is done in the old Tongan way, with snugly woven matwork in various designs, the harmonious beauty of it is not destroyed; but many of the *fales*, even in the villages well back on the island, are sided up with plain one-inch boards, with a doorlike opening before and behind covered by a hanging mat. Some of the lazier Tongans, too, if they have the requisite shillings, dodge the renewing of their grass roofs by using the white man's corrugated sheet iron— often leaving the soft-coloured woven matwork on the sides to accentuate the glare of the stuff from town. Yet taken all together, these weird combinations are not numerous enough to spoil the picturesqueness of Tongan villages.

* * *

Almost every day I wandered off to some village within walking distance from town. The village Tongans are still little-spoiled sons and daughters of nature. They meet the stranger with their quietly spoken "*Malo-lele,*" meaning literally, "Thank you, very fine"—a greeting with a melodious sound, and certainly not less sensible than our "Good-morning" on a rainy day. The "Aloha" of the Hawaiians and "T'Alofa" of the Samoans seem to have been lost here, along with some other Polynesian characteristics.

The natives on the two Tongan islands at which we stopped on the way down from Samoa—Vavau, and Haapai—responded almost always to my "*Malo-lele*" with "*Oe, malo-lele,*" meaning, "Yes, thank you, very fine." The "*Oe*" is supposed to give added cordiality. But when a Tongan on this island says "*Oe,*" he stops there. He answers your "Thank you, very fine" with a plain "Yes"—and that is a sure signal in Tongatabu that he desires to have the conversation go no further. On the few occasions when I have got the "*Oe,*" I have discreetly moved on.

The village Tongans are not exactly less cordial and good-natured than the Samoans. They are quite as willing to exercise their few words of English, like to have their children noticed, and are equally amiable in the matter of photographs. Yet Tongans, when not in the mood, do not screen their indifference with politeness. They have not the Samoan's inherent courtesy.

The almost universal dress in the villages is the waist-cloth, *lava-lava*, changed here only in name to *vala*—which is *lava* with the two syllables reversed. At this season it is unusual to see it worn without other clothing, even by the men. A temperature under 70—extremely rare in the daytime—will send the natives into any covering at hand. Against the bitter cold of night—once while I was in Nukualofa the mercury dropped to 58—they shut up their houses as nearly airtight as possible and wind themselves in tappa cloth.

The Tongans make more copra than the Samoans. They have to. Every male Tongan at his sixteenth year is allotted about eight acres of coconut land, and a little plot in his village for a *fale*. These, of course, he cannot sell—and he must pay rent whether he wants the land or not. It is a gift with a decided string to it.

Land rent, extra clothing, the demands of the church, and the cost of boards and corrugated roofing if their tastes happen to run that way—these compel the Tongans to make an appreciable amount of copra. It is well that they have to, for in the absence of indentured or imported labour of any sort the whole commerce of the Friendly Islands—and the preservation of the kingdom, for that matter—depends upon the copra turned out by the natives themselves.

The less debilitating climate favours them, and their allotments assure plenty of coconuts. Even at that they work only a small fraction of the time at copra-making. The Tongans are not forced out of the leisure class by the total of all the shillings required of them.

Like other natives who work grudgingly at civilized pursuits, Tongans will put in an incredible amount of labour on anything which serves directly their own ends. A shining example of this is in their making of tappa cloth.

A short club in a woman's hand, raised above her head and skilfully brought down five thousand times on a piece of young mulberry bark laid across a smooth log in front of her—this might make a square foot or so of tappa. Piece by piece it has to be put together with a gum of their own making, dried in the sun, and ornamented with designs carefully daubed on with a stick.   Who wants to calculate the hours-per-yard cost of tappa?

Even as an article for use about the house, tappa has survived the invasion of the traders' cheap cloths to a surprising extent, when the immense labour of making it is considered.   Tappa is one of the Tongan signs of resistance to civilization, and the resistance reaches its climax in the use of this native cloth as a winding for the dead.

The windings require great quantities of tappa.   In their villages I have seen a single piece laid out on the grass fifteen feet wide and one hundred and eighty-five feet long; another, of the same width, one hundred and fifty feet long.   Lengths of forty to sixty feet are common.

This incredible outlay of toil, simply because they will not have the white man's cloth around their dead—in our own lives, is there one example of arduous personal devotion to an ideal which remotely approaches this of the Tongans?

*   *   *

Another survival of an old Tongan custom is the women's habit of wearing decrepit mats tied around their waists as a sign of mourning. It persists even among the well-dressed native women of Nukualofa. The more shabby and ragged the mat, the greater is the wearer's sorrow for the departed.

Among the villagers living as Tongans have always lived, one thinks no more of this mourning custom than of our wearing of black; but frayed and dingy mats tied around the neat European dresses of girls and women on their way to Sunday morning church in Nukualofa strike rather forcibly at one's sense of the incongruous.

*   *   *

Kolomotua, of all the villages on the island, has no church. This is because the people of Kolomotua go to church in Nukualofa. Every other village of a few *fales* has at least two churches out of the six denominations covering the Friendly Islands.

The Tongans seem to have had about the same religious experience as the Samoans: a decline in chieftainship, a void to be filled, and the rise of a native ministry. They take to religion for obvious reasons, and they pass up the rest of civilization for reasons as obvious.

The inhabitants of the Friendly Islands were once anything but friendly. Warlike, fierce, brave—and as cannibals not far removed in savagery from the Fijians. Now, they all go to church. They *enjoy* it—and without their church they would be holy terrors. But the multitude of native preachers!

Getting contributions from members is a skilfully conducted business. Churches are stirred to rivalry in the matter of collections—not churches of rival denominations, but of the same denomination, and by their own pastors.

Such and such a church has collected so much; shall we let them get ahead of us? No! Then the contest is on.

The giver has the inspiration of publicity. Each donor marches up forward, while songs and chantings stir his emotions to a pitch of financial indiscretion, and lays down his money in full view. If it is not up to expectations, the native pastor is rarely backward in voicing his desire that the brother or sister come again. But many a donor gives less at first than he intends to eventually, so as to have the pleasure of one or two more parades to the front.

Raising money for the church stimulates copra-making and trade, and with it comes the eternal question, as in other South Sea islands, whether a church and a preacher for about every one hundred inhabitants are a necessary incumbrance.

But the traders like the copra, and the preachers like the money, and the people like the excitement—and the people are not very busy anyway.

The Tongan takes his Christianity back with him into the old Tongan atmosphere. To the call of the native tom-tom beaten with a club he gathers at a church built like a *fale*, squats on a native mat and listens to a native preacher in his native tongue, sings songs in Tongan set to native music, and works himself into the superstitious fervor of his ancestors.

That's the way he likes it. And as we civilized people have our Christianity served up in forty different ways to suit individual tastes, why criticize the Tongans and Samoans? *Laissez faire.*

There's an indescribable weirdness in the sound of the tom-tom giving its call in the still hours. A log six to eight feet long, hollowed out like a feeding trough and left solid at the ends—this is the Tongan tom-tom. Struck on one edge with a short club, it has just enough resonance to save the sound from being a noise. Even when a church has a bell, as in town, it also has a tom-tom—and the bell-ringer, after a few feeble jerks of the bell, falls upon the tom-tom with a vigour that proclaims his love for it. The *boom, boom, boom,* at night off in the villages takes one as nothing else can back into the primitiveness of the old Tongan days.

* * *

Of the forty-nine automobiles in the kingdom, all except a very few are of a certain make. In a car of this make I set out one summer-like day with the auditing agent of the largest copra company in the South Seas, on a tour of their buying stations. This kind invitation of the auditor gave me one of my most enlightening days in Tonga.

Over a well-surfaced road we ran for a dozen miles almost across the island. From there on for the rest of the day the roads were cleared trails through long stretches of jungle—so well cleared and open to the sun that at this season, when rains are few and little more than showers, the way is fairly passable. The absolute flatness of the country makes travelling easy in the dry season and a terror in the wet.

Vividly pictured is nature's struggle in the tangle of life underneath the majestically waving fronds of the coconut palms. Flowering plants and flowering bushes, even trees bearing large, richly coloured blooms, lend a gay covering to this contest for existence. Soil and climate in the tropics invite extravagant growth. Then, if a dozen plants try to live where one might do very well, it is their business to fight out the question of survival. The weak succumb, and the strong live. On a drive through the jungle we see only the joyous picture of the favoured ones which nature has selected to maintain the vigour of species.

Now and then we came to little patches of clearing, dug up by hand and planted to taro, yams, and perhaps a few bananas. But the one staple product of the island is copra; that grows with only the planting of coconuts wherever they are not already growing of their own accord.

In every village are copra-buying stations of rival traders—sometimes only two, oftener several, depending on the amount of copra produced in the district and the individual notions of the traders. They are all pretty much alike: a raised platform thirty to fifty feet square, on which the coconut meat brought in by the natives is spread out to dry; at one corner of it, a small warehouse for weighing, receiving, and storing the copra in its various stages; and the trading store, its shelves laden with tinned goods, bolts of gaily coloured cloth, matches, tinware, and odds of all sorts.

According to a law of the kingdom, all copra must be paid for in cash; then the native pays cash for his purchases in the store. The law fairly shines with wisdom. When the native had to trade his copra direct for goods, he found it confusing business to translate the value of one into the value of the other. Now, he gets the whole proceeds in money which he has learned to count; he can buy what he wants, and where he wants, or go home with his money if he wishes.

This law has taken the chief joy from the lives of un-
scrupulous traders. This and the fierce competition of
these latter days have put most of their kind out of business. If any survive, they tread the thorny path of
rectitude.

*   *   *

On arriving at a company station I would usually leave
the auditor to do his business with the agent—a native,
as these agents are almost without exception—and stroll
off for a look about the village. In one of the villages I
stopped at the cricket ground, where a group was about
to begin playing. Nearly every village has its cricket
ground, and in a kingdom where every day is a holiday,
the men spend much of their time in playing.

One of these men came forward to meet me and tendered me his bat. Never having had one in my hands, I
was glad to see it. I noticed that it was not at all like a
baseball bat.

But the man kept on saying something, and pointing
to the weapon in my hands. Finally it dawned on me—
he wanted my expert opinion on his bat.

I had to be either dishonest or disappointing, so I chose
the honourable course under the circumstances. I ex-
amined the bat carefully, balanced it, squinted down its
edges, gave it a thoughtful swing or two.

"*Lele*" (very fine), I remarked with conviction, as I
handed it back to the owner. Exultantly he turned to his
companions and shouted the verdict.

In a moment I was surrounded with cricket bats. Some
were fairly new, others evidently were the ancient dis-
cards of Europeans. Each one had to come under my
impartial judgment.

All the bats were found to be "*lele.*" A deep split in the club end of one had to be noticed, but I passed it off as a minor defect.

Of the company's thirty-odd stations on Tongatabu we must have visited at least fifteen that day. Something different was always bobbing up to make each village interesting.

At one of the stations, the company's agent was a half-caste son of an American whaling captain of some fifty years ago. He spoke no English, and his skin was quite dark; but I have rarely seen a stronger American face. The auditor pronounced him "the best man on the job." By all the signs, in his clear-cut features he had the inheritance of some fine old New England stock.

Again I was held by that intense fascination of the half-caste. An American who did not know his own tongue, with perhaps half brothers in business in Boston! His nephews, nieces—who are they? I know several descendants of whalers—could this man's politely bred relatives be friends of mine? His half sisters—what would they say if they were to meet him now? Well, if they said anything, it would have to be through an interpreter.

Then I fell to wondering whether he himself ever got into these speculations? Why not?—he knows about his father. But what does he know about his country? And what a joke it would be on some Back Bay family whom leather, or cotton, or wool has made aristocratic, if this man were to enter the sacred portals as a brother, or an uncle!

To such ramblings there is no end. The relentless auditor started the engine and we rode away. At the last sight of this American with a banker's face and a

Tongan skin, he was contemplatively watching us disappear. And I had to wonder again—is some vague picture of his connection with us shaping itself in his mind?

But probably he was thinking of his business with the auditor.

At the next stop my friend had to take a complete inventory of the goods in the store. I took pictures of a *fale* or two and a pretty girl, walked down to the seashore under the guidance of a native boy to some bat-inhabited caves in the coral rock, and wandered about the little place of less than a half-dozen houses and the inevitable church. The hour might have been more than sufficient for the sights at hand if it had not carried me into the lunch time of the pretty girl and her family.

Watching any person eat is a disillusionment, especially if one's admiration has been running above the ordinary; but watching a pleasant-faced Tongan girl eat is a positive downfall.

The family laid the meal out on palm leaves spread under the trees, and sat around it on more palm leaves, after the manner of village Tongans. Then they went at it. Taro, camellas (a kind of sweet potato), something that looked like breadfruit, and scraps of meat that might have been pork but probably was chicken—these were picked with the fingers from the steaming mess and literally packed into the mouths.

Taking in big pieces is less effort than biting off small ones, and Tongans seem fond of chewing with oxlike placidity. Once the girl got her mouth so full that when she tried to bite she could not get her teeth together —so she deliberately began over.

Having seen enough of a Tongan repast, I went back

to the car and sat in the front seat.   Soon the girl followed, glanced into the tonneau—and spied our lunch in the bottom of an open goods-box.

A Tongan can always eat, but that lunch had been provided by my host.   My interest in it was merely anticipatory, yet that was enough to make me alert.

Leisurely the girl reclined against the tonneau door, until one elbow rested on the box.   She smiled at me engagingly—then fixed her eyes on something back of me.

My eyes did not follow hers.   An instant's turning would have cost us at least a handful of biscuits.

I smiled back at her elaborately as I tucked my raincoat around the lunch box.   She may have been a daughter of the preacher in the church across the way, but I knew the meaning of that careless gesture toward our chow.

Yet after that glance at white man's food neatly wrapped in paper napkins, she was not to be so easily discouraged.   Strolling back to the remains of her own lunch, she soon reappeared with a camella, which she smilingly offered me.

I did not succumb to the blandishment.   After the native custom, this was an open bid for something out of our box.

This South Sea island custom of exchanging gifts is one of the most universal of the native practices which have survived the coming of white men.   I have seen tourists who could not be made to understand that they were leaving a trail of indignant natives behind them by accepting trinkets without paying for them.   They go home and prate to their friends about "the natives who came to us bearing gifts!"

The custom is carried to ridiculous lengths.   If a native pointedly admires anything in a friend's house, it must at once be offered to him—and he usually takes it. But he must be prepared to have the donor invade his own home and carry off his best possession.

Visiting between villages in these islands is often equivalent to a cleaning-out of the visited—and a return visit is a lugging back of mats, baskets, food—each intending to get a little the better of the trade.

It is a devastating custom. Some headway has been made toward checking it. I did the kingdom a service by not making a swap with the pretty Tongan girl.

* * *

As we rode along between copra stations through the jungle, my friend told me a strange, if unromantic, tale. Not far ahead of us on this road, he said, lived an American—a middle-aged man, and quite deaf. A supersensitiveness over his affliction was the reason for his being here. He had sought seclusion from humankind on the back end of a Tongan island.

Thousands of harassed men in civilization have dreamed of getting away from the world and all its worries in the same manner. It is a popular dream, this living under a coconut tree, with nothing to do but sleep and eat. A heavenly isolation in an earthly paradise. A great life for a cat—until he gets to longing for another cat.

Here was a man who had followed the dream to its reality. And of course he had not found the longed-for seclusion. Wherever people are scarcest, one is apt to be most plagued with company. The best place to hide from humankind is in a crowd. The closer the neighbours the less they speak.

If this man had taken a room in New York City, he would have had only to pay his rent by mail, eat in an automatic restaurant, and walk unhailed in the throngs on Broadway, to live a life of perfect isolation. But in Tonga——!

With half of the island peering at him, the recluse probably had not seen an American for an age. Should I stop and have a chat with him on the strength of a common citizenship? Or should I respect his desire for seclusion, his supersensitiveness, and pass by?

Stop, by all means. Show the old boy a glad hand, and shout the latest news from America. Give him something to think of for the next ten years. Make this one day different—he has three hundred and sixty-five every year pretty much alike. Stop, of course.

Then I switched over to the other view. This man came here to get away from a hundred million Americans. I'm one of them. What business have I to break in on him? He would know at once that I had been told his story—and that in itself would make him resent my coming. Curiosity—so he would think—and at that he would be thinking a half truth. No—respect his eccentricity. Stay away.

By the time I had got the thing into a complete muddle, my friend remarked, "Here is the place. Shall we stop?"

I stared in befuddled silence. A neatly planted little yard, and back of it a low cottage, not well in sight from the road. As I looked, a clear way to the house came into view, and in the centre of it stood the deaf American, regarding us fixedly: tall, gaunt, gray-haired, and as motionless as a statue during the few seconds of his revealment.

We passed by. The lone figure had no sooner been cut off by the foliage than once more I was torn by conflicting impulses.

Not speak to a compatriot way off here among a lot of uncomprehending natives? How would you yourself like to have another American pass you by in a wilderness some ten thousand miles from home?

It sounds well, I answered myself, but suppose I had fled into that wilderness some ten thousand miles from home to get away from people; what would I think of a man who, knowing my story, had the effrontery to come in on me uninvited? *I* should be the one to decide whether I wanted to see people—and if I did, I could go to Nukualofa, or back home.

Anyhow, we did not turn back. Indecision is one of the reasons why I would not do at all as president of a railroad.

I wonder whether the reader would have stopped or passed by?

* * *

Tongatabu has the distinction—or it would be a distinction if more people knew about it—of harbouring the most mysterious object in the South Sea islands. An immense trilithon, set up in the jungle near this road over which we were travelling, gives the archæologists a puzzle still unsolved, and excites the wonder of the few who get so far off beaten tracks as to see it. "Haamonga" is its local name, but the word explains nothing.

We came upon it shortly after leaving the American. Partly hidden by the luxuriant growth, it stands not more than a hundred yards back from the road. Two square-hewn pillars of coral rock, each five to six feet in thickness, stand nearly twenty feet high and as many feet apart; these support another huge beam of rock laid horizontally into deep mortises in their tops. How far into the ground the monoliths extend, or whether excavations would reveal anything more, nobody has tried to find out.

The great rocks are worn down by the storms of hundreds, perhaps thousands, of years. This trilithon resembles those of Stonehenge only in being made up of three huge stones; the clever mortising of the top stone indicates a craftsmanship far superior to that of the Druids.

The Haamonga stands as a relic from a civilization of which we as yet know nothing. Archæologists have not even guessed at its age. The only certainty about it is that the engineering feats involved are absolutely beyond the capacity of the Tongans. The Tongans do not even have a tradition concerning the Haamonga. Apparently, it is related to other hewn stones found in its vicinity, and to some immense stone tombs near Mua, a native village only a few miles away, but the origin of these is as completely wrapped in oblivion.

If the Haamonga were not so isolated it might excite more interest and encourage speculation. Nobody knows what it was for, or whether it formed part of a greater structure which has disappeared. Possibly when archæologists have solved the mysteries of our own wonderful Egypt in Central America, they may be able to tell us more about this monument in Tongatabu. For me, it marked the climax of a well-filled day.

* * *

In Tonga, as in many South Sea islands, kava is the national drink. In Samoa they call it "ava" because there is no *k* in their alphabet, but the beverage is the same.

In the old times, the kava root was first masticated to a savoury pulp by young girls whose mouths were supposed to be notably clean, and the resulting juice—or juices—mixed with water. The white traders liked kava, but their fondness for the drink was clouded by thoughts of the process. So the traders, although not specially given to reforming anything, brought about a reform in the making of kava. Nowadays, the root is pounded into shreds, then tied up in cloths, which are mashed, squeezed, wrung, and twisted in a bucket of water by as many brown hands as can get into it. The improvement in method is largely sentimental. Having observed the new way, I have a leaning toward the old.

I have drunk kava with as much relish as I would drink dishwater, which it resembles more closely than anything else. And what is more to the credit of my heroic nature, I have drunk kava after watching the natives make it. It was because I had to, or give mortal offence.

When used freshly made, as it almost always is, kava is not intoxicating; but because of some drug effect in it the kava-drinking habit grows on the drinker, until, in the case of Tongan natives at least, it becomes a widespread dissipation. Heavy drinking brings on a temporary paralysis of the legs—and of the legs only.

Imagine the effect. A man may be dead drunk from the hips down, while his mind is as sober as that of the proverbial judge. Kava is the only beverage which puts the right end of a man out of commission. It makes him safer to be at large than when he is sober.

The after effects of steady indulgence are a general weakening of the system and a scaling off of cuticle.

Kava drunkards can be distinguished by whitened patches of skin, especially about the legs.

Kava-drinking opens most native ceremonial gatherings. One might naturally think that the head chief would be the first to drain the coconut bowl; but good form decrees that two subchiefs must first partake of the liquid. This old custom—and indeed the origin of kava itself—is accounted for in one of their legends. This legend was told me by a man who had an ear for the picturesque in language. I shall try to follow him with a free version:

Back in the days when big chiefs held office through their skill at dodging poisoned drinks and the javelin thrusts of impatient ones in the succession, it was the habit of the chief to choose as a bodyguard from among his subchiefs the two whom he least mistrusted; and since this number enabled him to keep one tight eye on each, he felt comparatively safe in their company.

One day, these three, walking along the banks of a pool, saw a rat gnawing at a root strange to them.

"Ha!" said the chief. "Another edible root is discovered, methinks!" (This happened a long time ago.)

But the rat, they noticed, after chewing the root meditatively, often ran back to the water and drank with gusto.

"Ho!" said the chief. "The pleasure, I trow, comes in the mixing of it with water."

So he ordered the subchiefs to gather samples of the root; and beautiful young girls—not to repeat unnecessary details—were chosen to follow as closely as possible the prescription of the rat in making the new drink.

When all was done, the first subchief offered his master a bowl of the milky fluid.

"No," remarked the chief. "What is good for a rat may not be good for man. I shall watch with interest its effect upon you. Besides," he added significantly, "*you* offer it."

That was enough. According to the strained etiquette of the times, the subchief had to prove the innocence of his offering by drinking of it. He tasted, drank, finished the shell-full, and smacked his lips as the sign of a delicious after taste.

At that, the second subchief dipped a shell into the liquid and tendered it to the old man.

"Not so fast," said the chief. "You, if my memory serves me well, are the next in succession. Temptation is a dreadful monster. After you, my dear Alphonse!" he exclaimed jovially—in the Tongan equivalents.

Thereupon the second subchief drank heartily, and rolled his eyes as the sign of a ravishing after taste.

Satisfied, the old chief drank. And drank. And drank. The last half of the pailful he took sitting, but his mind was perfectly clear, and an eagle eye still followed each of his faithful bodyguards.

So kava was discovered. And to this day in all Tongan ceremonials, two subchiefs taste it before the head chief imbibes.

* * *

Luckily for the Tongans, our hectic struggle for property—the basic principle of our civilization—hasn't the ghost of a show of infecting their scheme of life. Their communal system, combined with the ridiculous "gift habit," bars them from anything more than a desultory imitation of white men.

They have no incentive to accumulate, because the

accumulation would at once be appropriated by others still lazier. If one kills a pig, the village helps eat it. The sound of pounding kava root in a *fale* is the signal for all thirsty men and women within hearing to flock in for a drink. The man who works on the dock and brings home a few groceries to his *fale* is at once visited by a crowd of appreciative neighbours.

Then why attempt to keep anything? Every man's allotment of coconut land and his obligation for it are fixed for life; he makes copra to pay rent, and just enough more to buy stuff at the trader's store which he can eat or use before some friend admires it away from him. After that, it's just as profitable and a lot easier to loaf.

Theirs is the hand-to-mouth life of birds and fishes. Churches, cricket, football, and iron roofs do not so much as make a dent on the mental attitude induced by this old order of living.

But what's the matter with it—for the Tongans?

Nothing. A desire for accumulation and ownership would bring with it all the crimes and ferocities which are inspired by an urge to gain, to hold—redoubled, in the case of these grown-up children, because of their child minds. The white man's ambitions, thrift, and greed don't fit in with the ways of tropical peoples. Missionaries have brought them religion, but not, thank God, civilization.

*   *   *

Religious schools educate natives to a life which can find little expression in Tonga—then the educators wonder why most of them go "back to the mat."

Where else could they go? Aside from the ministry and one or two positions in each of the larger villages as

Tongan house, showing mat-woven sides

Tonga's great Trilithon, "Hoamonga"

Scene on the Rewa River, Viti Levu, Fiji

Fijian house, Lautoka

traders' agents, almost no other work is open to them. They seem contented to fall into the life of their people —make a little copra off their allotments, play cricket, attend meeting, and live on the mats. Lucky it is when they can do this contentedly, because the only alternative for them is discontent.

But a few cannot go back so easily. In one village I met a Tongan girl who interested me as an example of what education can do for one of her kind. She had had instruction in English, and spoke the language fairly well.

She was back to the native way of living, and apparently making the best of it. But she did like to talk with me and show me her knowledge of English ways and English manners. Her "I beg your pardon?" whenever some expression of mine went over her head was as politely done as that of any finishing-school girl. She disliked to admit total ignorance of a word. If I used one which she did not know, she would say in her very distinct way, "I have heard that word—what is its meaning?" I caught myself talking to her with the same precision.

The girl seemed cheerful enough, but the undernote was of a wistfulness that told as clearly as words the impossibility of her situation. Instead of the native *vala* she wore a European dress—and it was clean, which in itself marked her as different. Shoes and stockings would have been out of place in the village. The cheap cotton dress was her only sign of variance from the ways of all other native girls.

She got me to take her picture with a girl friend; but without shoes and stockings she would not have it taken standing. Down on the ground they both sat, and over the bare knees of both she arranged foliage so that they would not show in the picture.

Intent on suppressing the Tongan in her, making her pose as like that of a white girl as she could, yet Tongan she was to the last drop of her blood—a girl at pathetic odds with her own self!

She told me that she was a Methodist and nineteen years old. Thoughtlessly, I asked her if she was married. I did not realize that it might hurt. She hesitated, then answered slowly, "No—not yet."

In Tonga, to be nineteen and not married is a calamity. Yet whom could she marry? Certainly not a white man —and I could not conceive of her marrying a village Tongan. For an English-taught girl like her, living with a Tongan father and mother was nothing compared to living with a Tongan husband. What on earth *could* she do?

I wish some missionary would explain this to me: in taking a Tongan girl out of her native village, educating her in English and to English ways, and turning her back to her village again, how do they make out that they are doing her *good*

*   *   *

One day is sufficient for viewing all the sights on Tongatabu; but a month of browsing around among its people grows more fruitful of humanly interesting touches as the days pass. In a hundred years, our exotic culture has broken through only here and there into lives shaped to resist it through ages of a different mode. Speaking commonly, the Tongan is a tough nut to crack

Usually, peoples born to be let alone are the most easily

meddled with, but the Tongan is stubborn where the Samoan is indifferent. That is why he alone of all in the South Seas has been permitted the form of an independent kingdom to play with.

It used to be said in the old days that one Tongan could whip fifty Fijians. And white men? There is no standing record of his prowess with white men. In those days, he merely ate all who came his way. Not with any particular relish, for the Tongan, like all other cannibals in the Pacific, complained that white men were "too salty." It may be that from this poor flavour of ours rose his deference to the pig.

When his broad, fertile acres are needed for the plough, and sugar cane and pineapple plantations have displaced the coconut palms, and along with them his easy living, will the Tongan settle back wistfully twirling his thumbs as the Hawaiian has, and as the Samoan will when his time comes? I wonder.

*   *   *

Once more I am on the *Tofua*, this time bound for Fiji. If this handy tourist-freighter were going direct from Nukualofa to Suva, the Fiji capital, I would be there in forty-eight hours. As it is, she has come from Suva to Nukualofa, and is going back by way of several Tongan ports and Samoa. For eight days, then, I shall be an ordinary tourist, among a hundred others fresh from New Zealand, "doing" the islands.

The *Tofua* is little, but her capacity is limitless. After every stateroom is filled with three, the second-class packed, freight hatches overflowing, and her decks heaped with lumber, she can take on a hundred or so natives and a few horses without shifting an anchor or displacing a coil of rope. This is because they—the natives—sit on the anchor, coil up in the rope, and sleep on the lumber. It is called "going deck passage"—a lark for the natives, whose journey will end on the second day out, at Vavau.

Up the gangway they came in a seemingly never-ending flow. Both forward and aft they made their way in two steady streams, quickly appropriating unoccupied spots on the deck freight and spreading out their mats as a sign of preëmption. A chattering, laughing, happy lot, this mob that flows perennially, by way of the *Tofua's* decks, between Nukualofa and Vavau.

Who are they?

"Visitors" from Vavau, returning home, loaded with the spoils of social intercourse and wreathed in contented smiles; and the "visited" Nukualofans, empty-handed but eager, now making a return depredation on their Vavau friends.

It's a great and exciting game, this "visiting" between Tongans. We had picked up the same sort of a crowd at Vavau on the way down from Samoa, a month before. Then, it was the returning Nukualofans who were loaded with "gifts"; the Vavauans carried little more than their lunch baskets.

Fifty Fijian deck hands, camped on the fore and aft freight hatches under awnings, made no appreciable increase in the deck congestion. They couldn't.

This carrying Fijian freight handlers was a recent innovation. The steamer had always depended upon local workers. But a few trips before, on its arrival at Nukualofa, the Tongan dock men demanded a stiff raise in pay before they would touch the freight. Dealing with natives on a tight little island in the middle of the Pacific, and Tongans at that, the *Tofua* capitulated.

On the next trip the Nukualofans cheerfully doubled their rate again—and got it. But on her third appearance a month later the doughty little steamer carried fifty big, woolly-haired Fijians, taken on at Suva, and to be dropped at Suva on the return trip to Auckland, with a goodly number of shillings tucked in their belts.

The arrangement suited the Fijians and it suited the Company. The Tongans? Theirs was a case of "two strikes and out." Each Steamer Day recalls to them the unwisdom of that second raise.

*   *   *

Getting in undamaged through the coral reefs to an anchorage off Haapai, our first Tongan port out from Nukualofa, is a tribute to the skill of any navigator, even when it is done in broad daylight. Our captain holds his job because he can make this and other harbours like it without scraping the keel of his little four-thousand-ton vessel—not because of any special amiability toward his tourists, nor because of pronounced fondness for Americans. His personal leanings were distinctly, at times loudly, the other way. If the two were to compete for his disfavour, I should say that the Americans would win over the tourists, although by a narrow margin.

However, in sailing the South Seas it is better to have an ogre—not that this captain is one, mind you—who can dodge the reefs, than a gallant who hits them now and then. Oddly, he seemed to tolerate me; and toleration, in him, shone by comparison like a consuming love. We got on without a hitch.

The little village of Haapai, made up of natives, here and there a trader, and the few necessary officials of the "Protectorate," is strung along the shore. Immediately back of it begins the coconut forest that covers the island.

Apia makes a gala event of Steamer Day. Nukualofa receives the boat with subdued curiosity, now that she has lost her job of unloading it. Haapai may wake up from her month-long rest after the boat has left, and learn that we arrived. Curiosity may be fatal at times, but lack of it is the sign of a dead one.

The tourists scattered about in the native village to watch the everlasting beating of tappa cloth, bought cards at the post office, or walked through the coconut forest to the windward side of the island—a half-mile walk—for a view of the magnificent surf. I dropped in on a trader whose acquaintance I had made on the way down from Samoa a month before.

In Haapai it is the same story as in every Tongan island. Without imported labour, just so much copra is made as the natives themselves are willing to make—which is mighty little. Therefore, according to this trader's view, business in Haapai was dead. He would like more opportunity, he said, for white men, and imported labour to show these natives a thing or two—bringing five times as much copra out of the groves, and so on.

The same old cry of the trader. Natives and the natives' country ought to be made useful—to the traders.

Now, why should I start an argument with this trader by venturing the opinion that the natives are better off with the white man's business quite as dead as it is? And what's the use asking him who invited him to come and who's urging him to stay?

I strolled off across the island, reclined on the clean white sand a long way off from the shell-gathering tourists, and lazily watched the five-mile stretch of huge rollers crash over the coral reefs a few hundred yards offshore; while the tropical sun and the gentle southeast trade combined to give me one blessed hour of the Tongan's carefree happiness.

A year of it? Well, a year of it would be like sitting down to a barrel of candy. I'm not a Tongan. And a Tongan, harnessed to our daily routine for a week, would want to die. Why can't we let each other alone?

* * *

Solid coral islands several hundred feet high are a geological anomaly, yet such is the Vavau group. Through some great upheaval, the coral-building insects suddenly found themselves lifted high in the air. It must have been a stunning surprise, after labouring for ages, merely to get up for a peek at things around low tide.

From a distance, these flat-topped domes of rich green impress one as no more than two or three large islands. On closer view, they separate as the channels of deep sea open between them. At their bases, new coral reefs have formed nearly to the surface, giving the waters a wonderful shading of colours, from the rich blue of the great depths to the greens and yellows of the coral shoals. These, merging into the variegated greens of the abrupt walls of the islands and the changing colours of the sky, make a picture unmatched, although perhaps not unexcelled, in tropical beauty in other parts of the South Seas. It is a masterpiece second only to that of our Pango-Pango.

Because the shore here is too abrupt and offers no foot-hold, the village of Neiafu is not the usual shore-line affair. As a pleasing novelty, its houses are perched against the hillsides and scattered about among the knolls and valleys back from the landing pier. Another full day on this beautiful island—we had stopped here on the way down from Samoa—was compensation enough for having to take the longest-way-around trip to Fiji.

On a trail leading off into the country, I happened upon a family starting out to gather oranges to sell at the steamer. Vavau is the only place in the world where I have seen oranges growing wild; here they grow in profusion off in the jungle. I suppose somebody knows how oranges happened to get all over several of these islands, and why, living wholly uncared for, they are so uniformly good. Nobody whom I met was able to enlighten me, so I had to take the evidence of the oranges themselves that they grow at haphazard and are delicious.

I followed this family down a lane, then off into the jungle. By the time I came upon them, a young man was up in a magnificent orange tree thirty or forty feet high, plying an axe with vigour.

"*Malo-lele*," I remarked to the waiting group.

"*Oe, malo-lele*," answered a pleasant young woman, stepping forward. "You come on steamer?"

This girl had attended one of the church "colleges" for a year in Nukualofa. Now, she was not distinguishable from the rest of her family, except by her knowledge of English. As we talked, there was a great crashing of branches, and down came half of the immense orange tree, yellow with its burden of ripe fruit.

"Why do you cut the tree down?" I asked the girl,

knowing perfectly well why, of course, after a month of acquaintance with the Tongan way of doing things.

"To get oranges," she answered, surprised at such an odd question.

To justify myself, I asked another: "But why don't you pick the oranges, let tree grow, get more oranges next year?" I always try to keep my language within the native understanding.

"Oranges too far, no can pick," she explained confidently. Then, with a wave of her hand, "Next year? Another tree."

That settled it. Not only next year, but next time they happen to want oranges, it will be "another tree." The girl's education in Nukualofa had not budged her from the Tongans' reliance upon an always provident nature. When the trees are gone, they will do without oranges. Luckily, they do not think it necessary to chop down coconut palms to get the nuts. They climb up for them.

* * *

In our tortuous wanderings among the islands on this trip we crossed the international date line twice, thus experiencing two Wednesdays and no Monday within a single week. Yet we did not approach within hailing distance of the 180th meridian, which one ordinarily thinks of as the international date line. The line crooks itself way off to the eastward here in order to accommodate the Tongan Islands, which their "Protectors" for some reason want to have on the same time schedule as the Fijis. The Samoas have the eastern date, the Tongas and Fijis the western—one day ahead of Samoa on the calendar.

In this connection our worthy captain played a neat

little trick on the labour unions of New Zealand. In going from Apia to Niuafoou, the last of the Tongan ports on our way to Fiji, we crossed the date line for the second time on Friday night, and should have skipped from Friday to Sunday. But this would have brought us into Niuafoou on Sunday afternoon—and the all-powerful Seaman's Union, which permits the marine commerce of New Zealand and Australia only for the purpose of giving its members jobs, will not work on Sunday except at high rates of pay.

So the captain reckoned our time at Niuafoou as Saturday, by the Samoan calendar, and worked the crew at week-day wages while it was Sunday a few hundred yards away on shore. If the unholy union men had discovered that they were violating the Sabbath without being rewarded for it, the captain might have been in more trouble than the game was worth. As it was, we had our Sunday next day at sea, skipped Monday, and arrived in Fiji bright and early Tuesday morning.

But this is getting ahead of the schedule. Two Wednesdays of steaming north from Vavau brought us to Apia.

Again the smiling faces of Samoans, with here and there one that broadened a little more extravagantly than the others whenever I was recognized as the strolling visitor of a month before. The women who then had had to pack up their souvenirs and leave the quarantined vessel to its fate were now strung along in the shade of the Apian way, dangling their wares before the eyes of eager New Zealand tourists. Steamer Day, which a month before had turned out a "dud," was on at full blast in Apia.

A walk out to a near-by village disclosed that the village had gone to town. Not a soul was in the bathing pools along the stream. I pleasantly renewed acquaintance with Samoan scenes, while the Samoan heat and Samoan flies unpleasantly renewed acquaintance with me. Within an hour I was back in town, greeting traders and business men with only a word or two on this, their busiest day of the month. After a luncheon at the hotel among friends —it is astonishing what a line of acquaintances one picks up during two months in the islands—I went back to the vessel. "Willie" was not on hand at the landing—I think it was "Freddie", this time, who took me out.

*   *   *

Many miles away from any other island, Niuafoou rises out of the Pacific, a huge and not wholly extinct crater without even the semblance of a harbour. Among its population of more than a thousand are four white people. Two are traders to look after the island's copra, and two are missionaries, supposedly with the double function of looking after the natives and the traders.

Landing at Niuafoou is often so difficult that the mail is dropped overboard in a sealed can; passengers booked to land go on to Fiji and wait a month for the *Tofua's* return trip. The sea, as it happened, favoured us with only a mild roughness. We had a quantity of supplies to land, besides a middle-aged Tongan chief of some importance, several of his friends, and a considerable amount of their belongings. Evidently the party had been making a Tongan "visit."

By the time the freight and most of the chief's spoils were on their way shoreward in the lighter, and everybody, including the chief and his friends, was expecting the craft to make another trip, the captain suddenly concluded

that he could not wait.   The sun was nearing the horizon;
our vessel must be clear of the reefs before dark.   The
chief and his crowd could stay aboard, said the captain,
with the sure prospect of a month in Fiji before the vessel
would again be coming this way; or, they could jump overboard and swim ashore.   It didn't matter which, to the
captain.

We were a good half mile out, but the old chief, not in
the least perturbed, took an extra notch in the belt of
his *lava-lava*, discarded his coat, waved a cheerful good-
bye, and hopped off the gangway into the sea.   One after
another his retinue followed.   Splash! splash! and the
most novel disembarkation of passengers that I had ever
witnessed was accomplished in perfect good humour.

I have seen men and women forced to make fantastic
jumps from vessels to all sorts of bobbing craft, and I
have seen husky sailors, to a chorus of horrified "Oh's!"
from women aboard, nonchalantly toss babies across
raging gaps of sea when a nearer approach of the tender
would have crushed it; but to behold passengers travelling
first-class take to the water and swim ashore—well, it
could happen only in the South Seas, and on the *Tofua*,
with a certain captain counting the minutes to sundown.

Our last act at this last of the Tongan ports was to take
aboard a stout rowboat which had been brought out from
shore.   The thing had a familiar look; inquiry developed
that it was a lifeboat, the only surviving relic from a large
American schooner, wrecked a few weeks before on the
reefs off to the southeast.   The crew had got ashore in
this boat.   Somebody had bought it, and now it was being
shipped to Suva.

There was something fetching about watching this

American lap-streak boat being lifted out of the rough Pacific midway between Samoa, the Friendly Islands, and Fiji, and laid down on the freight deck forward. After the dinner gong had called the crowd below, and we were headed into the setting sun straight away for Fiji, I stood for some little time at the rail under the captain's bridge, gazing with a sort of fellow feeling at that lonesome piece of freight. Hard luck for the trim little boat from the homeland! Instead of lying snug in her davits under the American flag, she probably will end her days at humble shore duty somewhere along the Fiji coast.

"What a rotten time that boat would have if it could be homesick," I remarked to myself, as I went below for chow.

CHAPTER V

THE FIJI ISLANDS

FIJI, the barbarous Fiji of story books, with its cannibals extraordinary—this Fiji passed for good and all fifty years ago, when Great Britain took over the Islands as a British possession. It had then been passing for almost as long.

I landed in Suva at a modern pier alongside huge freight sheds, and straightway fell into the clutches of two cannibalistic-looking blacks who wanted a shilling apiece for carrying my trunk forty feet. There's the white man's culture for you. I carried out the part by refusing to be squeezed. Then in a fine American car I was whirled off to the most palatial hotel, if not to the most palatable chow, in the South Pacific.

For one hundred and fifty years after their discovery, civilization made no impression on the Fiji Islanders beyond contributing bits now and then to their human food supply. Every attempt to gain a foothold ended with a slip into the Fijian kettle. This was their naïve way of absorbing immigrants into the native population. Nor were the Fijians especially grateful for the sailors and others tossed ashore to them at times by fierce hurricanes and hidden coral reefs. Like the Tongans, they found white flesh "too salty."

Yet these benighted Fijians—and the Tongans, to be perfectly fair to both—have made their humble contri-

114

bution to Science. Without their painstaking—or pains-giving—investigations, we never would have known the true flavour of white men.

To write seriously about the old Fijians, I would have to deal in horrors the like of which history never has had to record against any other set of human beings. It's a long, tough story, and I will only hint at the details of it. By some good people it is regarded as a great feather for the missionaries in Fiji that the rock used as a braining-stone for children devoured at their feasts was afterward made over into a baptismal font; and that a Christian church now stands on the very spot where Fijian chieftains once dismembered their victims piecemeal and compelled them to eat of their own cooked flesh. Others, I think, might prefer a cleaner trophy for a font and a less gory spot for the building of a church.

But we might as well let bygones rest. The white man's coming has reduced the Fijians to a singularly placid, aimless, churchgoing race. In my rambles about these islands for a month I found the Fijians the tamest lot of niggers outside of "South C'lina."

A dull month? Not a minute of it. Fiji is pulling off a human drama—or is it to be a tragedy?—as novel as was ever staged. Like all South Sea Islanders, the Fi-jians generally refuse to work the land for white men; so, as in other islands, the whites have brought in in-dentured labour—East Indians, in immense numbers. Now, throughout these islands three totally unlike races are braced against each other in significant proportions: 85,000 Fijians, 61,000 Indians, 3,900 whites. A rather prodigious triangle on a ticklish base; we will have a look around, then come back to it.

Suva is a small modern city; too small to warrant a tram line, yet big enough to have two weakly dailies and a mayor. Instead of traders' general stores, Suva has specializing shops worthy of a place twice its size. Good roads about the town and extending for a few miles into the country account for the considerable number of automobiles in Suva; but the great fertile island of Viti Levu has nothing better than a precarious horseback trail across to the other side, where sugar growing has become the island's most thriving industry. Long ago a road was surveyed, begun, and ever since has been hopefully talked about. The development of the island awaits it. Many excuses are given for the delays; the one good reason lies in the fact that Viti Levu is within eighteen degrees of the Equator, and things get done accordingly.

The distinctive feature of the Fijian men is the huge, built-up head of woolly hair. In Tonga one merely notes the kinky hair, flattened features, and dark skin as an infusion of negroid; in the make-up of the Fijian, Negro blood clearly predominates. His country lies within mingling distance of the New Hebrides, and only a little farther to the westward are the coal-black, woolly-headed Solomon Islanders, hardly distinguishable from typical African Negroes. If the inhabitants of Fiji ever were straight-haired Polynesians, they gave over most of their inheritance long ago for that of the peoples whose islands join them on the west.

I have wondered whether our American Negroes could develop such grand bushes of hair on their tops. Picture a Fijian dandy, dressed in a silk shirt, collar, necktie, a trim blue coat with the tip of a coloured handkerchief daintily showing at the pocket, a dapper cane, and no breeches! With all this display surmounted by his kinky brush, and his black legs with their hamlike feet swinging free below a native waistcloth, he would start a riot on Fifth Avenue. In his own bailiwick he merely excites the envy of those whose limit of dress is a shirt and a *sulu*—Fiji's name for the waistcloth of the tropics. It is a fact, too, although I did not have occasion to see this, that these dudes go to evening entertainments in Suva quite as faultlessly arrayed in the upper half of a dress suit.

But the pride of the average native is in his precisely trimmed forest of hair. A hat is out of the question, unless it were one the size of a half bushel. The particular Fijian spends considerable time every morning dressing his chief adornment, and if he can afford it he has it done daily by a native barber.

Suva's traffic policemen are one of the street sights. If a reckless motorist happens to look first at the officer's ladylike, snow-white skirt, prettily scalloped all around the bottom, he may not think it necessary to obey the signal to stop; but by the time his glance has reached the ferocious head he will be setting his emergency brakes with a jerk. The middle part of a Suva policeman is deceiving.

The European section of Suva is mostly English, or Colonial. If there are any resident Americans I did not hear of them during my month in Fiji. The customs and sports are English, as a matter of course. Across the way from the hotel are the spacious, well-kept grounds of Albert Park, given over to sports. The half next to the street, reserved for the English, is devoted mostly to tennis and cricket, while on an equally large field back of it, and set off from the Europeans' playground by a few straggling trees and a very obvious social line, the younger Fijians play football.

On Saturday afternoons both grounds are alive with players and spectators. There is a cheerful absence of our emphasis on gate receipts. Everybody strolls in who cares to see the games.

They say that cricket is an exciting game to watch when you have got into the intricacies of it. I have never been able to see any chance for intricacy in hitting a ball on the bounce, then running gingerly back and forth between wickets until somebody "shacks" the ball and throws it in, always to the home plate. Certainly there are none of the involved combinations in cricket which give baseball its ecstatic moments. But probably Englishmen would think our national game hopelessly simple. Both views are right; the most absorbing game for a middle-aged man to watch is the game which he played in his youth.

The thrills and the noise and most of the spectators are on the Fijian side of the dividing line. Here, as in the school football games in Nukualofa, white men always act as referees. There is no social mixing implied by acting as referee; on the contrary, this dependence upon Europeans to run their games for them seems to accentuate the white superiority. Perhaps the natives feel more sure of impartial decisions with white referees; without a doubt, too, they would be less inclined to dispute the judgments; or they may feel that Englishmen know more about the game than any of their own race. Quite likely all three of these considerations taken together make up the reason for white referees at native games.

Anyhow, the arrangement works perfectly; I have never

seen a dispute or a sign of hard feeling toward the referee, even when his whistle was stopping the game every few seconds for misplays. And, of course, it would never do for a white referee to display the slightest temper with natives, whatever emotions may be striving within him. It's all very businesslike.

In Fiji, as in Samoa and Tonga, the colour line does not have back of it the old sting of slavery which makes it so inexorable in America; but if it is any less effective among the common run of Fijians, I saw no evidences of it. There appeared to be a slight social unbending toward a few educated Fijians of high native rank.

The Indians mix with neither. Although they are a shade blacker than the Fijians, they are so utterly different in racial characteristics and tradition that they will have nothing socially to do with them. The Europeans, on their part, do not gratify in the least the Indians' desire for racial equality.

Each of the three races sticks tight to its own side of the triangle. There are remarkably few half-castes in Fiji.

The sixty-odd thousand Indians in Fiji need no more explanation than imported labourers anywhere in the South Sea islands; it lies in the disinclination of natives to work in European enterprises. They were first brought over in immense numbers as indentured labourers to work on the plantations; they multiply rapidly; they save money out of their incredibly small wages; and what is more to the point, they work.

Fijians taken as a whole will not work on the plantations. They will not work even on their own land so long as it will give them a living without working. But at certain kinds of intermittent labour they will work with surprising skill, intelligence, and industry.

On the *Tofua* we had ample evidence of this. Fijians are the best handlers of cargo I have ever seen, not excepting white dockmen at home or in Europe, as I have observed them. They run the whole business of loading and unloading cargo, from operating the hoisting engines to bossing themselves. In fact, one white boss would "queer" the lot, and not a stroke of work would they do.

It was fascinating to watch these half-naked ex-savages manage the two hoisting engines at each hatch of the vessel—never missing the exact coördination of the two which is necessary to lift the freight, swing it over the side or from the dock as the case might be, and deposit it without a bump in the right spot. A few silent motions of the hand from the Fijian overseer, who stood between the rail and the hatch, merely supplemented their own skill in swinging the huge burden across while it was in their sight above decks. Every man of them, down to the common stacker of freight on the hoisting tackle, did the right thing at the right time, with no shouting and a minimum of orders. They kept their minds every second on the job. They seemed to play it as an absorbing game.

Between ports while at sea, or between arrivals of vessels in Suva if they are stationed there, the men have long intervals of rest. That is why Fijians enjoy being handlers of cargo.

Our Fijians on the *Tofua* certainly rested between ports. The everlasting scrubbing and painting which seem necessary to keep white sailors out of mischief were not for them. A South Sea Islander can keep out of mischief by resting. He sits, and sings, and talks, and laughs.

Our Fijians put in considerable time practising for the *meke*—the native entertainment—which they give at least once on each trip through the Tongas and Samoa. On the evening appointed for the *meke*, nearly the whole fifty of them came up to the promenade deck and squatted in a close bunch in the midst of the expectant passengers. Those in the front row were bare above their *sulus* except for weird native ornaments around their necks and wrists; these men went through the rhythmic motions of the *meke* with their arms and bodies while all sang the native songs. Most of the men in the chorus honoured their brief mingling in the polite society of the upper deck by wearing an undershirt.

One cannot describe songs, much less the chantlike harmonies of the Fijians. The deep music rolling from that group of bushy-headed black men, timing perfectly with the manual interpretations of the picturesque row in front; in cadences and a tongue utterly strange to civilized ears, and on the deck of a ship ploughing in the darkness through mid-Pacific——

Well, one cannot describe songs. Once in New York I bought a grand opera ticket for five dollars from a grasping Jew, climbed up and upward to a seat mentioned on my pasteboard as "three quarters out of sight," or to some such effect, and through a fog of murmurings around me I heard the finest singers in the world doing time somewhere beneath the balcony rail. But they did not get me as these Fijians did—perhaps for the same reason that I would rather see a sunset than some great painter's hundred-thousand-dollar mutilation of it.

Among a generous offering of their own songs they gave us now and then a gospel hymn—in Fijian words, but set to familiar music. But the oddest of their side efforts were two or three songs with English words. English coming from these Fijians, and fairly enunciated, too, struck us like an electric shock. Officers aboard assured us that they did not know the meaning of a word they were saying. One of these songs, cribbed from the Samoans, carried the refrain, "I shall never forget you." They sang it with rollicking heartiness right after the collection.

When the cargo handler gets back to Suva—what becomes of his accumulated shillings?

He does not, sailor fashion, spend them riotously on himself. He hardly has a chance to. The old communistic system of the South Sea islands still has a firm grip on the natives of Fiji, in spite of long efforts to dislodge it.

Unless he is particularly modern, town bred and stony hearted, the Fijian coming ashore with money tucked into a fold of his *sulu* discovers a host of appreciative friends joyfully awaiting him. The communal pot is made to boil, and the communal appetite gets an impartial treat. It's a day of plenty for all when our Fijians land in Suva. Nobody has to work so long as anybody's money lasts.

Compare this happy-go-lucky attitude with that of the individualistic, thrifty, saving East Indian. He has not enough understanding of the Fijian on which to start a quarrel. East Indians and Fijians would not comprehend each other in a million years. Peace between them comes from having no point of contact.

The sixty-one thousand Indians do the real work of Fiji, raise most of the crops, get into small merchandising, bank their funds in the silver and gold ornaments on their women, and wait for a better day. Their sinister point of contact is with the Europeans. And there are thirty-nine hundred Europeans.

Luckily for his peace of mind, an Englishman is never alarmed until he has been properly surprised.

*   *   *

After a few days in the lap of luxury I felt a distinct urge to get out of it. When visiting a place, the best spot in which to see, hear, and learn nothing at all about its local life is the tourist hotel. No chance for chats with traders, or merchants, or island officials, or any of the local sort who drop in naturally wherever the less pretentious gather for refreshment. They of the imposing inn make sorties off to this and that in a big car, listen to the barkings of a chauffeur, and retreat to the sofas to talk over the experiences of the day with like adventurous spirits. They see the place, sure enough; and seeing it as they do, they don't know that they don't know it. But perhaps it is just as well. Knowing a place involves some personal effort.

To get away from Suva more than a few easy miles, one has to go by boat. The only advantage in taking the boat, that I did take over to Levuka, a night's run distant on the island of Ovalau, is in the fact that the other boat which makes the trip is still worse. I know, because, during my travels about Fiji, I had passage on both.

Levuka is the oldest European settlement in the Fiji Islands. Levuka was also the first capital under the British occupation, but an island of forty-three square miles could not expect to hold the seat of government against Viti Levu's forty-one hundred; neither did Levuka's few extra years of age long withstand the claims of Suva's better harbour on the big island. To-day, its glory is in the real affection which the older settlers hold for it in memory of the days when it was the white man's only refuge, and a rather uncertain one at that. And it still has the best part of the Fiji copra trade.

The town, nestled under jagged volcanic peaks kept riotously green by drippings from the trade wind, makes one of the prettiest pictures in the Fiji Islands. Only a single long street finds room between the abrupt cliffs and the sea. If this street were wider, most of the buildings fronting on it would have to be shorter. Levuka expanded lengthwise until it lost the capital; now it shrinks by shortening.

A walk along this thoroughfare discloses the reason for Levuka's fame as the coolest town in the Fijis. The southeast trade comes in directly over the harbour, perennially fanning its way into every open door and window. This is all very well, so long as it merely fans; but when it rises to the proportions of a storm, and the insufficient coral reefs which make the harbour fail to break down the seas, the great swells come ashore in Levuka, cross the street, and enter the stores—unwelcome and profitless customers. But this does not happen often enough to discourage the oldest inhabitants in proclaiming Levuka as the coolest town in the Fijis.

Another observation presses itself upon the visitor in Levuka. The town in which adventurous, if salty, white men first braved the appetites of the Fijians is now showing quite a line of Chinese stores. European enterprise is most in evidence in the copra and trading houses of the two big South Sea corporations which loom in every Island port. Europeans still control the place, but Chinese do most of its merchandising.

This drifting of Levuka's trade to another race is a reminder of like happenings in the older sections of America. One's ancestral farm is as likely as not in the hands of worthy but uninteresting Polaks, and the Main Street of many a man's home town now displays a solid line of unrecognizable foreign names. This coming along of the Chinese in Levuka is merely an indication of what they are doing throughout the South Sea islands. Long before the foreigners own us in America the Chinese will be running most of the islands of the Pacific.

* * *

Viti Levu's big river is the Rewa. A neat little day boat, the *Adi Raroga*—I can reveal the name of a neat little boat—goes up the Rewa as far as Nausori, the location of a sugar mill, after spending half of its time getting from Suva to the river's mouth. This first part of the little voyage is through the usual tangle of coral reefs; then come the inevitable sandbars of a shifting waterway. But these are mere trifles to a captain who has brought the same little boat around safely for a good number of years.

The name of this boat offers a lesson in Fijian spelling —or in the spelling which some early linguistic crank foisted for all time upon the Fijian language. Before every *g* must be sounded an *n*, as in Tonga and Pango; but this language calls as well for an *n* to do duty before every *d*, and an *m* before *b*. Until one gets used to it, he has to spend a little time scattering in extra letters before he dares pronounce a word.

"Adi Raroga," then, becomes "Andy Raronga," "La-basa" is "Lambasa," and "Nadi"—we shall hear more of it—sounds prettier as "Nandy." The originator of this system of spelling died before he could get adequately punished.

At the very start of the journey toward the mouth of the Rewa I felt the sensuous charm of the tropics. A bright sun and the gentle trade wind joined in making a perfect day. Receding astern were the ragged lava peaks off at the left of the harbour's entrance, every peak a livid green to its top and each cutting its own weird outline into the blue of the sky. Ashore, as the little city dropped behind, was rich tropical verdure, graced as on all South Sea islands by the waving branches of tall coconut palms. Seaward, great rollers broke into long ridges of foam over the coral reefs, and tumbled into still waters showing bright greens, yellows, and blues over the varying depths. Ahead of us rose the flat jungle growth of the delta country of the Rewa.

So I sat on the canopied deck and picked lazily at the different offerings as at a feast. Whichever way I looked was a tropical gem, each as unlike the others as nature could have managed it within the range of a single vision.

In the Rewa, we were constantly happening upon small Fiji villages as our little steamer puffed importantly around the bends of the river. Fijian men, women, and children, less covered than those in town, regarded us idly. Native canoes emerged here and there from under the overhanging growth, or slipped out from any of the numberless by-passes of the delta, and glided along the bank—perhaps to disappear again into another hidden waterway before we knew what had become of them.

They were picturesque craft mostly on prosaic business —laden with vegetables, fruits, or things gathered in the jungle; but one, at least, made me sorry that a passing cloud was spoiling a good chance for a snapshot. We swung around a curve upon a canoe rather suddenly, otherwise the damsels in it might have reached for covering; but caught as they were, they deliberately ignored us. In a moment we were drawing up alongside four buxom young women, clad only in their *sulus* and paddling along as unconcernedly as if we were a mile off. Into the absolutely untamed scene about us they and their Fijian dugout fitted perfectly. Fijians in Suva and Fijians off in the jungle are quite as unlike as Tongans in Nukualofa and Tongans in "the bush."

The Fijians of the Rewa delta have their spiritual welfare looked after by substantial missions, one managed by the Catholics and the other by the Methodists. Our first stop—a brief one—was at Naililili, the seat of the Catholic mission, and one of the largest Fijian villages in the region. In South Sea languages, many syllables in words and names are repeated once, but not often are there three in a row, as in Naililili. But one does not have to stutter to pronounce it; the word is divided for the purpose of graceful delivery into *Naili-lili*.

Fijian houses differ in shape from the *fales* of the Samoans and Tongans in having the ends squared off, instead of rounded. A minor difference—one which identifies a Fijian grass house at a distance—is the ridgepole made of a coconut tree, with its black ends protruding over the gables; but the distinctive feature, no matter if the house happens to be as sadly mixed with civilized architecture as some of those in Tonga, is the squared end.

Soon after leaving Naililili we were up among the rolling lands of the sugar country. The fascination of the delta and its primitive life dropped away before these returning evidences of the European. Nausori, which exists chiefly for its sugar mill, is as interesting as a half mulatto town in Missouri. South Sea island natives show at their worst in the vicinity of civilized commercialism as it is represented by a sugar mill.

It is a beautiful ride of thirteen miles back overland to Suva. This is the weather side, and the wet side, of the island. The luxuriant growth of every kind of tropical plant and tree known in the Fijis proclaims an abundance of moisture, while the rolling and at times precipitous country through which the good automobile road winds makes a picture as striking as any that I saw in Fiji.

Its climax came at the top of the last rise before dropping down into Suva. On one side we looked out over the great valley of the Rewa, and beyond it at the landscape's wavy, interlacing outlines, one after the other more dimly showing until the last of them vanished in the haze brought in by the trades. Before us extended the colourful waters of Suva's harbour, dotted with shipping of all the odd and usual kinds which make South Sea island ports. Once more, too, beyond the harbour's entrance were the grotesque lava peaks as in the morning, yet coloured differently this time by the declining sun; the oddest of them all, "Joske's Thumb," sticking up from among the others like the proverbial sore member.

Suva is on the island's weather side, but it is a bit uncomfortably sheltered from the trade wind by hills. Harbours have a way of locating themselves disregardful of the saving breeze—as in Apia, for instance, and now in Suva. But the climate of Suva is cool in September— the last of the Fijian winter—and the Fiji Islands claim the top record for all-the-year-round healthfulness in the tropics of the South Pacific. Europeans seem to find little difficulty with the Fijian climate.

In judging a tropical climate, one does not have to go wholly by its medical records. The best evidence of its temper is in the white women and children who live in it. Statistics may show how cleverly or poorly the doctors have warded off the common diseases of a hot country, but the white women and children tell without words or records what the steady heat and the high humidity of any particular island will do to constitutions better adapted to the temperate zone. Men yield their vitality quite as surely, but it takes years longer for a tropical climate to "get" them physically, even after it has got their "pep."

So in the tropics, *cherchez les femmes*. If they are pasty and their children spiritless, don't think that your own iron constitution will stand for long against the climate.

* * *

At nine o'clock in the morning the whistle of the *Adi Keva* gave a toot almost as big as herself. All aboard for Lautoka!

It is a two-day journey around to Lautoka, on the opposite side of Viti Levu. The two days of chugging along inside the barrier reefs would not be so bad if they did not in the nature of things have to include a night on the *Adi Keva*. Don't forget to say it "Andy." But then, what can one expect of bunks where some of the passengers are quite as apt as not to go to bed with their clothes on? Now, if *everybody* did, or *didn't*——

One way or the other, to relieve bedtime doubts on the *Adi Keva*, they ought to make it unanimous.

Thus began an eleven-day trip to the sugar country. Until noon we followed the route of the Nausori boat along the shore line and into the delta. But instead of going up the Rewa we turned off to starboard into one of the delta's many side streams; one which makes a short cut across the corner of the big island and leads to the sea on the easterly coast.

Again there was the tangle of flat-land growth; more villages opening up in little clearings around the bends; more natives idling ashore or serenely paddling their canoes, as on the trip to Nausori, and still as fascinating to see.

The crookedness of the narrow stream kept the boat lurching about in a way that started pleasant apprehensions that she might run aground, and the same number of mild disappointments when she did not. At two specially short turns, a Fijian deck hand swam ashore with a hawser, threw its bight over a stout stake, and the engine pushed the boat around against the pull of the straining line. It was quick work, with no stops; when the turn had been made the native slipped the bight, dashed across into the water ahead of the boat, and was pulled aboard by his mates.

The night was to be spent tied up to the dock at Levuka. Cruising for miles across the open sea in the *Adi Keva* may suggest possibilities for discomfort, but the barrier reef reaches out to the eastward here to include Levuka's island, Ovalau. In smooth water we plugged along unexcitingly through the last hours of the afternoon.

Levuka at night is not a stirring place. A walk alone in the stillness for a mile out the shore road, with the Southern Cross and myriads of unfamiliar stars shining down through the palms along the way, led me to contemplate the strangeness, the distance away, of this other world in the South Seas. Every white man here is an exotic, and every touch of his is an imposition—sometimes beneficent, sometimes not. In none of the islands which I have seen, and, so far as I have learned, in none of this wilderness of earth bits scattered over this waste of sea, has he succeeded in remoulding the natives to his notion of what life is about. They more or less good-naturedly repudiate him and his ways. His little achievements bear only the marks of his own wit and the labour of indentured yellow and dark men who yield to his methods through sheer necessity. If starvation did not threaten them at home, they would not work for him here for the price of a single meal.

For the leisurely traveller, the most fascinating of lands; but the white business man in the South Seas spends his days closed in upon a handful of his own race, uncomprehended by the peoples in whose islands he lives, and with never a sign of unbought coöperation from his imported menials. I should call it a dog's life.

Our boat was to leave port at daylight, so everybody had to spend the night aboard. By the time I was out next morning we were pretty well across from Ovalau to the east shore of the big island. A few hours more of unhurried chugging brought us up along the northerly coast, and to a change in the scenery. Going from the wet to the dry side of any South Sea island reveals the dependence of rank tropical growth upon an abundance of water. With anything like as much moisture as falls on the windward side of most of these islands, even our verdure of the temperate zone would take on a surprising richness.

The foliage of Viti Levu began to show a change in character as well as in luxuriance. From our distance offshore it looked more like that of some temperate zone, especially after we had rounded the northernmost point of the island and were going down the westerly side toward Lautoka.

But this sort of climate, if the soil is of the right kind and water for irrigation can be had, makes a great sugar country. Sugar plantations extend all along the shores of this part of the island and run back into the uplands. Centring this great agricultural region is the sugar mill of the Colonial Sugar Refining Company—the largest in the South Seas, and among the top few of the world's sugar plants.

Altogether, it is quite a place to be off here at the end of a horse trail. Suva's long-projected road across the island may some day be built to it. At present, a weekly mail comes by way of our little *Adi Keva*, and a small steamer from Sydney once a month stops here on its way to Suva.

But the C. S. R. is quite independent of public lines of communication. Its product goes out by its own ships from its own dock, and in the same way most of its supplies come in. Along the shore both ways as far as the sugar plantations extend runs its narrow-gauge railroad, with branch lines and movable tracks ready to tap every cane field in the district. The only telephone line across to Suva is owned by the Company. It owns about everything in the place, and has a full line of the usual necessities, such as electricity, ice, water; operates a good hospital, houses most of its employees after a fashion, and I have to thank the Company for good accommodation in its Rest House, which serves as the only hotel in the place.

On the little railroad, passenger trains are run both ways two or three times a week; and among all the railroad trains in the world these are unique in not charging any fare. They carry passengers, I was told, because something in the franchise requires it.

At first thought this seems like an astonishing piece of altruism on the part of a corporation; but one does not have to observe the C. S. R. long before he searches for a more plausible explanation. It is all in the matter of liability for personal injury. A passenger train competing on a single wobbly track with cane-carrying trains of uncertain schedules is not in the nature of things as safe as one on a well-blocked section of a modern railroad; and on modern railroads the damage suits eat great holes in the revenue.

So the C. S. R. dodges all possible liability by not collecting a penny of fare, even though it appears to have no accidents worth mentioning. At the speeds usual on its railroad, two trains coming head on could not have much of an accident unless at least one of the engineers was asleep. A clip of around ten miles an hour suggests caution, or decrepitude, or a natural hesitancy. The last two characteristics are not mentioned in the bright lexicon of the C. S. R.

Here one sees East Indians. Indians working throughout the mill, in the cane yards, on the truck trains, in the engine cabs. Those in the engine cabs displace at twenty-five to thirty shillings a week white engineers who were getting twelve to fifteen shillings a day. The wages for labour around the mill and in the cane fields are from a shilling and sixpence to a shilling and ninepence a day.

One and ninepence amounts to forty-one cents a day. There is a perquisite in the way of housing, which some take advantage of and some evidently do not. At first thought, forty-one cents seems to an American a shockingly inadequate day's wage; but this is Fiji, and these are Indians. The cost of living is not high in Fiji, but the one big reason for the forty-one cents a day is in the fact that these are Indians.

Centuries of precarious living have taught Indians how to exist on next to nothing. A little rice, perhaps a few vegetables; a room in the Company barracks, or a straw shack on the hillside; a few yards of cheap cotton cover the family. And some of them save money on forty-one cents a day.

Europeans never did understand Indians, and perhaps they never will. But at the beginnings of an understanding must lie the knowledge that Indians are not savages touched up by civilization; they are a civilized race forced down by circumstances. They had a civilization before we had shifted out of bearskins. Primitives live on next to nothing because they have never desired anything more; Indians live on next to nothing because ages of poverty have made them forget the desire for anything more.

Indians are supposed to be dark Aryans. The remoteness of their separation from the parent stock attenuates the relationship with us to an uncertainty. They have mixed with stocks with whom we have never mixed. Yet if given white skins, the regular, delicate features and aristocratic heads of many Indians would make them look like well-favoured white men and women. I say "look like," because I do not know Indians well enough even to guess what that other blood has put into their racial characteristics.

One day I went out among the straw shacks of the Indians, on the hillside back of the mill. The men, of course, were away at work; only the women and children were at home.

I always have my camera along when off in villages, partly for the purpose of taking photographs, and partly as an infallible opener of communication with the inhabitants. In the camera they see an excuse for me, a bit of flattery, and perhaps a coin or two. It diverts their attention from me to themselves, and tickles the human nature in them to a responsive mood. After that, one doesn't need more than the language of signs to get on famously. Often when overtaken in an interesting village by weather too dark for photographing, in make-believe I would steer them through the voluble business of getting all set for a picture, hold them in a moment of agitating suspense, and hand over the expected reward without wasting a film. A camera taps the fount of spontaneity even when it cannot take pictures.

About one of these Indian shacks, more pretentious than the others in having a straw awning built out over the door, was quite a group of women and children. Indians resent the approach of obvious visitors, probably suspecting inquisitiveness. One has to begin at once on the business of the camera.

At the trifling expense of three negatives and as many sixpences that group gave me a half hour of character study which no money could have bought without the pretext. The play of their interest in the proceedings was as finely cut as their features. The experience was so novel, after my months of doing the same things with peoples differently interesting, that I prolonged it by sitting down amongst them and changing to a fresh film—showing them carefully each move in the operation.

Many years before, in Jamaica, the cryptic attitude of indentured Indians there toward coloured natives had puzzled me; but the strange contrast of personalities in Jamaica had little more than impressed upon me the crude obviousness of the Jamaica Negro. Now, in Fiji, I was beginning to learn why Indians do not mix with Negroes anywhere. In their depths they have not a thing in common.

I wondered how people of such innate fineness could live so meagrely; but compared with the lives of their people in India, they were not living meagrely. They gave evidence of sufficient nourishment, which would spell affluence in India; and silver ornaments in the ears, noses, as well as on arms and ankles, indicated savings unheard-of at home. They were living in the lap of plenty on their men's forty-one cents a day.

These Indians reminded me that "plenty," anywhere in the world, is a relative term. The discontent of our well-to-do drifts in mostly from adjacent millionaires. An exacting mental attitude makes a limited income satisfy; shift that attitude ever so little, and one can live in poverty on twice as much.

I strolled along to an Indian home made mostly out of

battered sheets of corrugated iron, back of which I had
noticed a comely young woman. When I came upon her
she started to retreat, but the camera arrested her. I
assisted the camera by centring my attention on her two
little children—youngsters with as well-shaped heads and
features as any white children.

Between the camera and the children we were soon in
friendly negotiation for a picture. Her few words of
English, too, gave an opening for questions on my part,
and a display of mental agility on hers.

This young woman may have been of a common caste,
but she had features which under a white skin would
have passed as aristocratic. Their expressive play under
the strain of getting at what I was talking about kept
me at thinking up other things to talk about. Instead of
going to total blankness like a native when she failed to
comprehend, she looked humanly puzzled. When she
got the point, she flashed understanding. Her smiles
broke quickly, and receded as quickly before the next
question. Probably the interview was as difficult for her
as it was interesting for me.

There is something about an Indian which is not ob-
servable in any other person of colour who is not mixed
with white. At times, in watching the facial expressions
of this young woman, I felt a shock of recognition, as if a
European were masquerading behind that dark skin and
might suddenly reveal herself. The thing enigmatic in
the Indian make-up seems to be the bit of ourselves
lodged there. If they were not endowed with so many
of our Aryan characteristics we might understand them
better.

In this attempted new light, the tragic events of the

past few years in Fiji may, perhaps, be viewed a little more clearly. Strikes for better wages, religious and political agitations, fierce race riots and bloodshed, demands for an indefinite racial equality with the whites—anyone who cares can go into the details of them. Summed in a line, they all were manifestations of India's unrest; mostly engineered from India through Gandhi's representatives sent out to the Islands, and following with almost chronological exactness the rise and fall of similar disturbances at home.

With the subsidence of the Gandhi propaganda in India to a state of passivity, the troubles became quiescent here. A new outbreak in India will be a sure signal for another agitation in Fiji.

The Indians in Fiji seem unable to translate their indefinite longings into demands which have any steadfastness. A strike which starts and fails as a demand for higher wages shifts to varying degrees of appeal for racial and social equality. A strike for higher pay is met and usually overcome by pointing to the rings and necklaces and bracelets on their women as conclusive evidence that they are being paid enough so long as they can save money. A fallacious argument, of course, but in world-wide and effective use.

Another threadbare excuse for the forty-one cents is that the Indians are better off here than they would be at home. Aspirations for living conditions even remotely approaching the white standard are nothing less than rank heresy, in the view of the sugar companies and most of the Europeans. It is the same argument as that of the sugar planters in Hawaii and everywhere else: sugar is made elsewhere under living standards incredibly low, sugar must be made here under the same standards or not be made at all.

It sounds all right as an economic dictum, but it looks heathenish as a human proposition.

In the confused struggle I see clearly nothing but its unutterable pathos. Out of this welter I make only one point: these Indians in Fiji will never get higher wages until they have learned to squander all of that forty-one cents on their daily expenses. *They must raise their standard of living first.* When they are spending fifty cents a day and running into debt, they may get an advance to sixty.

But as for attaining a social relationship with Europeans —that will come when the white world has changed its age-old view of colour.

* * *

On the seashore near Lautoka is a Fijian village of the sort which one might expect to find so close to a great industry. The houses are all of the Fijian square-cornered pattern, and very few of them have desecrated the native grass roof or neatly matted sides with boards or sheetiron; yet the straight, laid-out roadways—used only as paths —and the regular spacing of the houses suggest a village planning which never came from the head of a Fijian.

The Fijians seem uninterestingly imitative of Europeans in the running of their villages, but I suppose it is because they have generous official advice, if not official urging of a more compelling sort, as to the way things should be done. The high authority of a district, which may comprise many villages, is in a District Commissioner, a European. Under him, and topping all native control from the chiefs down to the family councils, is the Fijian "Buli."

The Buli is the great man of his district, and among his functions is that of tax-gatherer. An annual tax of eighteen shillings is collected from all males.

The placing of this financial trust in a native shows the Britisher's confidence in the integrity of at least certain picked Fijians. But, now and then, as in civilized communities, they pick the wrong man. A delinquent Buli came to trial in Nadi (Nandy) while I was in Lautoka. This Buli had been collecting funds without turning them in to the government treasurer. After repeated urgings to settle, a complaint had been filed against him and he was to be brought into court.

The attorney for the defense, whose acquaintance I had made in Lautoka, gave me a pretty ride of a dozen miles to Nadi, and, at the end of it, a shining example of what the law can do to the goddess of justice when she ventures into court without a lawyer.

Nadi is a mere village, with only the few necessary white officials of the district mixed in with the Fijian and Indian population. In the little government house were gathered some fifty natives to listen to the trial of the Buli. On the bench was the District Commissioner—a white man, but not a lawyer. Another official, equally inexperienced at the bar, attended to the prosecution. Beside him sat my friend, the attorney, for the defense. I was the only other white man in the room.

Behind a little rail stood the accused Buli—agitated, disconsolate; and beside him was the official interpreter —a fine-looking young native with magnificent hair, who repeated in a deep Fijian rumble the essential parts of all that was said. Whenever the proceedings became a bit dry I listened fascinated to that subdued musical roar,

and so never had a dull moment. This Fijian's mono-
tone, coming from down in his toes—he had no boots—
had the quality of a rich organ note. I felt an almost
irresistible impulse to ask him to "sing it."

For some reason—probably to spare the poor Buli's
feelings as much as possible—the charge had been worded
as a "breach of trust," or in some such polite term for stealing. Justice was not at all particular about a little matter
of words; the case was clear, and this Buli was to be discreetly punished as an example to all the other Bulis in
the Islands who might have leanings toward the funds in
their charge. These laymen had the blindfolded goddess
all set to give a righteous judgment tempered with the
correct shade of mercy—when in bobbed this honest-to-
goodness lawyer on the side of the prisoner.

It was a bit disconcerting, but my friend of the profes-
sion let the prosecutor go ahead with his witnesses and
prove the first count in the indictment. The Buli had
collected money and failed to pay it over. The lawyer admitted the incontestable evidence. His client was guilty.

"But guilty of what? Not, surely, of anything so mild
as a 'breach of trust.'" Then he flashed a fat law book.
A crime of those dimensions, said the law, was nothing
short of embezzlement.

"Oh, very well," said the prosecution. "Drop the
first count, call it a dud. Let's go ahead with the others,
and charge embezzlement."

"Ah, but my client hasn't been indicted for embezzlement. That's a greater crime than the one mentioned in
the indictment. I cannot have him placed in more
serious jeopardy without due process of law." Turning
to the prisoner in the dock, and dramatically waving his

hand toward the door, the lawyer commanded, "You leave the room!"

Never before had I witnessed the discharge of a prisoner by his own attorney. If a lawyer-judge had been on the bench I think he would have asserted this as his prerogative. But the District Commissioner was too paralyzed with surprise to utter a word.

The prisoner, dazed, pattered his bare feet toward the door and vanished. He of the magnificent hair and bass-drum voice gazed after him—an astonished man suddenly out of a soft job. The natives stared uncomprehendingly. I wanted to laugh at the ridiculousness of the whole proceeding.

Then came a recess, and prolonged discussion, in which my friend, being the only man present with a full knowledge of the law, had decidedly the best of it. Before we took the ride back to Lautoka he had the District Commissioner wondering whether a man once placed on trial for a crime and discharged—no matter who discharged him—could again be brought before the bar for the same offence under another name.

All of which led me to observe that lawyers function quite the same in Fiji as elsewhere. If you are innocent, seek justice; if the law has caught you with the goods, hire a lawyer.

So the upshot of the trial was a pilfering Buli turned loose, for a while if not for good; if he is ever again brought to trial, he will face a heavier punishment than the original dispensers of justice had planned for him. Meantime, the news of his farcical escape will spread among 85,000 Fijians, who are supposed to have a wholesome respect for the white man's law; and the Buli of every district in Fiji who has tax money in his charge will have his primitive mind touched by an engaging but unholy suggestion.

Quite a forenoon's work for a mighty good fellow well versed in the law!

*   *   *

How will these 85,000 Fijians eventually fit into the destinies of Fiji's wabbly human triangle? It is an interesting speculation.

So far, they have amiably accepted whatever rules and regulations the British have imposed; and the British, with their usual wisdom as colonizers, have imposed very little on the more intimate habits and customs of Fijian life. If there is friction between the two races, it is not in evidence. The question of racial equality is not in the minds of either. They live too differently to have unpleasant differences.

Fijian life off in the villages is not much unlike that of Samoans and Tongans, except that it seems to be more under the observation of European officials. Fijians are more amiable than Tongans, and less cordial than Samoans. In personality, they are less attractive than either.

The women show the negroid infusion if anything more than the men. Some of the younger ones affect the bushy tops of the men, but very few of them carry it to such lengths of personal vanity. They strongly reminded me of three-quarter-blood negresses.

On the trips of the *Adi Keva*, going both ways between Suva and Lautoka, I fell in with enlightening passengers: traders, two or three of them left over from the old days; plantation owners, managers, sugar men—but one learns very little about Fijians from sugar men. Their point of contact is with the Indian. Wives of some of the men aboard, too, were not averse to talking about Island conditions with a frankness which now and then touched asperity.

The old traders did not picture the Fijian virtues in the usual high colours of Suvan enthusiasts, yet after discounting their opinions for the years of sordid contact with natives, the Fijian reputation seemed to come off fairly well. More particularly they dwelt on the Fijian's lack of gratitude for any favours done him, or for assistance when in distress. One trader of thirty years' experience whom I ran across in Levuka stressed this as an almost universal trait. Do a good turn for a Fijian, said they all, and he will come back time and again for a favour as something due him. No sense of gratitude—that was their verdict against Fijians.

The same charge is laid quite as generally against Samoans and Tongans. One hears of it constantly in the South Sea islands. But why call it ingratitude? This native attitude toward kindly advances is a manifestation of their universal communistic habit. All natives, accustomed to share in everything alike, regard the European's thrifty accumulation of goods as nothing better than an incomprehensible selfishness. So, when a white man loosens his purse strings to one of them, or helps him in any way out of his difficulty, that native sees no special virtue in the act. He looks on his benefactor as having merely come into the normal state of his own people. He *does* return for more favours, and he seeks them as his right—just as he goes into the home of a more fortunate native friend and wishes himself into the possession of that friend's surplus goods. He may be deeply grateful, in his way, for the conversion of his white brother to the Fijian sense of right living; but gratitude for something done as a *favour* does not belong in his scheme of life. He only seems ungrateful, when, as a matter of fact, he is showing his lively appreciation of the kindly act by coming back for more.

In the South Seas, one should tie a string to his good deeds—exact, perhaps, a promise to repay—as a sign that he and his chattels have not joined the communistic fraternity. He will then have the natives cheerfully in his debt for life.

The firm grip of this communal idea on the native mind was illustrated by a peculiar happening in Tongatabu. A trader of my acquaintance there had engaged as agent in one of his copra-buying stations a native who held a reputation for strict honesty; but the trader had not reckoned on the man's deeply communistic spirit.

This chap could not conscientiously bring himself to the European idea of holding goods beyond the reach of one's neighbours; so, whenever his Tongan friends came into the agency store and admired the tinned beef, or expatiated on the beautiful pictures around the fruit cans, he followed the time-honoured custom of his people and gave the stuff away. By the time the trader discovered what was happening, his man had depleted the stock to the tune of one hundred and seventy-five pounds sterling. Not much was left in the store.

Now, a discriminating view of this fellow's act would not condemn him as a thief or an embezzler. He merely responded to his communal impulse. Quite as disconcerting for the trader, of course, as though his agent were

a *bona fide* crook.   There should be some way of examining
native applicants for these jobs as to the state of their
communal impulse.

With South Sea Islanders, life is not worth while if not
easy-going.   Here in Fiji, in the midst of two imported
races almost constantly in social and economic strain, this
mass of 85,000 Fijians is singularly inert.   However their
sympathies may lie, they preserve a neutrality of inaction.
Undoubtedly, their allegiance is with the British, but if
serious difficulty between British and Indians should arise,
would it hold fast against the appeal of colour?   In their
fundamentals, the Fijians have as little in common with
one race as with the other, but in colour they are close
to the Indian shade.

It is an interesting speculation, this trying to place the
Fijian in the human triangle as it may come to be; and I
am inclined to think that their present inclinations do not
furnish a basis for even passable guesswork as to their future status, if Indians and Englishmen in Fiji should ever
come to grips.

*   *   *

Back again in Suva, after eleven days off around the
Islands.   Suva, the civilized, the citified, where Fijians
and Englishmen play games on opposite sides of an invisible line, and Indians play nowhere.   "September in
Fiji" has been realized.   October is in its early days—
October, the beginning of spring in New Zealand, five days
away to the South.

Once more the *Tofua* is in from her tourist-freight trip
through the Samoas and the Tongas, and for the third time
I get aboard her; this time bound for Auckland and a taste
of chilly weather, after seven months in the tropics.   New

Zealand and Australia figure in the schedule as a tonic, to be taken before going into more tropical months in the Philippine Islands; but all is grist for these wanderings in the Pacific, and we might as well see what we can see while the climate there is getting in its work.

Good-bye, Fiji—Islands of the top-heavy triangle. Close to one hundred and fifty thousand, alike in colour if in nothing else, rest on a little white base of thirty-nine hundred. It's a beautiful place and a glorious climate—for the tropics—and I wish all of you luck. But if things should happen to break loose in India, I would not care to be in Fiji.

CHAPTER VI

NEW ZEALAND

AT THE *Tofua's* rail, coming into Auckland harbour, the throng of round-trippers exclaimed joyfully as the vessel's slow approach brought each familiar object into view. I myself could not figure exactly as a home-comer, but after months of stopping and staying in little island ports lined with the shacks of half-savages, where my own kind were outsiders and comparatively few, this red-roofed, all-white town, with every home a regular house and in every house a civilized family, looked quite as good to me as America.

Beside me stood a young New Zealand lady, showing me the place from the vessel's deck. Here, a sandy beach, just across the harbour from their part of the city, where they go to bathe in summer; there, perhaps, a suburb where she has friends; off on a distant hillside, hopelessly mixed in with green trees and bits of red roof, she made me see her home.

And all the while I was thinking what a home-coming this must be for her. She and her sister had left Auckland in May, for the usual four weeks' tour of the Islands; but a critical illness of the sister had put them both ashore at Nukualofa—of all places—and into the very same house of the hand-pump waterworks and Tongan towel dispenser that was to harbour me through August.

There I met them, after they had had two months of it;

yet they could not have been marooned among a kindlier lot of white people than those on Tongatabu.

August slipped by, and in spite of the fortitude of the girl on the screened-off veranda bed, and the unceasing devotion of the other in caring for her, the monthly boat had to come and go for the third time without taking the sisters away. I sailed for Fiji, leaving them cheerfully hoping that the invalid could be carried aboard the *next* boat.

Sure enough, in October, when I boarded the vessel at Suva for Auckland, there were the sisters—happy at the prospect of home once more. Now, after five days of sailing, the almost five months of stress were over.

Carried aboard and carried about, yet now that Auckland was actually in sight the sick one wanted to walk ashore into her home town. And so she did, an hour or so later, assisted with her less than a hundred pounds by two big men. *That* was somewhat of a home-coming!

Then there was another, quite as intense in its way, yet different. Along the vessel's rail only a dozen feet from us was a young New Zealander, returning from Tongatabu to the parental roof with his bride. In low tones he was showing her the sights of the town, but in his manner there was none of the enthusiasm of the young lady who was showing her town to me.

Strange, that tense, apprehensive look, as he did his best to seem at ease at this time of all times most trying for a bride?

Not strange at all. His bride was a half-caste Tongan girl, and more than usually dark at that.

They had been living with her relatives in a Tongan *fale* next door to us in Nukualofa. Now he was taking her to see his father and mother. That, too, was somewhat of a home-coming, especially for father and mother!

* * *

I had been told by American travellers, devotees of a blatant sort of progress, that New Zealanders are fifty years behind the times. In one respect I could see, even from the boat, how backward they are. Judging from the acres on acres of neat one-story cottages scattered all over the countryside, they have not advanced to the stage of childless cliff dwellers. They still live in houses, and the kids play on real grass in their daddy's own yard.

Trees in Auckland's residential parts are neither large nor plentiful, as viewed from a steamer's deck, but fresh-looking green grass is everywhere, setting off the house colourings and giving a cheery aspect to the city. Auckland is green at all times of the year, strange as it may seem for a place in the latitude corresponding to that of Washington, D. C. Washington in winter may be buried in snow; Auckland in winter is picking oranges. Auckland's summer, if not always cool, is at least merciful— which cannot be said of Washington's. We who live on a great continent do not always realize the tempering effect of an immense ocean on the climate of the islands scattered about in it, even when they are as big as the two which make up New Zealand.

In the custom house at Auckland I had keys mentioned to me for the first time. Perhaps I had relied too obviously on the usual "nothing but personal effects." But when my key was within an inch of the lock the official remarked hastily, "You say you have nothing but personal effects?—well, never mind." That was the worst custom-house grilling I had had in□ all the□

Within a stone's throw of the do□ck is the s□ of Auckland's tram system; an el□aborate one□ of one hundred and twenty-five □thousand p□ cars are large, cross-seated, with an aisle throug□ □he□ No sign of that fifty years back in Auckl□nd's tra□ cilities.

Most of the trams begin thei□ courses by running up Queen Street—a broad thoroughfare well built up and doing within a half-mile most of Auckland's important business. It is a street for an□ city to be proud of, and the citizens know it; their only worry about Queen Street is that down in the business centre there is no room for more streets like it.

Auckland spreads out generously into her back country, but in coming down to business and the water front she gets pocketed between two big hills by way of Queen Street. The people already complain of traffic congestion, but compared with the absurd piling up of vehicles in all our cities at home, big and little, Queen Street looks deserted. Their early facing of the problem is assurance enough that Auckland will not always be so much of a one-street town. A proper rise in square-foot values will melt down the biggest hill that ever stood in a city's way.

A one-mile ride on a tram, and a stiff climb that seems longer but is much shorter, takes one to the top of Mount Eden, the highest of the numerous high points about Auckland. From this elevation is a bird's-eye view of this city of homes. According to present-day standards of living, Auckland surely has a disproportionate number of homes. She needs advice from our builders of articulated cubbyholes.

the city and across the busy harbour, on the islands the white-capped Pacific, toward the Americas more than twice the e Atlantic. To the south, it is not quite as Antarctic Circle as from Boston to Denver. ard, beyond the great arm of this "North Island" which is Auckland, the Pacific shows again—this time as a dim ribbon of blue between shore and horizon. Down in that horizon twelve hundred miles away is Australia. My next tropical venture, the Philippine Islands, lies twenty days by steamer off to the northwest.

Mount Eden gave me the sensation of being a considerable way from anywhere except Mount Eden. Distances in the Pacific are immense. Already I had spent forty days and nights on shipboard, getting to places—and my sea voyages were not half done. When they are done I shall have seen a mere fragment of the lands in this one ocean.

It is difficult to convey in words this idea of *expanse*. You can get it by standing on the top of Mount Eden.

* * *

Rotorua is New Zealand's brave imitation of Yellowstone Park—or that is what it was before the geysers all went suddenly to rest over a year ago. Now it is a Land of Hope. Those interested may also be praying that the subterranean waterworks will start up again, and soon.

A government tourist bureau in Auckland gives painstaking advice to every traveller who applies, free of charge, and sells rail, hotel, and motor accommodation at cost for all trips on either island. Travel worry is reduced to the minimum.

Rotorua is eight hours south by rail from Auckland.

For the benefit of the service I have forgotten how few miles it is. But aside from the slowness of the little narrow-gauge trains, the railway service was well above what I had been led to expect. Even New Zealanders, having either ridden on or heard of our transcontinental trains, assured me that I would find their railroads something terrible. But they had neither ridden on nor heard of the many thousand miles of branch lines in America over which in years gone by I had had to be shaken for a living.

The first-class coaches have comfortably upholstered seats, built for two on one side of the aisle and for one on the other. In being arranged so that all can be turned to face forward, whichever way the train is running, they are as many years in advance of the best European equipment as it will take Europeans to get rid of their *vis-à-vis* compartments. The road bed on the Main Trunk is good—there is not much except "Main Trunk" road in New Zealand—and quite as good, too, on the branch off from Frankton to Rotorua. My long-standing prejudice against branch lines in general makes this a high tribute to the track from Frankton to Rotorua.

This being New Zealand, we had to eat frequently. At the hotel I had refused to be wakened for tea and toast in bed, but stopping at way stations for tea between meals gave welcome opportunities for the stretching of legs. They held up the train for tea at eleven o'clock, dinner at one, and tea again at four, so that we would be properly braced for getting off in Rotorua at five.

After the luxuriant growth of the tropics, the verdure of a temperate zone seems rather subdued. Yet this in New Zealand was as rich in colouring as we have it in our best-watered regions in America. It was the bright new foliage of spring, set off beautifully by the fresh grass of the almost continuous pastures.

The source of particular delight in this prosperous farming country was the sight of the live stock grazing everywhere. This was only the beginning of the country's stock-raising and dairying lands—as fine as any in the world. Great, square-built cattle; swine as straight lined as the cattle and almost as long—huge bulks of flesh on little pegs for legs; sheep, big and broad backed, ready to deliver a heavy spring clip of wool; horses that were horses, good to see after the stunted scrubs of the tropics. Every animal in every lot, if not a thoroughbred, was so near it that I could not tell the difference.

It was the most satisfying pastoral sight I ever saw. Perhaps the contrast with the miserably bred and worse cared-for domestic animals of the tropics had something to do with it, but a neatness of farms and fences which we do not often see even in our own prosperous agricultural sections, and a decided attempt at architecture and beauty about the houses and yards almost unknown to the average American farmer, give the impression that New Zealand farmers are not only farming, but living.

Their abodes are often prettily designed and lightly trimmed bungalows. New Zealanders do not have our heavy-timber effects on their bungalows, nor those hideous truncated pyramids which we must charitably mistake for pillars. Our architects might at least give us hope by buying a book of New Zealand bungalow designs.

Rotorua is an inland summer resort. October is off season, as the weather soon proved. Getting away from the sea and up to an altitude of a thousand feet gives quite a drop in temperature, yet almost without exception the houses and hotels of New Zealand have no heat except the little that escapes from fireplaces. The orange belt terminates just outside of Auckland, and the region of light coughs and cold feet begins.

I do not know that New Zealand should be declared behind the times because her people do not keep warm in cool weather. Not another country except America has generally adopted adequate heating systems. Her mother country is no better off. Oxford, the centre of learning, has shivered through the centuries without learning how to be comfortable in winter.

There are two sides to this heating question. Without a doubt the non-heating countries waste energy and reduce efficiency by living in the physical and mental constraint of a chilly atmosphere; yet the conviction grows on one who has to endure it with them sufficiently long that we in America depend altogether too much on artificial heat, too little on clothes, and have a dangerously wide difference of temperatures between indoors and out. So I have to say nothing more about New Zealand's heating arrangements, except that the beds are invariably deep, soft, and delightfully warm. One can always go to bed.

My hotel, because it was not the biggest in town, had more guests than any other in this off season. It was of that happy first-rate kind which attracts the best people, while the loud and the lowly follow their inclinations to the more and the less expensive places. These were mostly New Zealanders. I almost hesitate to remark again on the unfailing courtesy and good manners of New Zealanders, yet a delightful trait has to be readmired on each occasion.

Upon this company an ironic fate had dropped one of that pestiferous species, the southern California "booster.' A well-enough chap when taken alone, but, like all of his kind, he was too eternally satisfied with himself to learn anything of refined usage through observation of others. In a parlour full of these polite ladies and gentlemen, he alternated between engagements with his toothpick and bragging about southern California; ending, always, by settling back in his chair and cleaning his fingernails with his jackknife. That nobody else was doing the like never entered his head. The well-bred modesty of others he took as his special chance to roar about his home town.

Why is it that twenty cultivated Americans can travel abroad without leaving much of an impression, while a single blatant dispenser of unseemly manners is accepted as typical of America? I suppose it is because the twenty, wherever they are, fit into the social landscape as cosmopolitans, while the one stands out like a billboard along a scenic highway—politely abhorred, but always read.

Another striking characteristic of New Zealanders is the purity of their English. Descended mostly from the English and Scotch who came here two or three generations ago, they speak the cleaner English of those days. It is not only the educated who use these clear-cut pleasing phrases, but nearly all, even those of little education who now and then make a slip in grammar. This shows it to be the language of the family life. Their speech seems to fit in with their manners. Slang would be in too good company with such unaffected politeness.

The region for miles around Rotorua is alive with the manifestations of subterranean heat. All about the town are steam vents, potholes of boiling water, bubbling mud pools. Medicinal properties are claimed for certain of these waters and pools, and some of the best of them are led into a great bathhouse, operated by the government. Here, for small fixed sums varying with the kind of service, one can get every variety of thermal bath ranging from steam to mud.

An interesting thermal district, two miles out served by a convenient bus line, is Whakarewarewa. The name appears on only the longer busses; most of them abbreviate it to "Whaka." The whole country is afflicted with Maori names even more difficult than those of Indians affected by parts of New York State and Michigan, but the people here cut them for everyday use to a handy syllable or two.

The mild wonders of Whakarewarewa are exhibited by Maori women guides. Our little party was advised to look up "Guide Beatrice," but Beatrice happened to be engaged with another party, so we contented ourselves with Guide Susan, a middle-aged woman of unusual intelligence. If Beatrice is better than Susan, she is a very good guide.

I was more interested in Susan than in the various thermal effects which she faithfully showed us for a shilling a head. I began my first-hand studies of the Maoris with Guide Susan. She was, I judged, at least half-white. Indeed, she told me that full Maoris are now few and far between, and gave it as her opinion that in twenty-five years there would be scarcely a full-blooded Maori in New Zealand.

The Maoris, New Zealand's inhabitants when white men came to the country, are straight-haired Polynesians, closely related to Samoans and Hawaiians. Al-

though they are known to have been rank cannibals—
addicted to the eating of human flesh for the sheer love
of it—and both Hawaiians and Samoans deny ever having eaten their own kind as food, there are students of
race who regard the old Maoris as the highest type of all
Polynesians; which is equivalent to declaring them the
superiors of any of the South Sea native races. Guide
Susan exhibited the mental alertness which is so often
ascribed to Maoris; but it would be impossible for anyone
to tell whether her quickness came to her through the
Maori or the white in her. No mixture of races can be
relied upon for the special characteristics of either one.

Susan merely stirred my desire to know more about the
Maori people. I saw the mud flowers, Devil's Kitchens,
Bride's Tears, and such in Whakarewarewa, but, for the
life of me, I cannot tell now what they were like. That
comes from being addicted to the study of peoples.

On the opposite side of town from Whakarewarewa is
a good-sized Maori village, Ohinemutu. Maoris are said
to have occupied this site from times before white men
came. Steam holes in the lime-encrusted surface, pools of
always boiling water, natural ovens heated to good cooking temperature by steam from underneath—these are
used to-day by the Maoris for cooking, washing, and
bathing, quite as their ancestors used them, perhaps centuries ago. Children, *sans* clothing, are always in one
or another of the pools; some woman is forever pounding
some tourist's garment to pieces at nature's washtub;
here and there, kettles buried in rags simmer over steaming holes in the rock. One can easily think of Ohinemutu
as a Maori village since the race began.

The most obvious manifestation of the Maori in this

village is the elaborate carving on the facings of the houses. The front of the house is usually recessed, making a little veranda under the roof. Decorating the sides of this open space and the cornice above are heavy planks, carved in fantastic Maori designs, painted a dull red, and adorned at the peak of the roof with a rudely cut wooden image.

In other respects, the Maori house has succumbed to white influence. These curious strips of woodwork, when set up as doorposts on thatch-built huts of the Maori days, must have lent a weird effect to the habitations; nailed as they are now against the front of commonplace little frame houses, they look like something from the past lugged into the present. The Maori church, too, prettily set on the edge of the lake, is an odd mixture of these carvings and a style of architecture that seems to have tried to express the Maori idea in European terms—with effects which might be described as stunning.

The inhabitants of this village are interesting chiefly as examples of what a few generations of inbreeding with whites of uncertain quality can do to one of the finest of the Polynesian stocks. They are a coarse-featured, weak-faced lot. Degeneracy is unmistakable in a high proportion. In my visits to the place I did not see one Maori whom I would consider as a full-blood. I met a good number of mixed bloods around Rotorua quite as well-favoured as Guide Susan, but they were exceptions to the general run. One cannot conceive of Hawaiians and Samoans as being even remotely connected with these people.

Some New Zealanders assert with evident pride that there is no colour line in their country—an assertion that can hardly stand against one of the deep-seated instincts of the white race.   But New Zealanders have gone against that instinct with an extraordinary disregard of what they were doing to their own race, as well as to the Maoris.   It certainly would never do to judge Maoris by the remnants which one sees in the ancient village of Ohinemutu.

The best one-day excursion out of Rotorua is what is known as "The Round Trip."   Several other trips are made in a day, which go out to something and back; this one makes a complete round of scenery, interesting all the way, and doubles back on itself over a few miles only of the motor road.

The first part of the ride is through great areas of re-forestation—or rather, afforestation, as these hills never were timbered to any extent.   These miles on miles of pine and hardwood plantings indicate that New Zealanders, instead of being fifty years behind, are stepping along in the front line with the most progressive.   The work was done by prison labour.   The land, cleared at the start of all growth, is kept clear, and the trees spread over the hills to their very tops like an immense series of carpets, shaded in greens according to their kind.   Wide fire breaks, kept absolutely bare, pass over the hills at regular intervals.   New Zealand intends always to have lumber for those pretty bungalows.

The trip combines motoring with two launch rides over a series of beautiful lakes.   At the top of a cliff overlooking the first lake, we left the automobile and walked down a steep path to the motor-boat landing, where an open launch, built to carry a dozen or so, was awaiting us. Our Chesterfieldian captain and guide was a Maori—by courtesy of a dark skin and the astuteness of the management. Under any other name he might not have drawn as well.

Across the first lake and over a high hill this captain and his crew of one escorted us to the second boat, in which they were to take us through the region devastated by the cataclysmic outburst of Mount Tarawera, in 1886. I dimly recalled having read at the time about this disturbance, but New Zealand in 1886 was even farther away from anywhere than it is now. Probably few Americans remember the event. Not only did Mount Tarawera belch forth from three immense craters literally mountains of ash, but huge fissures opened up in the region about and disgorged new ranges, hundreds of feet high.

The classic English of this guide was in itself an entertainment; when used to describe one of the world's most awful volcanic eruptions, it made us see what he had seen in the days following the destruction. Maori villages now lie buried under grassy hills; lakes filled and vanished, and other lakes were brought into existence by the sudden changing of the face of nature; mountains and valleys are to-day where lowlands were before. The quiet, well-chosen expressions of our Maori guide gave vividness to the fearful remaking.

Across a lake of fifty-six hundred acres that was a little stream in 1886 we chugged leisurely past these mud mountains, now deeply gorged by the rains of forty years. In fewer centuries than it usually takes the weather to wash down mountains, I suppose these will have let most of their substance slip into the lake.

Then what of the lake? I am not a geologist.

At the farther end the waters of this lake become warm, then hot. Out of the hills at the water's edge, great volumes of steam issue with a continuous roaring. Terrific heat is somewhere under this lake. It makes one wonder whether the big fireworks are over.

But nothing happened worse than a scalded hand. Our guide had told us at a certain spot in the lake *not* to test the water. One lady just had to do it—and found it boiling.

Reluctantly we left the boat and the Maori, and took on another guide for a three-mile walk up a steaming, seething valley to the top of the low range, where a motor was waiting to take us back to Rotorua.

On the way was Waimangu, the crater of one of the world's largest geysers, which once discharged periodically a huge column of water nine hundred feet into the air. Next to it is Frying-pan Flat, which in 1917 suddenly exploded and wrecked the surrounding country with mud and stones. The force of its discharge knocked the upper story off the government rest house, nearly a mile away and hundreds of feet higher, and killed part of the keeper's family. Luckily this was the only habitation within range of its fury.

Now, all the geysers in the Rotorua region are no more than steam vents; hissing angrily, but never performing. Everybody is sorrowfully wondering when or whether they will become active again. Nobody knows.

Still, things happen suddenly in this region. Mount Tarawera blew up without warning. Once Waimangu shot its nine hundred feet of water unexpectedly, and carried off three people in its boiling flood. Frying-pan Flat had never done anything unseemly until it went off with a bang that tore up the countryside. And every hole in the earth hereabouts groans, growls, sizzles.

I advise the Rotoruans to stand in a safe place, and hope.

* * *

Waitomo Caves. How many Americans who were never here have heard of them? I had not; but within the space of a hundred yards in a cave not especially remarkable, a few million glowworms stage one of the most uniquely beautiful sights in the world.

From Rotorua it is a short day of zigzag travel by two trains and a motor to Waitomo Caves, but as the whole thing is done on a government ticket, and one fetches up in time for a good dinner at the government's hotel miles off in the hills, after nothing more disturbing in the day than the hold-ups for morning and afternoon tea, the journey is an easy one.

After dinner and an hour of rest, heavy, spiked boots were put on, and the party hobbled down under the bright stars of a moonless night to the entrance to Waitomo Cave. Limestone caves, I was told—not being posted on the matter of caves—are usually, if not always, the ancient waterways of subterranean rivers. Often the river has cut its way through to some other fissure in the soft rock and formed a new tunnel out of it, leaving the water-worn chambers of its old path to be decorated, perhaps through long ages, by the limestone drip from their ceilings.

The river which formed Waitomo Cave still runs part of the way in its original bed. It enters the cave mountain on one side, and emerges a hundred feet lower on the other; but the entrance for visitors is through a fissure conveniently opening about halfway between.

I have had little cave experience with which to compare

the limestone effects in these subterranean chambers. Once, years ago, I struggled through two miles of the then newly discovered "Cave of the Winds" in the Black Hills, South Dakota, but in my travels I have somehow omitted caves. These cavernous rooms and crooked passages were to me new sights, except as I faintly recalled my one previous journey underground. We wandered through a profusion of stalactites and stalagmites of all shapes and sizes; drapery formations exquisitely coloured; pillars like alabaster; and other forms shaped like nothing at all by the ages of lime-water drippings.

Astonishing, grotesque, sometimes beautiful; but all of it wonderful beyond expression in its incredibly slow building. A hundred years adds a paper thickness, or quarter of an inch, according to the nature of the drip; here its finished work is displayed in tons. A fair conception of the ages spent on this accomplishment ought to be a cure for human impatience. The chief entertainment of the party seemed to be to make out ducks, twins, sheepsheads, pulpits, in these stones; yet some, perhaps, got from them a sermon on the immensity of Time.

Finally, down a steep passage, we came to the underground river—and to the Glowworm Cave. Glowworms have attached themselves to every bit of the roughly vaulted ceiling over the water. Each worm lets down a single line six or eight inches long, slightly adhesive, like a spider's web. The rays of a light turned obliquely toward the ceiling reveal these as a multitude of glistening silver threads, so nearly even at their lower ends that they look like a beautifully trimmed decoration. Their spacing indicates a glowworm intelligence; none are close enough to interfere, yet they are rarely more than three or four inches apart. There seems to be precious little room for newcomers.

The glowworm, with his light turned on, sits motionless at the top of his sticky line and waits for some careless insect to trip a wing against it. With these millions of expectant diners, it is hard to imagine enough insects finding their way into the cave, or rising from the water, to make this scheme for collecting food much of a success. The uncertainty of it would be a nervous strain on anything less placid than a glowworm. They may become accustomed to long waits between meals, but if one's line were an inch or two shorter than the others, the vital question for that worm would be, will he *ever* get a meal? Or suppose that another, in a rush of luck, should capture two mosquitoes within a single month—what would he do with them all?

Orders to get into the boat and remain absolutely silent put an end to these practical speculations. All lights were extinguished; then, by means of a wire drawn taut from point to point along the winding cavern, the guide drew us noiselessly up stream.

In the stillness we seemed to be gliding into another world. Each point of light shone as a star in a miniature heaven. The silver threads became invisible; all surfaces vanished, and the even spacing of the glows made the rough vaulting appear as a smoothly rounded canopy, filled with stars. Moving as we were without sound or impulse, we lost the sense of motion, the spectacle seemed to pass slowly over our heads.

As we moved, the perspective of that uneven surface overhead was, of course, always changing, while we were seeing only points of light. The effect was a curiously beautiful undulating motion in what the eye was mistaking for a starry heaven.   In the shifting panorama, clusters of stars were moving unevenly, and drifting into each other; all over the canopy was this constant reshaping of the pattern.   Now and then, a hanging spur of rock, covered with lights but itself invisible, seemed as a bright constellation moving weirdly across the little firmament, putting out one by one the glows beyond, while in its wake other glows appeared as mysteriously.

Suddenly we awoke from our imaginings to a change in the view.   Without a sound we had pulled out of the cave into the clear, still night, and were looking at stars in a real heaven.

It was a shifting of scene so absolutely unique in the world's panoramas that we met it with a gasp of astonishment, as if well-behaved stars in a staid old heaven were a novelty.   But we did not want to be disillusioned; back again the boat took us to our mimic sky.   We watched the myriad points of light go through their droll contortionings in reverse, all the way to the underground landing.

It is a spectacle in which one could easily be disappointed.   One's own mood might not be right for it.   A single babbling fool who has always to be exclaiming how "fine" it is, especially in places where silence lends enchantment, could spoil the effect.   And some would see only a lot of glowworms anyway.   But as a half-hour's feast of imaginative beauty I have seen nothing in years of travel to equal the Glowworm Cave in Waitomo.

* * *

Back again in Auckland, ready for the sail across to Australia.   Whiling away time, I went to the Museum, to see the Maori collections, and the famous paintings of old Maoris.

One does not trust paintings to reveal human limitations—it is their usual business to conceal them; so one can leave the Maori paintings with the feeling that they are exceedingly well done, and that the old boys hideously overdid the tattooing of their faces. Tattooing has gone pretty much out of style with the present-day Maoris, but many of the women still have an ugly moustache design about their mouths, dripping down at the corners in an oddly suggestive way.

I went into the public library to see the American papers. It appeared to be a very well-equipped library, and the large newspaper room had files all the way around its walls and several times across, stocked with papers from everywhere—except America. The management told me that they had no call for American newspapers.

Off in the islands I did not expect to see our papers, but in Fiji, on the direct route of the liners through Honolulu and with two dailies of its own, I rather hoped to find at least one of the two good Honolulu dailies, if not a San Francisco paper. But the Carnegie library there, carrying English, Canadian, and Colonial papers, had none from America, and neither of the Suva dailies exchanged with Honolulu or any other American city.

Colonials in the Pacific do a fair and increasing business with America, but they do it without taking enough interest in us to look us up on the map. In Tongatabu, an intelligent trader thought that the woods of our Southern states were full of chimpanzees. Another business man, when he heard that I was from Boston, wanted to know whether Ohio was not in Boston. He was a local agent for an automobile firm in Toledo. A New Zealand church dignitary asked me if we had not made a pretty good thing out of Ceylon.

Whenever I broached a hobby of mine to New Zealanders, that all English-speaking peoples in the world ought to get together in a closer friendly understanding, they seemed to regard it as a commendable idea, but too novel to warrant any expressions offhand. And a surprising lot of them held the view that, during the early part of the war, sentiment in America had been disposed against the Allies. The bellowings of a few wild Irishmen in America, reprinted in the English papers, had fixed this view in their minds, and not one of our own papers was on the ground to dislodge it.

Is it not about time that we became better acquainted with these virile, kindly, and altogether interesting cousins of ours 'way off in the Pacific?

CHAPTER VII

AUSTRALIA

I WENT to Australia loaded with warnings and advice from all along the line.

"Australia hasn't much to show a sightseer," admitted a Sydney travelling man in the South Sea islands, "but when it comes to business—say, some day she'll show the world!" I hastily denied being a sightseer.

"You'll not care for Australia," declared an American on the *Tofua*. "It's too much like the Middle West." As if I could not care for the Middle West. I was born there.

"Sydney is a windy place and full of dirt," observed a lady from Brisbane.

"Brisbane never got started. When she does, she's as likely as not to back up," remarked a jocose chap from Sydney.

"Melbourne is a nice old town—for funerals." This from a booster for Sydney.

"When you come from Sydney to Melbourne you will notice a *great difference* in the people," a precise Melbourne lady told me confidentially.

Puzzled as to just how they were different, I asked a Sydney lady what the Melbourne lady meant. Her answer was printable, but it showed hasty judgment.

What I heard in New Zealand about Australians would

have to be put into an appendix.   An appendix is a book's collection of suppressed details.

Australia may not have much to show the visitor, but her census figures and a look at the map will give him something to think about.   Less than five million people occupy an island continent of almost exactly the same area as the United States; directly north are the world's most congested lands, where one billion people struggle daily for enough to eat.

Hordes crowd the islands of the Straits right down to Australia's edge.   Java, a long, rakish island off her northern shore, would make one good eyebrow on the face of Australia; yet Java has thirty-five million people.   It seems an irony of fate that the most populous bit of land on the earth should lie next to its most sparsely settled continent.

Yet these five million Australians declare solidly for an all-white population.   They tell the billion yellows and browns, in no uncertain terms, that they shall not enter. With something like fifteen thousand miles of undefended coast line, Australia has no great army and navy.   Just one word stands between Australians and the billion yellows and browns: England.

The situation is enough to stir the imagination of any traveller; but as a student of race I had a still more lively interest in seeing the Australian people—a people whose beginnings are without a parallel in white colonization.

In 1788, a shipload of convicts from England was landed in what is now Sydney's harbour; thereafter, for fifty-two years, Australia was the dumping ground for England's criminals, men and women, and for a good one half of that time convicts, both in bond and liberated, were its chief population—the most unpromising mess of humans ever dropped upon a fair landscape.

The best story of those times is in a well-accredited book, "Curious Facts of Old Colonial Days," by James Bonwick, F. R. G. S. A few quotations from the book will convey an idea of this perfect hell of a start for the peopling of Australia.

A social state wholly without women may sink to the depths, but a scarcity of women leads it to more active deviltry. In the Australian penal settlements, the brunt of this situation naturally fell upon the women convicts:

> Both male and female prisoners were commonly forwarded to-gether; the officers and soldiers selected companions for the voyage.

On landing, it was the usual practice to "assign" the women as servants or labourers to anyone who might want them; the significance of this is bluntly told by an eye-witness:

> They were disposed of by Potter, the bellman, as so much live stock. I have seen them afterward sold—one of them for a gallon of rum, others for five pounds, and so on.

There were two principal camps: the first at Sydney, the other established later in Tasmania, across from the present site of Melbourne. Those female convicts at the "Botany Bay" (Sydney) settlement who had not been "assigned" were taken to the Paramatta factory—a woollen factory built for them a few miles out from Sydney—"to work and sleep, where the women have no other beds than they can make from the wool in its dirty state; and they sleep upon it at night in the midst of their spinning wheels and work."

No wonder that, for forty years, the Paramatta factory

was, as the Sydney *Gazette* of those days pronounced it, "a hotbed of depravity."

When female convicts in the service were found showing signs of approaching maternity, they were sent to the factory, which was much more of a lying-in hospital than anything else. No attempt was ever made to discover the father. The children were brought up by thirty resident convict nurses, engaged for the purpose, and transferred to the orphan schools when arrived at the age of three years, should they live as long in such a place and under such care.

Thus the population grew. Without belittling the horrors for some of these convict women, it is fair to observe that they were usually described as willing allies of the men—from inclination or previous habit, or through drink, which was universal, or because it was the easiest way to any humane consideration.

Any man so desiring could "get an order to the matron of the factory for a wife." These factories were in both settlements: "As the authorities were always glad to get the women off their hands," the questions asked were not troublesome. There was no compulsion, but so desperate were the women to get out of the factory that they usually consented, even with the knowledge that they might afterward be converted into "an article of traffic."

After twenty-five years of the penal settlements, was there ever a dark age in Europe so dark as this?

All those ties of moral order and feelings of decency which bind society together are not only relaxed, but almost extinct. . . . Sales of wives, public and private, were common. One of some attractions brought her owner fifty ewes; another, five pounds and a gallon of rum; a third, twenty ewes and a gallon of rum. . . . In 1809, almost the whole Australian population was living in a state of unblushing concubinage. . . . Cases not infrequently occurred where the master employed his assigned servant as a prostitute, and reaped the wages of her deeper degradation.

Sodom seems to have been outdone. The Vicar General of Australia dramatically exclaims:

There is another class of crime, too frightful even for the imagination of other lands; . . . crimes that, dare I describe them, would make your blood to freeze.

The state of public safety must have been near zero. In Tasmania, crimes on an average through a series of years were 97 to 1 above those in a normal English population:

One half of those that die in the colony at the present time perish directly or indirectly through drunkenness.

In that twenty-fifth year, the Governor made what seems to have been the first attempt at reform in the conditions:

"No fresh female convict will in future be assigned to any settler or other person unless he is a married man." But, the record says, "This order was little heeded by the officials who had the administration of affairs"—evidently for the very good reason that officials had first pick of newly arrived women convicts.

Ten years later, in another spurt of virtue induced by a clergyman known as the "Fighting Chaplain," the then Governor issued an order

commanding all officers, on pain of dismissal from the service, to be united in matrimony with those with whom they had been publicly living, and by whom, in many cases, they had a family. This struck terror into the community of officials. They wished to retain their position, but not to be fettered by the marriage tie. They conjured, and they blustered; they presented memorials, and they condemned the tyranny, but all in vain. . . . The "Fighting Chaplain" was not to be driven from his entrenchments, nor seduced from his duty. Gradually and sulkily the discomfited chiefs gave in. Their mistresses were made wives, and their children legitimated in the eyes of the law.

Other spasms for the uplift of Australia emanated from England. The disproportion of the sexes—about 4 to 1—was appreciated as standing in the way of any beginning at reform:

After a while, some good people in England sought to rectify the evil by the shipment of free, but destitute, young women.

Imagine the effect of shipping "free, but destitute, young women" into that maelstrom:

One of the female immigrants wrote thus to a friend in England: "Out of two hundred and sixty-eight that came out with me, I verily believe that there are not more than twenty who have any claim to a good name, being driven to the most wretched and loathsome debauchery."

Another trial of the same kind was made with a specially selected group of girls; but such were the conditions on the transports that virtue seems to have had difficulty in getting even as far as the shores of Australia:

A dozen [young women], sent out by a religious society, were christened by the sailors "The Twelve Apostles." Dr. Cunningham informs us of a goodly proportion of that chosen band being found in a matronly way by the reverend inspector, who visited them on arrival.

This pictures the Australian people as they were in the neighbourhood of one hundred years ago. The shipping of convicts ceased in 1840. Australia's present-day population has mostly arrived since the discovery of gold in 1851, and unquestionably it is rich in the virile, constructive types which usually venture into new lands; but there is no escaping the fact that this later influx was superimposed upon the most desperate beginnings ever known in the history of white migrations.

Who wouldn't be curious to see this great country of the

Antipodes? Now we are steaming into Sydney harbour, for a look at Australia—and the Australians.

* * *

Everybody admits that Sydney's harbour is one of the prettiest in either of the temperate zones. Once through the portals at the entrance, its waters spread irregularly into a great number of bays, formed by as many rolling, green promontories covered with red-roofed houses. Sydney harbour is pleasanter to see than many others as well favoured by nature, because its capes and islands are used for residential purposes, instead of garbage plants, boat yards, city prisons, and the like. The smokes of commerce are mostly about the city itself, at the farther end of the harbour.

Sydney impresses one as just enough unlike a big American city to have been built somewhere else. By taking in the suburbs back of it, the cottage-covered hills all the way down both sides of the harbour, and the populous beach resorts on the ocean side, Sydney counts up almost one million people. Her metropolitan air showed first in the price for transferring luggage—four shillings per trunk if you bargain in advance, and anything up to ten if you don't.

Sydneyites display a healthy common sense, not characteristic of many great ports, in making popular use of their harbour and its beautiful frontages. Several wide streets lead down through the business section to the Circular Quay; from this crescentlike arrangement of slips, lines of attractive ferries ply to every suburb and resort on the harbour.

What a delight it must be for Sydney's "tired business

man," in the sweltering weeks around Christmas and New Year's, to slip off almost directly from the roar of town for a quiet sail out to a pretty cottage home on the shore! This sounds like a rhapsody, but in Sydney it is a realized fact.

Sydney's big down-town park is something to make her coming generations rise up and bless the donors of it. It must have been set apart in her early days, else one hundred and thirty-odd beautifully green acres, embellished with trees and flowers, would not now be lying right alongside the heart of the city's business and sharing the water front with it.

A closely centred business district, with the relieving Circular Quay at the end of it and this high, rolling expanse of quiet a few minutes off at one side, feature an otherwise not too interesting town. Most big cities give the impression that they "just grew." A careful look at Sydney arouses the suspicion that her layout was deliberately planned.

On these pleasant spring days—it is the middle of October—I made frequent escapes to the water. Halfway down the harbour is the Zoo, on a great hillside where dens cut into the rock in a way to resemble caves and grottoes display the animals to unusual advantage. My chief interest in zoos is to see the animals fed. Not being much of an eater, I get an appetizing thrill out of seeing others wildly interested in food; and there is always something delightfully incredulous in watching lions, tigers, leopards, and panthers rage with anticipation for half an hour before dinner, even if it is too much to expect that I shall ever know their ecstatic desire for nourishment.

But the wild denizens of this zoo behaved astonishingly.

As the hour approached, their natural indifference turned to apathy. The meat man had actually to stir them from an unbecoming lassitude.

And no wonder. What seemed like half a side of beef was given to each sizable creature, while hyenas, wolves, and the like were fed enough to gorge a lion. Into the den of three immense tigers the meat was dramatically let down through a hole overhead. They looked at it with the sad eyes of a man whose plate has been too much heaped with cabbage. Then it was dangled enticingly lower, just out of reach. Nonchalantly one of the tigers strolled over, rose to his splendid full height, missed it by about an inch, then lay down and refused to become interested again until the keeper virtually announced, "dinner is served," by dropping the huge chunk on the ground.

I sought the meat carrier. "If you want to make a show of feeding the animals, why don't you put some snap into it by letting them get hungry?"

"'Ungry?" The moron had to entertain this for a moment before its meaning dawned.

"Ow!" He said it with a dropping of the jaw as if I had pinched him, but Australians do this in ordinary conversation. "'Ungry! Well, now! I did wonder w'y stryngers kyme 'ere to see 'em fed." By this time the full flood of my suggestion was upon him. He eyed me with rising suspicion.

"*Starve* 'em? 'Ungry? Gawd!" he exclaimed, for want of a vocabulary to meet the new thought, "It's wicked!" And he looked wicked. At twenty paces I glanced over my shoulder. He seemed to be deciding between bowling me over and calling the local police. I hastened to the boat.

Another delightful harbour trip, twice as long, is to Manly Beach, the city's largest and best open-sea resort. Against a fine crescent of sandy shore the prevailing east wind drives heavy breakers. Even in these spring days of October many bathers were enjoying the surf, under the eyes of life guards and the usual gathering of onlookers. Australian beaches have a wide fame for the variety of their bathing costumes—especially for certain varieties. Except that some of them were enticingly stretched on, there were none to indicate that Manly Beach has anything to show Waikiki or any of our speedier resorts in America—but, only because at all of them, some women's bathing suits have already fetched up against impassable limits.

*   *   *

Armed with a card from the Jockey Club, I went by tram out to see the apple of Sydney's eye, the Randwick race course. Speaking of trams, who ever heard of city street cars run on the plan of a steam railroad? Sydney's trams are built with that European relic, the *vis-à-vis* cross-car compartment; the conductor is not in sight, nor is there any way of signalling him.

"How do I get the conductor to let me know when I reach my street?" I asked a lady next to me.

"Ow, you down't," she replied affably. "You watch the street nymes."

"Ow, I see"—I had been in town for several days—"but suppose I happen to catch a fleeting glimpse of my street, how do I signal the man to stop?"

"You down't. He stops at styshuns. and you get off at the nearest one."

Which, for me, meant the next one beyond, if any.

In the business section every street crossing is a regular stop, whether or not anybody wants to get on or off. In the outskirts, the stops are a long way apart—otherwise, a car halting half the time for nobody would get nowhere. The system may have its advantages, but they are not obvious at a glance.

Getting back to the Randwick course, horse racing is the great Australian pastime. Perhaps it would be more correct to say that betting on horse races is the great Australian pastime. The government itself gets a big revenue from a percentage on all bets placed. By the time I arrived in Australia, hundreds of thousands were either going or preparing to go to Melbourne for the biggest meet of the year, which ends with Australia's top racing event, the Melbourne Cup.

Railway accommodations were not to be had. Every sleeping place in Melbourne had been engaged for months, down to the last billiard table. For these reasons I did not get a chance to verify the Melbourne lady's remark about the "great difference" between Sydney and Melbourne people.

But if Melbourne has the greatest race, Sydney boasts the finest race course in Australia—the Randwick Course. I was shown into every corner of the immense plant, from the Premier's suite to the jockeys' weighing-in room.

In its arrangements for vast crowds of people and a multitude of racing horses—these are always running races, and always on turf—Randwick is built up like an institution. The three huge amphitheatres offer nothing remarkable in their sea of benches—we have bigger capacities in many of our stadia and baseball pavilions; but nothing of ours compares with the luxurious appointments in the maze of rooms and halls built in underneath. For an hour we wandered through suites for state and city officials, suites for the Board, and suites for members— all beautifully finished and furnished and spread with ·fine rugs; parlours and rest rooms galore for ladies, dressing rooms for ladies with all conveniences of the boudoir; dining rooms for ladies, for members, for special guests, for the public. I began to wonder whether they came to see the races or to spend the day below decks dolling up and being fed.

Watching the horses race is incidental with Australians. They are here to bet. Scores of bookmakers accommodate the small fry, but the chief excitement at the Randwick track is its huge automatic betting machine, the totalizator.

Who knows what a totalizator is? I didn't. On an immense facing set well up over the heads of the crowd are forty numbers, representing the horses, in easy view of the tens of thousands who can find standing room in front of it. Under each number is an indicator which shows at any instant the total number of unit bets placed on that horse; hence the name, totalizator. A unit bet is ten shillings, but one can bet as many units as he pleases.

I happened to see this machinery in operation while it was being tested by the experts, in preparation for a coming meet. The bettor steps up to a booth, puts down his money, and indicates his horse; the operator presses certain buttons; then a complicated little machine not only prints a ticket showing the number of the horse and the units bet, but it automatically adds the bet to that horse's score up on the totalizator, a hundred feet away.

This machine keeps humans strictly out of all contact

Maori mixed-blood girl and Maori wood carving

Igorot women road-workers, Baguio, Philippine Islands

Pines Hotel, Baguio, Philippine Islands

with the betting record, for the record's own good; and the devices for holding the jockeys to the path of rectitude make those of a high-class girls' boarding school look like invitations to crime. Human frailty gets one hundred per cent. credit at race tracks.

Australians are ready to lay stiff wagers on anything. They will bet as to whether a man standing on the curb across the street will start off with his left foot or his right. They will bet on which of two pigeons will fly away first; and if both fly at once, they will match coins to see whose bird won.

In all their games of chance they frankly play for the money. There is none of the silly subterfuge of our auction players who put up little stakes—"not for the money —oh, no!" but because, they say, it makes them "play a better game!" Friends, sniping at each other's small change! And into a great game of golf on a glorious morning with jolly good fellows, our money-steeped business men have to inject a few car fares, "to make it interesting!"

Pin-money sports. Australians gamble and admit it.

*   *   *

Everybody who goes to Australia goes to Australia's country show place, the Blue Mountains.

To Katoomba, in the centre of this inland resort district, it is a slow train ride of about four hours. Like New Zealand, Australia has a system of well-managed tourist bureaus which make travel easy for strangers in the land.

The Blue Mountain region is not mountainous in the usual sense of the word. It is an extensive plateau in which great gorges and cañons have been cut by the corrosive action of ages. Instead of riding through valleys and looking up at mountain peaks, as one ordinarily does in mountain scenery, we were most of the time riding on plateaus and looking down into gorges. Many of the gorges are impressive, some of them beautiful in spite of the dull green of never-ending eucalyptus forests. And, best of all, there is no better way to get acquainted with Australians than to live for a week in one of their little hotels and knock around with them on the oddly built busses—capacious Australian bodies set upon American chassis. Sometime they may take to manufacturing their own complete cars, but at present you are urged to try a Buick, or a Hudson, or a Packard, or some other reputable American car which you never could recognize except by the hubs. Fords abound, but they do not appear to have been raised to the dignity of busses. Australians want something bigger and heavier.

Here, again, I took to visiting caves. They make quite a point of it in this region, possibly because there is not so very much to see above ground. A day's journey by motor takes one to the famous Jenolan caves, through any two of them which may be selected, and back to Katoomba. Possibly my new friends were "pulling my leg"—this is Australian slang for "stringing" a newcomer —but they explained "Jenolan" as derived from the name of the discoverer of the caves, J. E. Nolan. It must be said for this collection of caverns that they outrank in size, variety of formations, and generally wonderful limestone effects those in New Zealand, yet I would not give up the mental picture of that one hundred yards of the Glowworm Cave at Waitomo for all the astonishing sights in these caves of J. E. Nolan.

That bit of slang pertaining to the nether limb got me into an embarrassing few moments. I had always connected pulling one's leg with attempts to extract money, or favours—never having heard of its Australian meaning. Now, if the young lady to whom I was making conservative statements about automobiles in America had turned to me in the soft twilight of the veranda and remarked sweetly, "Oh, but do you really think I can believe that?" I would have understood her. Well, she expressed herself sweetly, but not in those words. Imagine my surprise. I certainly was *not* pulling her leg; neither had I tried to borrow money from her. Both literally and figuratively her remark seemed to be uncalled for.

"If you mean——" I began heavily, and hesitated, not having the slightest notion of what she did mean.

That girl was quick. In a flash she was back to safer English. "Do tell me about those automobiles," she prattled. "Are there *really* so many of them in America?"

* * *

The Australian mode of speech should be able to stand a little good-natured comment. Let a member of the Melbourne University staff introduce the delicate subject. Discussing the criticisms which travellers direct at their way of talking, he was quoted in a Sydney paper while I was there as saying:

Our critics are quite right; the Australians as a rule really have an awful accent. The ugliness of some Australian accents is a misfortune, but not a crime, and no visitor from other lands has a right to be annoyed by it.

I hasten to agree that we who travel in foreign lands have no right to be annoyed by any vocal sounds which come within the law.   And also, that the Australian way of torturing the King's English is not a crime; but in the interest of a language hallowed by Shakespeare and others, couldn't it be made a plain misdemeanour, punishable by thirty days in a school of elocution?

As early as 1814, in the twenty-sixth year of the convict colony, a school teacher remarked on the "stammering tongues, repetitions, and improper accent" in New South Wales.   It is reasonable to assume that the present medley of accents is to some extent a survival of those early days, mixed with the various dialects of later immigrants from all over England.   Many educated Australians speak good English, of course; but one often hears a half-dozen accents in a single group of intelligent people.

While in Katoomba I asked a lady at an afternoon tea whether she thought they would serve cocoa instead of tea. Her blank look led me to repeat.

"Ow!" she remarked, smiling on me indulgently, "you mean *cow-cow*."

Say "cocoa" with two distinct droppings of the jaw and the mouth spread wide, like a ventriloquist's dummy, and you will have it.   More practice along this line should enable you to "gow to the ryalw'y styshun to tyke a tryne, and come howme in the ryne with a cowld in your showlder."

A lady who had seen me about the little hotel for days finally asked me, "Are you an Austrylian?"   This was her highest flattery to an obvious foreigner.   Everybody there had been plying me with questions about America for a week.   But I fell for the taffy.

"No," I said, looking as pleased as I could on short notice, "I'm an American."

"W'y, isn't it strynge!" she exclaimed. "You down't have the American voice. I would tyke you for an Austrylian."

Of course, we are famous the world over for our terrible voices, and I suppose I should have been elated at having been tyken for an Austrylian; yet the lady's compliment did not fill me with a new joy.

* * *

"A White Australia." White, in this national slogan, has always stood for more than colour; it implies equality, responsibility, unity of ideals and purpose. How well has Australia attained this ideal?

These people impress one with their generally intelligent appearance. Well-shaped noses and firm chins on so many men and women indicate a good degree of racial strength. I never saw a higher proportion of strong-featured young girls—which plainly tells of strong-featured mothers, as well as fathers. Australia's virile men must still be marrying that kind of women in preference to the soft-faced and overfine—luckily for coming generations, since mothers contribute a full one half to the race's inheritance.

This is one side of the racial picture. Now for the other. It looks like an aftermath of Australia's convict beginnings.

Just before I left Australia, Melbourne had a police strike which for two days left the city practically unguarded. It was an almost exact duplicate of Boston's police strike—the one that indirectly made Calvin Coolidge president of the United States. One might expect something better than Boston's wild nights of looting from this all-white city in a new land; yet for two nights Melbourne was at the absolute mercy of her own savages.

These are newspaper headings, and extracts from the account of the affair:

MELBOURNE IN TUMULT

EXTRAORDINARY HAPPENINGS
"LARRIKINS" TAKE CHARGE OF CITY
WHOLESALE PLUNDER AND DESTRUCTION
PITCHED BATTLE IN STREETS
TRAGIC SEQUEL TO POLICE STRIKE

Wild scenes of rioting, which occurred in Melbourne on Friday night, were eclipsed on Saturday. As night fell, unruly crowds took charge of the centre of the city, and unprecedented incidents of savagery and looting occurred. . . . Several deaths have occurred, and many criminal acts are reported from the suburbs. . . .

A total of 78 shops were looted. Clothing stores were singled out by the raiders, 21 of these being stripped. Next came jewellers, 15 shops having been ransacked. . . . The looting was at its height when a man emerged from the midst of the crowd and proceeded to smash in the windows of the Leviathan Stores with a hammer. He was actually cheered as he proceeded with his destruction. Packs of Larrikins then entered the windows, loading themselves with articles of clothing, and throwing the expensively dressed dummies into the street, where they were quickly stripped. . .

Many wild scenes of spoliation and callousness were witnessed, and these, instead of striking the onlookers with sorrow and shame, were greeted with shrieks of hysterical laughter and bursts of cheering. . . .

Boston's police strike startled the world by disclosing the feebleness of civilization's grip. Melbourne's was of more significance in confirming the disclosure. "A White Australia" sounds well, but what point is there in preserving white skins for the race if half-men are to be inside them?

Australia is demonstrating nothing new in her failure to realize a workable human equality. Every civilized country is heading straight for the same failure by breeding its half-men at twice the rate of its competent citizens. We in England and America are now supposed to be bred down to about 20 per cent. morons. Whatever the right figure is—and it might be half that—an overwhelming mob of potential outlaws is in every big city, merely awaiting failure of the police.

Equality under civilized conditions is fast proving itself to be an impossible ideal. Civilization specializes in human *inequality*. Business must have it, and culture thrives on it. Culture has always risen highest when bestowing its benefits on the fewest. A socially wicked state, of course; but an ideally levelled-off social order would develop a civilization as flat as itself.

Australia is finding her "All-white" experiment mighty inconvenient. For one thing, it has put her securely under union labour's thumb. "Slow up!" is an Australian labour slogan that bids fair to kill labour itself by killing business. At Brisbane, our vessel, bound from Sydney for Japan, had its cargo handled by middle-aged, fat, intelligent white men. They took all day for shifting freight which our Fiji natives on the *Tofua* would have handled in two hours. Every detail seemed to be arranged to make the job last; a great ship was held up by a little handful of dockmen.

The cheapest labour in the world loads the ships which come to Australia from her fierce business rivals north of her. The cheapest labour in the world makes the goods which those ships bring in. How can Australia compete, with her middle-aged, fat, intelligent white men?

The bursting populations on the north look hungrily at a continent held by five million white people. They feel that its great areas are not being utilized, because these white people do not use it as they themselves would use it—to breed a seething population of the half-starved.

Is Australia scared? Well, rawther! But then, there are the big guns of Mother England!

* * *

The first week in November, and now aboard the Japanese liner *Tango Maru*, bound for Manila, sixteen days off to the northwest. The name suggests a gay craft; but twenty-eight first-class passengers could hardly make a riotous showing on a good-sized vessel. It was an agreeable little party, off for an uneventful cruise in the stillest waters of the Pacific.

A day ashore at Brisbane, and only a distant look at Thursday Island, at the northernmost tip of Australia; these were the two excitements. Days up the coast of Australia inside the Great Barrier, formed of numberless shoals and islands; days of going almost westward in the doldrums between New Guinea and Celebes; then past Ceram, through the straits of Molucca, and across the Line in a temperature of only eighty-three.

Deck games, as usual, and the Captain's tea party, which was unusual, celebrated the crossing of the Equator. And still it was two more days of sailing off east of Borneo before we had a first glimpse of the Philippines—Mindanao, the big South Island, the home of the restless Moros. After a quite sufficient number of days at sea, we were to get half a day ashore at Mindanao's port, Zamboanga.

CHAPTER VIII

THE PHILIPPINE ISLANDS

IMAGINE the Philippine group as transplanted to regions familiar to us: the north tip of its biggest island would rub against New York City while its southernmost bits of land were in the warm waters off Palm Beach. The range of latitude—a thousand miles—is as great as that between the north of England and the south of Italy.

But the Philippine Islands have no such differences in climate as these comparisons suggest. Their whole stretch is inside the tropics. A better measure of their extent from north to south is the distance between Havana, which is always hot, and Panama, which is always hotter.

In America, cities brag of their populations. In the Philippines, the big rivalry is over temperatures and humidities.

When you are perspiring in the mugginess of Zamboanga, and they tell you how much cooler it is there than in Manila, your overworked pores incline you to disbelieve them. And when, in the water-soaked atmosphere of Manila, the Manilans cast aspersions on the heat of Zamboanga, you regard them sorrowfully because you know how much cooler it is in Zamboanga.

So it goes. While in any one of the coast towns, it is difficult to believe anything worse of the others; hence, the impression that, when it comes to the weather of their respective bailiwicks, all men are liars.

The almost glassy calm of our long journey up from Australia deserted us as we approached the harbour of Zamboanga. Landing on the pier from a bobbing little steam tender was a feat for the agile; but an imminent prospect of drowning gives even to the aged a momentary sprightliness. Everybody made the hazardous leap in safety.

Zamboanga is a flat old Spanish town partly made over by Americans, and peopled mostly by unimpressive little natives ranging all the way from yellowish to dark. These Moros of Mindanao illustrate the advantage which a new religion gains in a heathen field by being first on the ground. Mohammedan proselytes beat the old Spanish priests to this big island, and as a consequence the Moros to this day are followers of the Prophet. If their faith shades off into paganism here and there, it does so no more than other faiths which have been impressed upon pagans everywhere.

All the available motor cars were at the dock to meet us. We seemed to owe it to the town to visit the waterworks, a few miles out, and other objects of less interest about the place. When our two hours were up we were permitted to get out and see Zamboanga. It was like attending devotions in the morning of a holiday and enjoying one's self afterward with a clear conscience.

But why should I write about the Moros? Zamboanga is the only town of any special interest on my whole itinerary which I "did," tourist fashion, in a day's stopover of a steamer. The place gave me only impressions of people and things with which all of a winter in Luzon was to make me intimately acquainted: little brown people about as featureless as rabbits; thatched-roof houses, built high up from the ground on posts, and set against one another as South Sea island houses never are; non-descript store clothes on all natives in a climate made for the *lava-lava;* and a primitive race unmistakably aping the gregarious ways of the white man, instead of sticking to village life in "the bush."

The stay in Zamboanga began with a shower and ended with a shower.   In between, the weather was threatening. We boarded our steamer for the two days' sail to Manila, and gracefully slid out into the embrace of a typhoon.

I have seen worse gales on the Atlantic, and more imposing seas—although none so viciously short and steep except perhaps in the Mediterranean—and quite as many inches, too, of rainfall per hour, in various tropical downpours; but never have I seen the three together in such a hell's concert as we had on those two days going up to Manila.   Most of the time it was difficult to tell whether the tons of water shooting horizontally through the rigging were seas breaking over us or the spillings from heaven.   The speed and the shriek were pretty much alike for both.

The worst of the storm we took abeam.   The vessel, heavily laden with freight, was unusually steady.   She took on such a list that she couldn't roll, but she "heaved" bodily, with a jerkiness and lack of rhythm that raised doubts within various of our seasoned passengers about the ultimate joy of living.

My attempts to cheer the cheerless ones did not make a hit.   I remarked on the steadiness of the vessel: no roll, no pitch—I ignored the "heave"—not much of a storm, this, compared with *some* I had been through. "Why, once, off the Azores . . ."

If you want to restore the fallen pride of ladies who have succumbed after fourteen days of living on even terms with the sea, don't belittle the cause of their undoing. Make them think that nothing short of the wickedest storm ever known could have so mistreated them. Then they will settle back in cheerful despondency, ready to like you as soon as they feel better.

We arrived off Manila toward evening of the second day. Harbours are ordinarily regarded as places to get into when the sea is rough, but the entrance through the breakwater at Manila was made so narrow that large vessels cannot safely go in during a storm; so we anchored outside all night. After bucking a typhoon for two days, one expects something better of a harbour.

Next morning, our ship blew in against her dock with a gay abandon that snapped off a few pilings. We landed in a pouring rain and drove to the hotels in a deluge. It was Manila's worst typhoon in three years, so they told us. Parts of the town were under water, and the railroad, washed out for miles, would not be running for a week.

I outlived the week. For one who is neither a sport nor a boozer, and cares nothing for decaying Spanish churches or a hectic night life feebly imitative of Broadway, a week's incarceration in steamy Manila is quite a while.

Manila is a flat old Spanish town, partly made over by Americans, and peopled mostly by unimpressive little natives ranging all the way from yellowish to dark. *Vide* Zamboanga. The terse description fits both places—except that Manila's almost three hundred thousand give her a near-metropolitan air and a much larger collection of unimpressive little natives.

Manila retains the Spanish atmosphere. Most of the streets have Spanish names—"Calle" this or that—and the money is the peso, with centavos for cents. The value of the peso is half a dollar.

Manila's Main Street is the Escolta. Every enterprising shopkeeper tries to get on it; and because it is not more than four blocks long, abnormal rents prevail. Those who cannot find space on the Escolta locate as near it as they can, along the cheaper side streets, and advertise, "Walk a few paces and save a few pesos."

This sounds fetching, but the American population of Manila, as in New York, loves to see the name of its Fifth Avenue on its parcel deliveries. The Escolta does a greater proportion of the high-priced business and has more bad debts than any other spot in the city, except, perhaps, society's favourite resort, the Manila Hotel. This hotel, I was told on the best of authority, carries the permanent mark of society's favour in the shape of anywhere between forty thousand and eighty thousand pesos in unpaid "chits"—I O U's—for dinners, parties, and drinks. A conspicuous element in Manila society measures its speed by its outstanding chits.

The Walled City—detached not only by reason of its ancient wall, but quite as much by its ultra-Spanish atmosphere—is the most interesting part of Manila. Along its narrow streets one has glimpses through doorways of spacious *patios*—once the lounging places of Spanish families, now mostly piled high with goods or lined with Filipino artisans making in primitive fashion all sorts of utensils. Filipinos and mestizos everywhere in the walled city, but Filipinos and mestizos led for two centuries to the life of Spaniards, and still living a slovenly imitation of it.

The streets of Manila fairly swarm with shady-skinned men, women, and children.   When I was young and confined at my job indoors, I would look out at times and idly wonder how so many people could be walking up and down Main Street during business hours.   In Manila, I wondered at first whether anybody at all had a job.   But a look into shops, offices, and all manner of buildings reveals everywhere a decidedly full complement of employees; those on the streets represent the overflow—bent on errands, going somewhere, or merely overflowing. Inside and out, Manila swarms.

An excellent trolley system serves the city and extends to the towns for several miles up and down the coast. You can ride in the after part of the car for ten centavos, but aft is second class, and all there are Filipinos.   You pay two centavos more and ride in the first class, forward, where the crowd is only nine tenths Filipinos.

I learned—too late to save my reputation—that whites who are at all pretentious do not ride on the trolleys.   Riding first class, forward, at two centavos extra, doesn't redeem you from the imputation that you are a social cipher. It is almost as *de trop* as going afoot.

Next to flies, the most obvious insect in Manila is the humbug.

Transportation here is tied up with social intricacies. The different means for getting about, stated in their order from high respectability to disrepute, are: automobiles, *calesas, carromatas,* street cars, *carritelas,* and afoot.   Of course, the known rich can ride in any old thing, or even walk, but there are very few rich in Manila; what you mistake for affluence is small money talking big.

At four pesos an hour one buys the impregnable social armour of a motor car. If your outstanding chits are becoming top-heavy, you simply cannot afford to ride in anything else.

A *calesa* is a two-wheeled vehicle with a top, drawn by a horse not quite so little as the ordinary, and driven by a man in semi-uniform. That is, he may vary as to pants. You have to order a *calesa* from the stable by telephone. This inconvenience adds to its respectability. You can drive from any place to any other place in a *calesa* and still be recognized by your friends.

A *carromata* is a played-out *calesa*—rig, horse, and driver—reduced to roaming the streets looking for fares, and parking, when it parks at all, in a nose bag, or under some Filipino's house. It is the handiest vehicle in Manila. You take a *carromata* when your credit at the stable is gone and you still have thirty centavos. But you mustn't get out of a *carromata* in front of a high-class shop, or the Manila hotel, or at the Club, if anyone is on the veranda. It is less dishonourable to walk from the nearest corner.

Next comes the street car. I cannot picture the heinousness of riding on street cars in Manila without incriminating myself.

A *carritela*—now we *are* getting low down—is an exhausted *carromata* outfit made over to carry stuff in behind. Natives use it as a carry-all, and white people for transferring baggage. On leaving the city, you *can* ride to your boat on the seat with the tough-looking driver, your trunk stowed in back—but you don't, unless the sheriff is after you with a large bundle of chits. In that case, a *carritela* is a complete disguise for a white man.

The lowest form of transportation is going afoot. One cannot decently walk more than three blocks in Manila without a doctor's certificate. Still, there are those who brave social opinion for the sake of the healthful exercise. I know of one young man who walks to business every morning; but everybody worth knowing knows that he is manager for his house. It stands to reason that he must have at least thirty centavos about him. When he gets to be a partner in the firm he may also walk home at night.

*   *   *

What are these little brown brothers whom we Americans have had the doubtful luck to inherit from the Spaniards?

Centuries ago, Malays from the westward fell upon the original Negritos in these islands and took possession. Nine or ten of the eleven million present-day Filipinos are derived from these Malays, somewhat mixed in blood with with their Spanish conquerors, and with Chinese. The other million or so—the only ones who really count in island politics—are *mestizos*, a term applied to half-castes or better, whether the infusion is Chinese or White.

Filipinos are remarkably unlike South Sea Islanders; alert, eager for city life, while islanders are placid, indifferent, aloof. Filipinos in the city make a showing of bustle and ambition which might be mistaken at first sight as evidence of at least a modicum of brains, were it not for the clear evidence of their faces.

Those faces! By long odds the weakest of any I have ever seen on native peoples. Features so insignificant that noses, eyes, mouths, and chins impress one as objects of utility rather than as indices of character. Lines of strength in a Filipino's face are sure marks of the mestizo. Those who visit America are mostly mestizos, and we, not knowing the difference, listen to their florid oratory and think of Filipinos as a smart people.

In these islands I followed my usual habit of getting into conversation with old-timers. The wrong way to begin with white traders anywhere is to ask questions; just offer a few groping, slightly inaccurate views of your own, and the Man who Knows will earnestly set you right with a string of facts and near facts which you never could have pried away from him with a questionnaire. Here are phonographic bits from the old-timers:

"The Filipino people? No such thing. Eighty-four varieties of natives—*and* the mestizos, the itching fingers of the whole bunch."

"Brains? Natives? Say, ask me something reasonable. Mine's a mint julep."

"Here's the difference between them: the Filipino is hopelessly a child, and the mestizo has just enough brains to fall short of being a man."

"Mestizos? Mine isn't fit to print. Ask some American congressman who's dropped in here and been fed up and toted around by 'em."

"Filipinos are half child and half devil. Better stick to the child side of them." These are the exact words of an American who ought to know; he had lived with a Filipino wife for twenty-five years.

A composite of the Filipino: "Don't expect him to think. Tell him what to do and how to do it, and tell him often."

A composite of the mestizo: "Rises sometimes halfway up to the quality of his alien blood; no head for business or trade, has a gift of gab which education aggravates, wants a sit-down job, but prefers politics."

Incidentally, I learned that every last man in the previous legislature was a mestizo; not a Filipino bigger than a cipher in the whole political machine; Quezón, the chief "Filipino" agitator, is three quarters Spanish, and Osmeña, a still abler politician, is half Chinese. "These are the men," as one of my informants put it, "who are shedding great words for their beloved *Filipinos!*"

From all of which I gathered that the righteous answer to the Filipino problem is not necessarily in the mestizo noise.

* * *

In the Igorot country, one hundred and eighty miles north of Manila and five thousand feet above sea level, is Baguio, the great health-dispensing resort of the Philippine Islands. It is the place to which white people of every description go to cool off and recuperate. Ilocanos and other lowland natives are gathered there—mostly hand-picked for the various kinds of service required in a place of this sort. Chinese and Japanese, too, at anything from shopkeeping to market gardening; and Igorots, the backward "Little People of the Mountains," all over the place. Just the spot for observing all sorts and conditions of life in the Islands.

As soon as the railroad had recovered from the effects of the typhoon, I went to Baguio.

The seven-hours' ride through the lowlands to Damortis reveals again the striking difference between life in the Philippines and life in the South Sea islands. No easy living here off coconuts and breadfruit; there are altogether too many people for the "bounteous nature" life. Besides, Filipinos are rice eaters, and rice demands the most intensive and laborious cultivation of any cereal grown. Everywhere on the level ground along the way were rice paddies—great and little patches of muddy water, in which each individual stalk of rice has to be tucked down in the mud by hand, and later on gathered by hand, and threshed by hand. The work is perennial —the threshing of the last crop laps over on the planting of the one to come.

Rice eating certainly is an unfortunate habit in a climate that induces laziness.

Huddled together in the towns, or bunched in groups in the little native villages along the way, were the thatch-roofed houses of Filipinos. These houses lack the symmetry and uniform character so noticeable in the *fales* of South Sea Islanders. They lean against one another in a haphazard way, with an unlikeness of shapes which somehow falls short of displaying individuality. Their elevation on posts rising five or six feet from the ground probably lessens the discomfort of the rainy season; it also gives shelter underneath to pigs, chickens, miscellaneous junk, and sometimes a scrubby little horse or two. Yet, in the very confusion of their lines, these rows and clusters of native habitations have a certain picturesqueness, if the brown, matted-straw effect is not too much disfigured by prosaic boards.

"Damortis! All out for Baguio!" We made for the motor bus that was to take us up the five-thousand-foot rise to Baguio. The native driver met us contemplatively, counted his passengers over several times, backward and forward, to make sure of the right number. There were three of us.

"No 'nuf for bus," he announced.   "Bus no go."

"What! No bus!" we threatened in unison. After seven hot hours in a train, with Baguio in prospect, a night in this little sea-level town was unthinkable. "No *bus?*"

"Yes, no bus," he replied, unmoved—then pointed toward the other end of the platform. "We go that."

Oh. Instead of a lumbering, noisy bus, we were to have an up-to-date Peerless touring car for the greatest ride in the islands. We carefully deflated our emotions, the other male passenger merely breathing into the boy's ear, "Young man, you came within an ace of hearing something derogatory."

"No, I came Cebu," he answered, pleased at our interest in him. We let it go at that.

As the motor entered the mountain gorge and began its climb up the perfectly graded highway, whiffs of cool, fresh air from higher up gave us an exhilarating sense of escaping to a more friendly climate. A picturesque escape it was, twisting and turning on a smooth, narrow road notched out of almost vertical walls, with a dashing stream most of the time below us.

The stiffest grade and the grandest scenery are in the "Zigzag," the last thousand feet of the rise. At the gate facing the zigzag the engine was given a rest and its boiling water changed for cold, in preparation for the final, gruelling lift to the top of the island, where Baguio nestles among pine-covered hills. A fitting end, in the shadows of twilight, to this great fifty-kilometre ride from Damortis to Baguio. It is a journey from the tropics to the temperate zone. The quick shift from tropical verdure and sweltering heat to Baguio's pines and clear, crisp evening air is an experience nothing short of delicious.

I awoke next morning with a curiosity to see Igorots—a curiosity whetted by a glimpse of them in the twilight of the evening before—little, dark figures stepping aside for our car. What were the men wearing besides an abbreviated shirt?—a shirt obviously too short to perform the offices of a single garment, and with nothing to tuck itself into.

I looked out through a cluster of pine trees over an extensive flower garden, worked by ten gardeners. An extravagance? The ten of them, including their keep, cost less than one son of Italy on your own front lawn. Here, next door to China, begins the Orient's amazing cheapness of labour, of human life itself.

Those Igorot gardeners! Apprehensively I scanned the brief shirt—and sure enough, beneath its dirty fringes appeared the descending loop of the "G-string." Modesty was saved—by a thread or two!

One doesn't get through several months of living in the South Sea islands with more than a flagging interest in nudity; but the first glance at that inadequate strip of cloth, striving to do its duty, would arrest the eye of the most seasoned observer.

The cheap store-shirt dangling futilily above it accentuates the ridiculousness of the outfit as a human covering. Why the shirt?

Evidently some of the Igorots ask the same question. Off beyond the garden was a road construction gang, laying a new highway at the back of the hotel grounds; several of the labourers, *sans* shirts, were resplendent in their dark-brown skins, relieved only by G-strings; and somehow they seemed more clothed than those with more covering.   A sort of psychological paradox, this.

That road construction gang, like all others which I was to see in the Igorot country, was two thirds made up of women.   Little women, some of them seemingly not more than four feet high, wielding spades almost as tall as themselves; dressed in the universal one-piece garment of the tropics, tucked in on itself at the waist and hanging to the knees.   Above the waist they were more or less ineffectually covered by a brief jacket or a once-white blouse.

The sight of these women working on the highway was rather startling.   Throughout the South Seas, women do most of the drudgery in the native villages, but never had I seen one at public labour of any sort, even in places where their men condescend to work for wages.   But I was getting into touch with Oriental customs without knowing it.   Hong Kong, where women are used as beasts of burden indiscriminately with men, is only two days away.

A walk through the hills of Baguio is not at all like the moist drag along Samoa's Apian way; no dodging from shade to shade as in Fiji or steamy Manila.   In this cool, bracing air and never-failing sunshine—winter is the dry season—one pays the climate the highest of compliments by forgetting it.   Along miles of winding macadam roads new vistas of sharp-peaked ranges and immensely deep gorges are constantly opening as one walks or rides.   We are above the earth's heaviest mile-thick layer of air and vapour; the sun strikes hard when it is overhead, but somehow fails to heat.

Camp John Hay, one of the most comfortable of Uncle Sam's army posts in the tropics, is at the outskirts of Baguio. Army posts often lend picturesqueness to an undeserving landscape and a social glitter to the deadest of towns; but judging from tales of the high doings here in the vacation season—March, April, and May—this town shines with its own luridness. In the season, every social light and shade in the Philippines flits across Baguio.

In the winter months this perfect climate is wasted on a handful, merely because the heat in the lowlands is then tolerable. The outstanding social functions in this off season, aside from the inevitable teas, are the Friday night sparring matches at Camp John Hay. Although neither is my favourite sport, I go to sparring matches with less reluctance than to tea fights. So, apparently, do many of Baguio's army officers and civilians, with their ladies, judging by the looks of the ringside on Friday nights.

All battles are between natives. Two Ilaconos usually put up a fair game of skill; two Igorots are apt to mix their skill with a primitive enthusiasm which adds to the excitement; but if you want to see a fight loaded with an earnestness which looks like murder, pit an Ilocano against an Igorot. They haven't been permitted to hunt each other's heads for some time, but in those happy days their faces never could have expressed a more wholesouled desire to decapitate.

If evenly matched after the first two or three rounds, the bout is further enlivened by changing the regulation soft gloves for pairs considerably harder. Then there's a *real* battle. I have seen ladies in the front rows smilingly move back a seat or two when little red spots began to show on their white dresses, while the ring was a whirl of two brown bodies in scanty clouts and the towering white referee, whose lively job it is to see that they fight fair. And they do fight fair. Precious few decisions are given on fouls, and what looks like attempted murder shifts at the stroke of the gong to an air of complete docility. Nobody gets hurt—the occasional knockouts are more the result of exhaustion than any violent blow—and, more to the point, they carry no grudges outside the ring. Pretty good little sports—but a rough game.

Picturesque little Igorots! Flocks of their tiny women are always trekking from the barrios (native villages) to the Igorot market in town, each with a heavy basket of produce supported on her back by a stout, grass-woven band laid across her forehead. Homespun waist cloths and scanty jackets, with the stripes running horizontally, and if not carrying a baby tucked under one arm, they are likely to be strumming a piece of split bamboo with one hand against the palm of the other—their only musical instrument. Out of it they get weird variations of sound by manipulating a single hole in the tube below the split.

The big day in the Igorot market is Sunday. Sunday means market day to these little pagans quite as it means joy-riding to Christian peoples. For a day, two days, or sometimes three, Igorots have been trekking in from distant valleys, some with two-wheeled bullock carts loaded with vegetables, others packing on their backs a few pesos' worth of stuff to sell. On Saturday nights the great open market-place is a veritable camp ground; Sunday morning the buyers flock in, as well as near-by sellers with their packs and baskets. There is no shouting of wares; as in the South Sea island markets, everybody sits and waits and talks. The buyers are Filipinos and Orientals—white people buy almost entirely from Chinese provision stores. This is emphatically a native market.

Everybody smokes, and everybody "rolls his own," only in the case of Igorots the tobacco is rolled into big cigars. Women manage a ten-inch cigar as dextrously as the men. One of the chief products offered in the market is native-grown leaf tobacco, and the sellers of garden stuff, as soon as they have sold their goods, become buyers of tobacco. They also flock into the more permanently housed stalls of the market building and spend their newly acquired pesos and centavos for print cloth and utensils—store goods, such as they cannot conveniently make for themselves.

Then they start on the long journey home—Sunday night, Monday, perhaps running into Tuesday for the more distant ones. Some of them spend half their time getting to market and back, but their stuff has to be sold as it is grown, and they must get bright cotton yarns for the making of their women's two-piece suits and the men's one-piece G-strings, and have money enough left over to pay taxes on their little plots of ground. Happy little natives they seem to be, but theirs is not the unworried life of the South Sea islanders—there's a difference between the two of about three hundred and sixty-five days of hard labour in the year.

Americans have made Baguio the cleanly, well-laid-out resort that it is. All over the hills are neat cottages, vacant in winter, but filled to the last one during the dreaded spring months in Manila—March, April, and May. Many firms and organizations in the lowlands maintain rest houses here for their fagged-out employees; teachers' camps and missionary retreats give welcome relief to the overworked from the hot regions down below; hospitals take care of the sick in a way that they could not be taken care of in the heat of the lowlands. Baguio does the Samaritan business of the Islands—for a consideration.

A white man's town in its essentials, Baguio has not a white man's store of any account in it. All the best shops are Chinese or Japanese, and the others are run by Filipinos, for Filipinos. Rich Chinese own most of the business section, just as they own large sections of Manila and other towns. White men do not seem able to compete with Chinese merchants, even in Manila, except in lines which cater almost exclusively to white people.

We hear at home about Japan having her eye on the Philippines; if so, that is about all she has on the Philippines. In contemplating her possible seizure of the Islands it is well to remember that Japanese thrive nowhere in the tropics, while Chinese thrive everywhere on earth. But nobody considers China, in her present chaotic state, as contemplating the seizure of anybody's territory. She will do well to hold her own.

All inside service among the white residents of Baguio is done by Filipinos from the lowlands—mostly Ilocanos, with a sprinkling of Tagalogs from Manila. Igorots, except in rare instances, are considered as not having sufficient intelligence to be properly domesticated. Ilocanos assume a superiority over Igorots which is partly warranted; yet, knowing Ilocanos, it is difficult to imagine Igorots as having much less brains.

Simple-minded, plus! Filipinos have the peculiar "smartness" of the light-brained. They are bright, alert, attentive—*if they want to hold their jobs*. So are children of ten, if they are doing something in which they are interested. Give either Filipinos or children distasteful tasks, and they sulk. The similarity between the two grows on one as the months roll by.

The great Filipino ambition is to get away from the hard labour of the country and into some service in town. Nothing unusual about this—it's a world habit. But this flocking into the few big towns of the Islands makes competition fierce; generations of experience have taught the Filipino that he must step lively to hold his job. One can cultivate brightness without much brains.

At Baguio's best hotel—the Pines—we had too many waiters, only because there were too few guests. They were a picked lot, of course, but too many Ilocano waiters is a positive affliction, just as too many enthusiastic boys of ten trying to caddy for you would be a positive affliction. My entrance into the dining room was always the signal for a grand rush to my table. I generally managed to shoo off all except one or two.

No sooner has the young man brought on one course than he is impatiently eager to bring on the next. The necessary detail of eating each course is lost to the Ilocano; what little mind he has is strictly on his job.

These men had been taught that, when a guest lays down his fork alongside his knife, it is a sign that he has finished; but it happens that I have a contemplative habit of doing just this several times during a meal. At my first few meals I was constantly in agitated pursuit of my vanishing plate. Finally, I arranged with the waiters that when I was really through with a course I would push the plate forward with my thumb. This centred their interest on my thumb and gave me peace.

But with this I established a new signal at that hotel hereafter, if a guest at any stage of his eating happens to push forward his plate with his thumb, nothing but quick action will save his dinner.

In the course of time I wanted a new supply of writing paper. The printing shop of a group of Belgian missionaries accommodates the town with paper, so thither I went. The priest in charge took me into his stockroom and we picked out the kind of paper wanted; he turned to one of his young men and told him to count out two hundred and fifty sheets. Then he and I stepped into his little office, and waited. Talked and waited. Finally, the priest, remarking on the slowness of the boy, went out to investigate.

There were the sheets, counted out; not even wrapped up. The young man had done exactly as he was told. He had seen me buy the paper, he knew we were talking not fifteen feet away, but he had not been told to wrap it, or to bring it in to us.

The priest returned, smilingly shaking his head. "You've got to tell these boys every single step from A to Z, and tell them every single time, or the thing doesn't get done." This from a man who surrounds himself with the likeliest Filipinos—those who are seeking education and seem to have an ambition born of at least a touch of brains. Then he told me of an incident that would have seemed incredible if told by any less serious man:

A few days before, this priest had wanted information from a man at a distance. He chose one of his brightest young men and drilled him thoroughly in what he was to do. Knowing the Filipino failing, he was at great pains to go into the minutest details; not a single move in the whole procedure was he conscious of omitting.

His man departed—and failed to show up during the forenoon. In the afternoon, the priest sought him.

"Did you go and see that man I told you about this morning?" he asked.

"Yes, sir."

"Well, what did he say?"

The Ilocano gave a correct and satisfactory account of his errand. "But why didn't you come and report to me?" asked the priest, at a loss to understand the man's action.

"Oh-h!" said the fellow, as a wave of dull comprehension came over him. "You didn't say to come and tell you!"

The priest assured me that this was not at all an unusual example of Filipino intelligence. The chap would have gone to his grave with that information in his breast if his employer had not sought him for it.

Another childlike trait in the Filipinos is their proneness to weep when their feelings are hurt. They are exceedingly sensitive to criticism; but I had it pointed out to me by white employers that a Filipino will take a sound berating without crying if he is caught stealing, or lying, or in any act which deserves censure. It is when he thinks the harsh words are undeserved that he bursts into tears.

One day a gentleman at the hotel, out in his automobile with his family, spoke sharply to his chauffeur for some delinquency; at which the man, a father of six children, began to weep, and wept copiously all the way home. No condolement would stop him. He drove an embarrassed but mirthful family safely through a flood of tears.

Once I met a labourer coming down the main street of Baguio, his spade over his shoulder, sobbing like a child with a deep grievance in its heart. I did not learn the cause of his sorrow.

They are as childlike in their simple joys as in their griefs. It is a common sight to see two grown men strolling along the road holding hands. More than once I have seen native soldiers in this affectionate attitude. If for a moment they had to disengage themselves, their hands would again seek each other, like those of lovers out for a walk in the moonlight.

Their troubles vanish quickly into the past, and the morrow is of little concern. Thus they dodge two thirds of the white man's worry by having to meet only what's in the day at hand. "Childhood's happy hour" laps over into most of a Filipino's years.

The mestizo—he of the recognizable Chinese or white infusion—is the most significant human figure in the Islands. The mestizo of the Philippines, like the mixed-blood in the South Sea islands, is a racial misfit, an "in-between" unsuited for close relations with either white or brown; but because there are so many of his kind here he forms a separate class—and a dominating class, so far as the real Filipinos are concerned. He functions as an "in-between," exploiting the Filipinos as much as he dares under the watchful American eye.

Why don't we in America hear more about the mestizo in all this agitation for independence? No understanding of the question can be arrived at without knowing the mestizo for just what he is. When we step out, the mestizo will step in—and if anyone doubts what sort of independence the nine million Filipinos will get from the mixed-blooded outfit in these Islands, he has only to come here, observe, and draw his own conclusions.

* * *

Road-building is the chief industry of Baguio. Igorot road gangs usually have Ilocano "timekeepers"—bosses, in a way, over a dozen or so Igorots, while all are under the eye of a white foreman. If an Igorot wants a job under an Ilocano, he must learn enough of the Ilocano dialect to get on with him understandingly, just as all Filipinos in Manila must learn to talk Tagalog. Ilocanos are above bothering to learn Igorot dialects. There is a large Catholic church in Baguio—for Ilocanos, and Igorots rarely see the inside of it. Of course, no church anywhere bars people on account of colour or previous condition; Igorots are as welcome in the Baguio church as Negroes would be in a white meeting-house in Georgia.

I was interested in watching these Igorot road gangs at work, and always stopped to pass the time of day with the white overseer if he happened to be about. Everything is done with shovel and wheelbarrow by little men and women. They are cheaper than cattle, even if it takes several of them to do as much as a caribou or a bullock. Caribous—great rat-coloured beasts with immense flat horns turned back in a disarming fashion—and bullocks from the Orient, their necks hung low, are too expensive to be used on road work. Igorots, both men and women, are paid a half peso per day, with an allowance of rice and dried fish which costs from fifteen to twenty-two centavos. This makes the average total pay about thirty-five cents—one tenth the wage of a labourer in America.

I have also watched road gangs in America. These little people seem to do about as much work as the same number of Italians at home. The women rest rather frequently, often holding up their spades as shade against the hot sun. No notice is taken of it—that is, until the resting threatens to become a habit; then the boss suggests a little more activity, and they buckle down to work. I saw no harshness; the wages, like all wages in the tropics, are based on the cost of native living instead of on the work done, and thirty-five cents for these people who live on a trifle of rice and dried fish, wear no clothes worth mentioning, and stick their little huts against the hillsides, is a good wage. Happy little Igorots!

* * *

The Igorot habit of eating dogs troubles many of the white people, especially the ladies—more especially ladies who are new to the Philippines, and to everything else not strictly patterned after the home town.

Until recently, the dog market was a big feature of the Sunday market, sometimes as many as two or three hundred dogs being disposed of for the Sunday afternoon festivities. Now, the selling of dogs in the open market is prohibited. The Igorots have to get their dogs—mostly brought up from the lowlands—at some rendezvous of their own.

It's a dog's life for a dog in the Philippines. Allowed to multiply without restraint, and compelled to forage for themselves, they reminded me of the thousands of nobody's dogs in Constantinople, back in the days when that city was overrun with them. Foraging for scraps in a land like the Philippines, where the natives eat every vestige of eatable creatures and leave no scraps, makes life a difficult problem for dogs. Those that do not die of starvation arrive in the Igorot country with scant flesh on their bones—but this makes little difference to the Igorot; he is more interested in the parts of an animal which are usually discarded.

I was always relieved to see one of these dogs being led off by an Igorot. It foreshadowed a useful end to an unhappy existence. There is no unemotional reason why a dog, *per se*, should have special immunity from the hazards of the dinner table above that of chickens or pigs; it's all a matter of custom and taste in foods, if one can look at it that way; and being accustomed to chickens and pigs, none of us would eat dog unless in the most straitened circumstances.

But some people who have never experienced dogs except as household pets object to dog-eating on more elevated grounds. They invest their dog with near-human attributes, even to the extent of alluding to themselves in its presence as "mamma," or, in rare instances, "papa." They would regard the eating of their canine member of the family by savages with almost as much horror as if it were one of the younger children.

Such a woman happened into Baguio shortly before I arrived there. She was a nice old lady from Boston, where dogs are conversed with, and the dog-eating pained her to the quick.

She agitated among town officials and the like. The misery of dog life was not a part of her plea; the thing that bothered her was the cannibalistic feature involved in eating a friend.

One Sunday, while walking on the road just outside of Baguio, she met a construction foreman whom I knew. We will call him Jim. She stopped Jim—he has the good-natured look in his eye that appeals to ladies in distress. He told me the story of his experience with her.

She dilated on the wickedness of eating dogs—as dogs, not as food for the Igorots. He tried to show her that a dog is more interested in the way it lives than in the way it dies; but it was no use. She couldn't get the idea of a nobody's dog. She was trying to put over the Back Bay status of dogs in a country where a dead dog is better off than a live one. Had she been a missionary, she would have brought over civilized standards *en bloc* and tried to make them stick on the Igorots.

As she talked, and he politely condoled, along came an Igorot leading his Sunday dinner. This was "2 mutch," as Artemus Ward says. That dog must be saved. She had no use for it—no—but would the kind man buy it and save its life?

Jim bought it—for a peso and a half. Hardly had the lady's words of gratitude died away when another Igorot hove in sight, with the inevitable family repast.

Same emotional business of rescuing dogs from ig-nominious end. This time Jim paid two pesos. Dogs were going up.

Jim was now scanning the road apprehensively. There was a limit to his buying dogs, even to please a lady. Hastily observing that he must be getting on home, he managed to escape with only the two. The lady had the proud consciousness of having saved two lives.

"What became of the dogs?" I asked Jim.

"I dunno," said he, gazing off into space. "They disappeared about the time when my Igorots were having a dog feast."

The dog situation in that part of the Philippines would be a disgrace to a civilized people. Like all primitives, the Filipinos are cruel to animals—with a cruelty that was not softened under their generations of contact with the Spaniards. Teaching of the humanities is not to be expected from a people whose idea of sport is to see blindfolded old horses gored to death by bulls in a ring.

Possibly a few decades more of American influence will bring the natives to decent treatment of domestic animals. Wonders have already been achieved for the scrubby little cab horses in Manila. The society of the long name has many problems awaiting it in the Philippines, but dog-eating is not one of them. That's one for the missionaries.

* * *

Winding in and out for seventy miles or more through the mountain-tops northward from Baguio is the Bontoc Trail. Skilfully laid out as a foot trail by American engineers in the early days of our occupation, it follows at a uniformly ascending grade the contour of the ranges. Sometimes for miles it is a mere notch hewn out in the almost vertical walls.

Now, the Bontoc Trail is being gradually converted into a single track for Fords and near-Fords; no car with a long wheel base could possibly make the curves on the Bontoc Automobile Highway. And it should go without saying that not even Fords can pass each other along the way; it will be run on the block system, with turnouts arranged at convenient intervals.

The Mayor of Baguio—who is also engineer in charge of this work, and a genial sort of Pooh-Bah in the Mountain Province—invited me to ride with him over the new highway, just completed to kilometre 37. I thought of that agitating Olokele Cañon ride in the Hawaiian Islands, and accepted with pleasure.

It may seem odd to speak of "foothills" up a mile high in mountain-tops, but the beginnings of the Bontoc Trail are in foothills as compared with the precipitous ranges to which it leads. Before many kilometres have been covered, one is looking out over the valleys of the Igorot country—looking *down*, as the ascent continues, on thatch-roofed houses clustered in little villages at frequent intervals, usually set off in the landscape by bright, vari-coloured patches of garden, or the glistening silver of flooded rice paddies. Some are still in the morning shadows, seeming in this clear atmosphere almost black where the ragged patterns of shade and sunlight come together. These high contrasts, the exhilarating mountain air, scary curves, and sheer drops flirting with the offside front wheel—there's a sufficiency of palpitating interest in even this more staid portion of the Bontoc Trail.

At kilometre 22—one doesn't speak of miles in the Philippines except as one forgets—there is a comfortable rest house, where meals are served on advance orders, and lodging can be had for any who want to spend a few days in a wilderness of mountain scenery. We had got to it by ascending a thousand feet and dropping almost as much; the rest house twenty-two kilometres out of Baguio is at about the same altitude as the town.

Here begins the main ascent of the trail up through the peaks. Beyond this point, private cars are not yet admitted. After an early lunch for ourselves, and refreshment for the faithful Dodge in the shape of gas and cool water, we set out on the steady climb. The grade is so even and constant that one would hardly sense the extent of the rise were it not for the heated protests of the motor. Again the valley scenes became more downward than distant; once more, little pack-bearing Igorots and Bontocs—there is not much difference between the two—could be seen labouring up the steep trails from their homes below, to take the level road off to Baguio, and to Baguio's market-place. Hundreds of feet of climbing, and twenty-odd kilometres of walk each way—all this, and the work of raising the stuff, for the few pesos to be had in exchange for what little they could carry in on their backs. Poor little happy children of the hills!

The fear of automobiles has been so thoroughly drilled into these little pagans by the shrieking of horns and drivers that they frantically hugged the vertical inside wall or hung well over the precipices as we went by. They are keen at giving motor cars a wide berth—but when a motor fits the whole berth as snugly as on the Bontoc Trail, they cling to the edges and gaze at the oncoming monster like scared rabbits.

The widening of the original trail is done mostly by cutting the notch still deeper into the mountain wall; in some places, a few feet can be added by building up at the outside edge, but the more dependable surface is that which is got out of the mountain itself by cutting it away. In a country where the downpour is sometimes as much as twenty-six inches in a day during the rainy season, made ground and uncemented retaining walls on a mountain road do not inspire confidence.

If Baguio's mayor, and the same Ilocano chauffeur, and this identical Dodge had not made the trip several times before, and returned as undamaged evidence that it could be done, I should not have enjoyed the experience as much as I did. When the kilometre posts showed us to be in the thirties, the crooks and curves were hair-raising. At times we seemed to be cheerily driving off into space; a sudden swish of the wheels would fetch us about at right angles and still on the trail, always to my surprise.

At these approaches to yawning vacancy, too, the chauffeur's habit of driving out to the very edge struck me as needlessly endangering the front wheel; but I soon discovered that by going close to the edge *before* making the turn, he didn't have to go *over* the edge beyond the turn. He went on the theory that two narrow escapes are less annoying than one sure miss.

At kilometre 37 we came to the last turnout; only that morning completed; not fifty feet beyond, the Igorot construction gang was hacking away at the vertical wall and dumping rocks and dirt over the precipice. Beyond them stretched the original trail along the mountain-side—a broad even footpath, worn smooth along the middle by a generation of Igorot and Bontoc feet, and prettily over-hung with vines and luxuriant foliage, undisturbed during twenty-odd years. Almost too bad, it seemed, to make a raw little roadway out of this picturesque mountain path, but progress demands a quicker means of transportation to and from the Bontoc country, and the only way to get it is by widening the Bontoc Trail.

The altitude at this point, according to the Mayor, is close to seven thousand feet. It is the highest stretch of road accessible to automobiles in the Philippine Islands; and since this last kilometre or two had not been previously traversed, even by the Mayor, I joined in the honour of having attained the highest point ever reached in the Islands by a motor car. But the honour is not so overwhelming when one considers that the Mayor achieves a new altitude record in this same car every time he goes up to inspect the job.

About two kilometres beyond the finished roadway the old trail leads through a notch; there it takes up its windings among the peaks on the other side of the range, ascending for many more kilometres, until finally it begins its long drop into the north country. The Mayor and I walked those two kilometres to get a view off through the notch at the ranges beyond.

The walk along the untouched trail was most pleasantly restful, after the strenuous motor climb up the newly made road. Here, the path runs nearly at a level. With clinging green things, Nature has so beautifully healed the long, man-made scar that the old trail seems more like a handy thing of her own devising.

Here, too, we were well up into the tops of the peaks. They rise above only a few hundred feet, while the depth of the valley below is thousands. I say thousands, because, when we were peering over the edge at a spot where the wall rose sheer from the valley's bottom, I asked the Mayor if he didn't think the drop was at least two thousand feet, and he obligingly said yes, he thought it was.

The ride back to Baguio was as novel in its scenes and thrills as the journey out. Doubling back on any road has vastly more in it than merely seeing the same things twice. Nothing is the same going back, come to think of it. You go up all the hills you previously came down, and descend those which you had to climb. Riding the opposite way, you see the back side of everything first, which gives, or should give, a distinctly different impression, especially when it is considered that most motorists who go only one way over a road don't turn around to see the back side of anything. Then, too, if you go out in the morning and come back in the afternoon, the shadows are all the other way, which makes a different picture of everything in the landscape. And nobody, anyhow, can see more than a little part of all the interesting things along a road by going over it once in a motor car.

It is rather fun going back the same way to see how different everything can be. On the Bontic Trail, there will never be any of the usual wrangling in a motor party over which way they shall return. But it is just as well. Anyone coming down from the mountain peaks in a declining sun who cannot pick new beauties in the scenes of the morning has no business to be going up in the morning.

*   *   *

Back in Manila, after three months in a climate that discounts any in America's winter resorts. Baguio's winter-time is a succession of brilliant days, but her dry weather is never a drought. Every night the dew falls so heavily that it drips off the roofs like a gentle rain; through the almost rainless months nobody would guess from the appearance of the verdure that heaven's only contribution is an occasional shower.

Most travellers who wish to arrive in China and Japan

Igorot woman weaving

Caribou—Philippines

Chinese women pulling cart, Hong Kong

Chinese woman carrier

for the spring months think that their only way to avoid the northern winter is to start early and stop over in southern California. But why not start early and stop over in Baguio? Why stick around the commonplace when the unusual is more inviting? The one reeks of America at its most blatant stage; the other offers the charms of a new land filled with strange peoples.

Baguio has its quietest season during its best weather, because Manilans are not driven out of their town by the heat until March. Don't go to Baguio in winter if you prefer hectic resort life. It is a delightful haven for those who want peace, and want it at prices not dictated by a tourist line-up.

From Baguio to Manila it is a short day's run by motor over good roads. Probably no country on the Equator offers facilities equal to those of Luzon for seeing the tropics by motor. Excellent highways run all over the best parts of the island, and a complete road guide explains every twist and turn and point of interest.

All this awaits the traveller in Luzon. Americans should get acquainted with their greatest and most perplexing dependency. I am not writing for the Philippines, but for Americans who ought to visit the Philippines.

Back now in Manila, as I started to say when thoughts of Baguio interrupted me, to take a few short trips to points around the capital; to Malabon, to Fort McKinley, to Pasig, and to the Pagsanjan Gorge, before going on to China and Japan.

The places up and down the coast from Manila strike one superficially as little more than continuations of the big town; but Pagsanjan Gorge has individuality of its

own, in as pretty a bit of tropical scenery as I found anywhere in the Pacific.

Four hours of riding in a comfortable train, and a night's
lodging in a neat little Filipino hotel in Pagsanjan, give
one the advantage of an early morning start up the river
to the Gorge, when the light effects are best and the sun
is merciful. People make the wet trip in bathing suits
if they have them; if not, anything else will do. The
natives of Pagsanjan—no white people live in the place
—are accustomed to seeing ladies and gentlemen walk
the streets to the river bank in strange outfits. I went in
my pajamas, topped with an immense native hat bought
for the occasion, and straw slippers—a rig that would
have got me arrested in America.

At the river bank two Filipinos and a stout canoe
awaited me. For the first half hour we paddled upstream
in smooth water. Along the banks, through the town
itself, great quantities of coconuts were impounded, getting a soaking preparatory to having their husks removed.
Nowhere else in copra-making regions have I seen the
nuts soaked before husking, but they say that the shuck-
ing is thus made easier. It is not easy to believe this after
watching the celerity with which the Samoans strip coconuts in their exciting contests, but there must be something in it, or the soaking would not be done—unless,
possibly, it is a hangover custom from the days of the
Spaniards.

Beyond the town, the journey up the placid stream
gives a fascinating panorama of native life. A stillness
broken only by the rhythmic touch of the paddles; luxuriant tropical foliage down to the water's edge, and little
native houses half buried in it along the steep hillsides;

women, pictured in bright cloth and brown skin against the never-ending green, fill their buckets with water, or, squatted on tiny rafts moored to the bank, beat frailty into somebody's wearing apparel; an occasional raft loaded with coconuts glides past, poled along by men who regard us none too happily; one bank lies in the morning shade, the other glistens in the sun—the passenger in the canoe lazily shifts the scene for himself by a mere turning of the head. The spell of the tropics gets one in this beginning of the Pagsanjan Gorge.

Then a rippling in the surface of the water, and a slight quickening of the paddle strokes, suggested something ahead as a reason for these two strong men, and the stout canoe, and the pajamas. We came to a swift drop in the stream between great rocks, but the men, paddling violently, got to the top of it.

More rapids and skilful paddling; then a veritable cascade up ahead—ye gods! how can they drive this canoe through it, with three men aboard?

They don't. Right into the foaming waters they force the canoe, jump overboard, and invite you to step out on a huge boulder in midstream. In lively pantomime they indicate a line of rocks, inconveniently spaced by nature, over which you are supposed to play the goat up to still water. Off they go, dragging the boat up the cascade by main strength.

In the advice regarding pajamas, nothing had been said about agility; but no matter now if you have a settled conviction that your hopping days are over, you *hop*— grateful each time that the wabbling spell on the rock achieved leaves you upright.

In relating my adventures to friends, I do not often

mention this cascade, because the next one was enough worse to make a better story. It was just as well that my men spoke only one word of English, otherwise I might not have had the relief of thinking that each waterfall was the last one. The paddler astern was a silent man, but the one forward turned around at least three times during the morning and said, "boo-te-ful," with a wave at the scenery.

And so it is. The stream narrows as one ascends, and the hills approach the perpendicular until they become two vertical walls of rock, rising several hundred feet above the water. Here the verdure cannot stick to the walls—but it drapes them from the top with long hanging vines, and every little crevice that can hold a bit of soil decorates the forbidding gray with a bouquet of green.

Throughout its length, this gorge seems more like a huge cleft in the solid rock than a channel that has been cut out by erosion. At its head, the cleft ends abruptly; way up the rocky face the little river dashes out from the foliage and drops with a roar into a great round pool. No ordinary human goat could follow it into those mysterious recesses. The trip is done.

"Shooting the cascades" is less work and more exciting than coming up through them. But the two steepest ones cannot safely be "shot"; the passenger hops —hopping down seems more uncertain than hopping up —while the paddlers let the canoe down through the rapids.

If you go to Luzon, don't fail to see the Pagsanjan Gorge; but first, practise hopping on round-headed boulders in the back yard.

Natives, natives, swarming everywhere—this, to me, is the most impressive sight in the Philippines. Nine out of eleven million, mostly little weak-faced humans with mentalities of children.

Mestizos, comparatively few in number, but permeating the mass, and dominating it from the mestizo political machine in Manila down through every town and village. Also impressive—in a different way.

Now the cry goes up for independence. But *whose* cry is it?

The mestizo's. Anybody who knows will assert that 90 per cent. of the nine million Filipinos don't even know what the shouting is about; those who do, tell their white friends confidentially and fearfully that they do not want to fall into the hands of the mestizos—they want the protection of white Americans. But they dare not say so out loud in a country supposed to be struggling for independence.

And the antagonism to General Wood—another mestizo game in which the Filipinos have no interest. In Manila I had to get my passport renewed at the Governor's office. I approached a *carromata*.

"To the Governor General's office," I said.

The cabby looked blank. "General Wood's office," I explained. No better.

"General Wood." He didn't know the name. He could have taken me to any office building, business house, or street number in Manila at one mention of the name, but he had not heard of General Wood.

I tried again. "Governor's office.—Governor of the Islands.—Governor Wood.—Wood.—Wood!—Wood!!"

He never had heard of the man. I tried the same line

of questions on *three more* bright-looking cabbies, with the same blank result.

It was disappointing.   As a downtreader of the common people, General Wood seemed to be a total failure.   The piners after liberty right in his home town didn't know their worst enemy.

The fifth man said he knew.   Perhaps he was a mestizo. Anyhow, he took me to the Governor General's office and back for a peso.

Filipinos swarm into the city, yet they learn next to nothing of its intricacies.   They stop at the elements of shopkeeping and trade, and in all mechanical pursuits are second-raters.   A contractor of long experience told me that on simple carpentry work he paid Filipinos one peso fifty per day, while to Japanese on the same job he gave five and six pesos.   "This makes the Filipinos sore," he said, "but what else can I do?   The Japanese at six pesos are cheaper for me than Filipinos at one-fifty.   Filipinos have to be told everything and they have to be told every time."

"Have to be told everything and told every time"— this is the universal comment of employers in the Philippines.   Yet there are a few enthusiasts who still stick to the false idea that a generation or two more of education will fit these people to look after themselves.   Education never did endow anyone with brains, and never will.

* * *

Nine million Filipinos, dependent on somebody's protection.   Suppose we were to give independence.   The big plum of political control would fall squarely into the mestizo lap.   By no stretch of the imagination can anyone who knows think that any bit of it would get past the mestizos to the Filipinos.

Then the right answer to the question of independence lies in the right answer to this: Which would give the Filipinos the fairer treatment—the mestizo political crowd with its mestizo ramifications into every hamlet, or a picked group of American administrators sent out from Washington?

The answer stands out plainly in the long record of the mestizos in the Philippines. This is merely an attempt to show the American people what the real question is, lest they be fooled into thinking that independence for the Philippines means independence for the Filipinos.

CHAPTER IX

HONG KONG

BROADLY speaking, China is a place where five women hitched to a loaded cart do the pulling of one horse and are much cheaper.

Hong Kong is a British colony, and it should not be spoken of as China; yet in its wholesale use of humans as pack animals Hong Kong is China, up to 100 per cent.

Just as Filipinos swarm into the towns to get away from work in the rice paddies, Chinese coolies fall over each other for inside jobs as servants to avoid the never-ending carrying of dead-weight burdens on the streets. Not much is on wheels in China except rikishas and heavy carts; bare shoulders with a pole across and a basket on each end of it are less expensive than wheels.

In the Philippines the unit for moving dirt, bricks, and the like is an Igorot and a wheelbarrow; in China they spare the wheelbarrow and put on another Chinaman. Cheaper. When a wheelbarrow gets out of order it has to be mended; when a Chinaman gets out of order he is replaced.

But this is introducing Hong Kong wrong end foremost. One should speak first of the city, rising well built for miles along the shore line against the striking background of its great mountain island. A mountain dotted all over with villas, interspersed with abundant foliage and crisscrossed by roads and pathways leading up steeply to the heights; this is the Peak—Hong Kong's aristocratic refuge from the sea of Chinese below.

From Kowloon, the port on the mainland where steamers dock, our hotel tender steered its perilous way through a maze of junks to the great Island City. So overwhelmingly Chinese is Hong Kong's population that it seems like a substantial white man's town given over to natives. Old-fashioned stone buildings of several stories, high-studded, with sidewalks and a profusion of balconies recessed into their fronts; arcades and archways along the shore, swarming houseboats bumping against the piers, rikishas going both ways at a lively trot, coolies beyond numbering going all ways at once, and mostly lugging something—this is a first impression of Hong Kong.

I "did" Hong Kong's extensive shore line aboard a trolley. As in Manila, this is not socially permissible, even in the first-class forward, but one who is devoid of aspirations can do such things comfortably without a permit. Besides, riding in a rikisha behind a panting man is a habit which one who prefers to regard humans as humans has to acquire gradually by seeing others do it.

Hong Kong is not China, but it is a fair introduction to the country where the cheapest thing in the landscape is a human being and a bit of good soil the most precious. Its panorama of burdened men and women is amazing to an Occidental. The flood of Chinese seems never to end; neither do the myriads of laden baskets dangling from poles across bended necks—each neck back of a pop-eyed face, tense with the jerky gait of legs bearing close to double weight.

What do they carry?

Everything that is usually carried on wheels in countries where men and women are not cheaper than axle grease. Is a new villa to be built on the Peak? Sand, brick, mortar, tiles are lugged up from below in the little baskets. A strong coolie man can carry as many as fifty bricks at a load—twenty-five in each basket; women manage half as many and earn half as much.

Perhaps you find yourself meeting a continuous line of coolies whose baskets are filled with broken bricks, scraps of old mortar and glass mixed with dirt—evidently worthless débris. If at all curious, you follow back along the line as you would trace a string of busy ants—back along winding streets, through the everlasting crowd, across alleys, under archways—until, it may be half a mile away, you come to a building in process of being torn down. Worthless débris, of course, but it has to be got out of the way, off into some gully on the mountain-side. This is another thing that coolies are made for. One big truck would do the work of a hundred—and cost more money.

Another dead-weight load for the coolies is the sedan chair, hung midway on two long, slender poles, and borne by coolies fore and aft. Quite a weight it is, for two men —never less than two hundred pounds, and never less than three hundred with a big man as passenger—but it pays far better than carrying bricks and sand and débris. Nobody prefers to ride in a chair, with its funny little bounce, bounce, at every step of the coolies, to the smooth running of a rubber-tired rikisha; it is a necessary conveyance "between levels" on the mountain-side, and in paths too steep or alleys too narrow for the rikisha.

The rikisha is the almost universal conveyance. The

principal difference between having a man in the shafts instead of a horse is that he responds to "go-on" instead of "gid-ap," and you don't use a whip. Otherwise, the sentiment toward the coolie hardens with time into about the same casual regard for him as for a horse. "It's too hot to walk—let's ride," comes as naturally as "Let's take a car." A man takes you, himself, and a rikisha at a trot for the distance which was too hot for you to walk. But for your own peace of mind you carefully forget that he is a man; he's a coolie, without human limitations. They say it is a comfortable feeling when you get used to it— but I didn't get used to it in the two months of my stay in the Orient. In spite of the ease and luxury of it, there was always a man in the shafts.

It is something of a fad in Hong Kong for well-to-do business men—sometimes the English, but usually Chinese—to have their own elaborate rikisha outfits, quite as they would have had a span of high-steppers and an expensive rig in the days of the horse.

"High-steppers" is the right name for these rikisha men of the banker crowd. Young, athletic, three of them to a resplendent nickel-plated rikisha—one in the shafts, two pushing at the sides with one hand and waving with the other. Down the street they come with long, graceful leaps, their snow-white robes fluttering in the breeze and each shouting, "Ah-h-h-uh! Ah-h-h-uh!" assuming grandly their right of way over all ordinary mortals.

And they get it. The Chinese scatter, even white pedestrians step lively. Then, at some imposing front, the outfit quickly swerves to the curb; down go the shafts, while the two pushers bring the rikisha to a not too sudden stop—so skilfully done that the dignified passenger is lifted to his feet by his own momentum, steps off to the sidewalk, and vanishes within.

From the level of these aristocratic prancers, rikisha men range all the way down to the panting, stiffened hacks whose trot at best is little better than a walk. A rikisha man who can no longer trot is done for. Numberless overheatings and heart strains make his active years short; yet desperately he keeps on, hopping up and down in a futile way that may fool some tourists, but never a Chinese patron; keeps on hopping his imitation trot, knowing that for him is waiting the bare pole across the shoulders, with not more than a woman's load—and a woman's earnings—in the little baskets dangling at the ends. Lucky, too, if he has this much left in him; nobody but a Chinaman knows what comes next on the way to the coolie oblivion.

* * *

Motor vehicles seem almost outlandish in this "do-it-by-hand" country. A few foreigners and fewer Chinese have private automobiles; perhaps altogether not as many as are for hire to the incessant run of one-day sightseers off the many steamers which make the port of Hong Kong.

It is a pretty motor ride around the island to Repulse Bay, for luncheon or afternoon tea at the exquisite hotel there. The road swings up at once to the city's "second level," then gently rises and falls for twelve beautiful miles along the mountain-side until it touches sea level again on the opposite side of the island. In the stretch of sea between Hong Kong and the mainland, steamers and sailing vessels, little and big, are seen making their slow way through the dark-brown masses of anchored junks and sampans—the water homes of Chinese by the hundred thousand.

China feebly meets the housing problem for a little fraction of her surplus population by setting it afloat. Afloat, but not adrift; they put down their mud-hooks and tie up to each other, and live more or less happily ever after. It is a life of never-ending motion with little chance to move, but the fresh air must make it preferable to the unspeakable crowding in a Chinese city. Hong Kong, for a city in the tropics, has a raw, chilly winter, but dwellers on the junks and sampans make themselves shapeless and comfortable, after the Chinese fashion, by piling on cheap cotton-padded coats, one over the other.

If work is to be had ashore, the sea dwellers consider themselves more fortunate than those who live on solid ground; it is only the coming of the typhoon that fills them with terror. Then, great masses of the bobbing homes break adrift and are carried out to sea or dashed against the shore. The last typhoon made wreckage of the floating city and drowned its inhabitants by the thousand. But in China, what matter a few thousand Chinese?

Hong Kong's Peak—the mountain-top—seventeen hundred feet at its highest, can be reached by a circuitous motor road, but the quickest and most convenient way to get there is by the cable railway. Two tilted cars balance each other at the ends of a cable looped over a big wheel in the power house at the top; as one goes up, the other comes down, both on the same track except at the spot midway, where they have to pass.

On these reserved heights the wealthy foreigners have peace and quiet—a serenity, I thought as I strolled about, not wholly a matter of contrast with the confusion down below. Why does the self-same air of deathly stillness pervade the more expensive residential sections of cities everywhere? Here on Hong King's Peak, as on the stately avenues of the rich in many other lands, I saw wealth, felt luxury, surmised joy, and wondered about happiness.

The silent homes of the well-to-do. Is it because they are so nearly childless, or did wealth come too late to bring laughter with it, or are the people behind the polite barricades too old in experience to find pleasure in making any of the usual human noises?

Anyhow, a collection of money-made homes is a mighty poor place for observing the antics of humans. I soon got off the Peak.

* * *

Robbers and pirates. A trip out of Hong Kong by water is an adventure in Chinese banditry. Trains on the railroad to Canton had been discontinued because of inability to cope with robbers. All local steamers go armed and, in a way, armoured. Pirates operate right up to the limits of Hongkong—so near that, a day or two after I arrived there, a local ferryboat to one of the suburbs on the mainland vanished one night. Vanished so completely with its eighty-five passengers that its capture by pirates was accepted as a melancholy but monotonous fact. Because the passengers were all Chinese, conjectures as to its fate dropped after the first day to paragraphs on the inside pages of the dailies.

A whole week passed without so much as a clue in the hands of the police. Then, one morning, sixteen coolies, not worth holding for ransom, came back to Hong Kong from the pirates' stronghold in the mountains, bearing letters from the remaining passengers to their relatives, coupled with demands from the bandits for ransoms varying from small sums in the cases of the poor to several hundred dollars Mex. (The Chinese dollar is based on the Mexican, which is worth fifty cents, and foreigners add "Mex" to distinguish it from the American dollar.) If not paid within a given time, the captives were to be put to death.

This got the incident once more on the front page—for a day. Pirates aboard had overcome the officers and run off the ferry. Nobody doubted the fate of the captives whose ransoms were not forthcoming. The affair was dragging along when I left a few days later, and I never heard what happened.

An interesting daylight trip out of Hong Kong is by boat to Macao, the old Portuguese seaport forty miles down the coast and across the mouth of the Canton River. Interesting, and safe as well, judging from the precautions taken. Every Chinese passenger has to run the gauntlet between two lines of soldiers, who thoroughly pat and punch his anatomy in search of firearms. The pirate scheme is to have accomplices aboard, who at an agreed spot seize or kill the navigating officers and deliver the vessel to the band lying in wait on another boat, or near by on shore.

Seeing the line-up, and supposing that it was for all passengers, I walked into it. The politely suppressed smiles of the Chinese soldiers made me aware that I had committed a *faux pas*. A foreigner is expected to stroll down the pier and get aboard as if he owned the vessel.

Aboard, every deck was completely barred off forward with heavy iron gratings, like those used in jails. In this cage forward were the officers—Englishmen—and behind similar barriers aft, all the Chinese passengers were held under guard. At every padlocked gate were East Indian soldiers, with loaded rifles and orders to use them on anyone who might attempt to pass either barrier. Amidships, free to peer at the secluded officers forward and the isolated Chinese aft, were the first-class passengers.

The effect of these arrangements is either reasuring or terrifying, according to one's sex and disposition. There were no first-class women passengers on our boat.

Macao has a reputation for being the toughest seaport along the China coast. A two-hour stop in the place should hardly be made the basis for judgment, even if it did disclose rather convincing evidence.

My rikisha man in Macao got his job with me on his assertion that he could speak English. What he really could do was to halt every now and then before some entrance, explain the place in bad Chinese, and add, "You go in?" After experiencing a stocking factory and a fire-cracker works, as well as the inevitable places where they tried to sell me something, it seemed safe enough to accept his "You go in?" without further understanding.

My careless "Yes" finally got me into a place of entertainment not bargained for; but every situation is grist in this browsing around among peoples. Some coin of the realm placated the charmers for my hasty exit.

Another of the rikisha man's surprises was a large opium factory. This impressed me more than anything else in Macao. Great cauldrons of the stuff cooking over what seemed to be slow fires, and rows of women rolling the finished product into neat little packages ready for marketing, gave a sense of *quantity* to a drug which is usually considered in the minutest terms. How much of this immense output gets into illegitimate trade I do not know; the well-meant gesticulations of the Chinese attendant, and the fluent "You go in?" of my English-speaking man, did not take me far into the intricacies of the opium traffic.

The final sight on this rikisha-conducted tour was a Chinese gambling house. Macao is famous for its fan-tan joints. Mah Jong may be the great Chinese gambling game for private groups, but fan-tan, like faro and roulette, suits better the purposes of a gambling house because it is played by the house, while the patrons merely bet on the outcome.

Fan-tan, which I had supposed was played with cards, is a simple guessing affair over a pile of Chinese brass coins, scooped out at random from a much larger pile and dumped before the dealer in full view of all the bettors. Nobody knows how many coins there are in the pile.

After the bets are placed the play begins. With a short stick the dealer carefully flips away from the pile four coins at a time; of course, after the removal of the last full four, there will remain on the table either none, or one, two, or three coins. It is on these numbers—zero, one, two, and three—that the bets have been placed.

The little stick keeps the dealer's hand away from the pile of coins and gives every player a chance to see that neither more nor less than four are removed at a time. The dealer plays fair—but who wouldn't, with forty slit-eyed Chinese gamblers watching his littlest move?

It is a game in which the excitement starts at zero and rises to 100 per cent. toward the finish. The pile, at the beginning, has some fifty or sixty coins; not until it has been reduced to about fifteen is there any chance to count those remaining on the table, but from the first flip of the stick expectancy seems to grow. The suspense is aggravated by the deliberate coolness of the dealer—he refuses to speed up with the excitement. This gives the agitated Chinamen the impression that he slows down as the pile diminishes. It is merely a trick in relativity.

* * *

"Night life" is quite as much a source of brag in Oriental cities as it is in New York. The only kind that interested me in Hong Kong was the kind that is mentioned least—the night life of the homeless Chinese.

Crowd as they will into their holes-in-the-wall and junks and sampans, there simply is not room enough for all under cover. Thousands crawl at night under any shelter that offers.

The arcaded sidewalks along the downtown streets are strewn with sleepers after ten o'clock. Walk through any of these streets at about nine, and you will see these Chinamen, each with a little bundle of matting, loitering about some doorway, or recess under a show window, which he has chosen for a bed. But he must wait until the store closes. No Chinaman is permitted to lie down in front of an open shop.

By quarter past nine, shutters begin to be drawn over the windows, doors are locked; before the shopkeeper has turned his back, mats are down with weary Sam Lungs and Yung Wings rolled up in them for the night, while the tramp, tramp, of the multitude goes on within a foot of their heads until the wee sma' hours.

The arcade keeps off most of the rain, if there is no wind; their greatest trouble is with the dust kicked into their faces by the constant shuffling of sandals along the stone sidewalks. They meet this difficulty in various more or less ingenious ways; some attach strings to the outer edge of their mats and draw them well over themselves by tying up to the gratings of the windows; others pull a separate mat over their heads, or cover their faces with cloths. A few make rather elaborate beds, with perhaps a padded quilt inside the mat, and something rolled up under the head for a pillow; but a single mat serves the large majority. The more luckless, without mats, pull their ragged coats about them and lie down to forget it awhile in sleep.

Strolling at night on these arcaded streets of Hong Kong is a veritable walk among the sleepers. I have counted thirty-eight within a single block. Many of them are said to be Cantonese refugees, escaped from the desperate conditions prevailing up-river. If they call this an escape to something better, why wonder at the appalling number of bandits and pirates in China?

* * *

Up-river to Canton. Every visitor to Hong Kong wants to see Canton, the most typically Chinese city in South China; but in these days of outlaws, and despotic Chinese "generals" whose unpaid soldiers are almost as lawless, many visitors can easily be persuaded not to take the journey.

Yet the very fact that the trip is dangerous has made it comparatively safe. They have stopped the trains because they cannot protect them. Every vessel goes prepared for the worst, so nothing happens; and sensible travellers, when they get to Canton, don't run around the city alone. It is safer to do Canton under proper protection than it is to stroll in some parts of New York City with a fat satchel and a countrified air.

CHAPTER X

CANTON

ON THIS occasion I gave myself over to the polite captivity of tourist conductors, only to avoid the sterner methods of possible bandits and pirates. A reliable agency in Hong Kong arranged to have their Canton representatives meet me at the boat, provide an escort sufficient to take me into the most Cantonese parts of the city, and deliver me, reasonably whole, back at the boat.

The ninety miles up the Canton River is a night's run. Because the trip was made at night, and through a region particularly infested, the steamer was more thoroughly protected than the one on the day trip to Macao. Forward, every deck had two gratings instead of one, set about twenty feet apart. In the space between were the armed East Indian guards. Thus the officers up forward had a double steel protection, besides soldiers who could not slip away from their jobs even if they were so disposed.

The first-class cabins for foreigners were just aft of this barricade. A rush forward by the Chinese astern would have found us in the thick of the disturbance, but heavy gratings, guarded by soldiers, held the swarm of Orientals to that end of the boat. Of course, they had been searched for arms before getting aboard.

With these precautions in evidence, none but a nervous

person would let apprehensions break in on a night's rest. I awoke in the babel of Canton's water front on a dull day, cheered myself with the reflection that taking pictures is next to impossible anyhow in the little streets of Canton, and breakfasted under the appraising eyes of three Chinese of the better class from the tourist agency.

One of these men was to be my courier; another attended to the matter of sedan chairs and carriers for this courier and myself, while the third, a well-educated man, seemed to have come to give me advice and see the expedition off.

"Keep with your men, and don't show money on the street," he said as we got under way. "Take the guide's advice about going into places. Just be discreet, and you will have no trouble."

Instead of the usual two carriers for each chair, we had three. One big fellow on my chair evidently had orders to plant his feet in my tracks whenever I got out to walk. I couldn't turn around or stop quickly without bumping that huge coolie.

An escort of seven men struck me as adequate, unless our conspicuousness might in itself be an incitement to deviltry. But the trouble with Canton, as with most other Chinese cities in these disturbed times, is not so much open violence on the streets as lawlessness under cover—much of it winked at, too, by pilfering Chinese officials. They say that in Canton you can get a man murdered for fifty cents Mex. This may be an exaggeration, but it is unhealthy for Chinese citizens to protest the high-handed acts of those who have assumed despotic authority, from Sun-yat-sen down to his unpaid soldiers who coolly help themselves in the provision shops.

From the partly Europeanized water front we went at once into the narrow streets of the Chinese—streets so narrow that a rikisha cannot get through them; the crowd had to edge its way single file past our sedans. Turning some of the corners was an artful business. The constant "Ah-h-h-uh! Ah-h-h-uh!" of our six coolies seemed to be taken for granted by those who had to flatten against the walls or shop fronts and perforce watch us go by.

Hatred of foreigners is said to be ingrained in the Chinese masses; but if it is, they show it only spasmodically. These Cantonese on the streets displayed toward me what might best be described as a wooden indifference; but they say a Chinaman can be thinking a number of things behind that inscrutable face of his.

For hours we wandered among scenes which have no counterpart outside of China. Shallow pockets in the wall serving as shops; pockets a little larger in which the fabricating of all things Chinese, from sandals to hairpins, went on in plain view; jewellery sellers and jewellery makers, rich shops and shops for the poverty stricken— all with only this single reminder of the ways of shops at home: places making or selling the same kinds of goods were in clusters. Workers in copper and brass might occupy everything along a short little street, while around the corner was a solid display of footwear, or silks, or provisions. Then we might go on through to another string of workers in copper and brass or iron or wood, and beyond again into a nest of retail pockets in the wall.

In the streets of jade and ivory, the fabricating is often done in the back part of the shop and the selling at the front. This is an innocent trick of trade not confined to the Orient; they show the interested foreigner how it is done in the fabricating department, then expect him to buy in the selling end of the establishment. The visitor not only feels a slight obligation to buy, but he takes an added interest in the thing he buys because he has seen one like it made.

These workshops, with huge ivory tusks from India or Siam strewn over the floor, or chunks of jade in the rough, worth perhaps thousands of dollars, lying carelessly about, impress one with the genuineness of the wares for sale; yet there are persons of experience who are skeptical enough to assert that, in spite of the profusion of ivory and jade in the workshops, articles of bone and coloured glass somehow get on the display counters.

High-class shops of this kind, as well as shops where the best Chinese embroideries and old silks are sold, take on a half-European air from the fact that they cater to the tourist trade, as well as to that of the rich Chinese. Shops and streets of this grade make up an infinitesimal part of Canton's fabricating and retail business, for the very good reason that Canton, like all Chinese cities, has an infinitesimal proportion of rich Chinese. Of her two and one half millions living on next to nothing, a full half million exist in junks and sampans on the river and its various inlets—the human overflow from a mass crowded, beyond any Occidental conception of crowding, in the little streets of the city.

It was through this sea of humans that we floundered most of the time. I came to see the Cantonese. I saw them, but the smells nearly conquered me. In the feeding alleys they were bad enough—thousands standing about eating rice with chopsticks amid the ageing refuse from other thousands of eaters who had come and gone before—but the odours were in greater strength and variety in the living sections of the city. The fetid exhalations of the unwashed, four-foot streets with offal from the swarming holes-in-the-wall dumped along both sides of it, oozing filth into the narrow pathway between——

Smallpox, always prevalent in China, was especially bad in Canton while I was there. They are a tough lot not to die of it wholesale in such surroundings, but I suppose it is these surroundings for generations that have made them a tough lot. I see now why Chinamen can live anywhere else on earth.

We visited gardens, pagodas, temples, joss houses. My intelligent young courier was free with information, and not at all sparing in his comments on the Sun-yat-sen régime, which was driving the Cantonese to poverty, hunger, and desperation. Other self-imposed Chinese overlords are doing the same thing in nearly every province of China. In some of the temples of Canton, horses of the army were stabled next to the shrines where worshippers knelt at their devotions, while soldiers were quartered in all available spaces about them. Disrepair and decay everywhere were eloquent of the twelve fearful years of China's Republic. One has only to look at China's people to know why her attempt at a republican form of government is such a ghastly failure.

The stabling of horses in the temples is an indignity and a damage which might some day be repaired; but the usurping dictator, squeeze the merchants for taxes as hard as he may, cannot begin to extract enough money to keep his ambitious schemes afloat. One of the largest and most famous of Canton's temples was being torn down by his orders while I was there. The bricks and other material were to be sold for what they would bring, and the land, the most valuable in the city, disposed of at fat prices to keep his tottering army a little longer on its feet. Yet nobody dares protest.

But not so many weeks before, Sun-yat-sen had carried his hand a little too high. He threatened to seize the Chinese customs, which are administered by foreign nations for the benefit of China's foreign loans. Lying off the piers I saw the answer to his bluff: a fleet of up-to-date war vessels, bearing the British flag, the French, and, prettiest of all, the Stars and Stripes. From Hong Kong and Manila and other parts of the Pacific, they had been rushed to Canton as the only sort of argument that a man like Sun is capable of appreciating.

He appreciated it. He gave up his designs on the customs and took to wrecking temples. According to my well-informed courier, he will soon be selling the public parks of Canton. It is a situation inconceivable except among a people without guts.

Shameen. If ever there is an uprising or an overturning in Canton, we shall hear considerable about Shameen.

It is a little island in the Canton River lying up against the city; so close, that only a narrow canal separates the two. And the canal is spanned by three or four bridges.

The island of Shameen, perhaps a third of a mile wide and twice as long, is reserved exclusively for foreigners. No Chinese are permitted to live there. It corresponds to the Peak in Hong Kong and the Legation Quarter in Peking. It is the foreign refuge usual in all Chinese cities.

But what a refuge! All right, of course, so long as the Chinese will is to keep hands off. In other words, while no refuge is needed, Shameen serves as one admirably. But suppose there comes a time when the present million of hungry and desperate Chinese across that canal become two million? Or suppose the present million get a leader? Incoherence is not a safe thing to bank on always.

Guards and iron gates are at the bridgeheads—but what of that? The canal is two thirds full of Chinese houseboats. Swing these end-on across it, and there would be no canal. On the Canton River side of Shameen, the water is half black with sampans and junks, loaded with Canton's half-million overflow.

Once they take the notion to swarm the place, Shameen would be alive with Chinese inside of an hour. It is the most unprotected bit of protected white man's land I ever saw. Of course, war vessels from Hong Kong and Manila and other parts of the Pacific would be rushed over to Canton—in time to pick up the remains and collect indemnity.

I spent a pleasant hour walking about Shameen with my courier, after the six coolies had been dismissed. The quiet, the European air of the place, the stately buildings, the vacant streets—one could almost forget China, in Shameen. We came to a small landing, where a sampan or two were taking on native passengers for the opposite bank of the river. I suggested that we cross over and have a look at things there. The young man shook his head.

"You are safe here," was his only response. All done with our wanderings in Canton's swarming little streets, and now he had me safe in Shameen. He had still to deliver me at the boat for Hong Kong, and didn't propose to take any risks which were not on his schedule. I was rather pleased that he felt his responsibilities.

Back to Hong Kong by the boat, after as complete a day as I ever put in at sightseeing. Sightseeing! Of course it is ridiculous to see Canton in a day; but Canton at present is no place for one who has the habit of just browsing around. It is too sinister, too impending.

* * *

Travelling east or west in the main thoroughfares of the Pacific is made easy by the great steamship companies. It not only seems easy after some months of picking one's irregular way through the South Seas, but it really is.

Four of the largest trans-Pacific lines issue interchangeable through tickets. This might appear at first glance as an unholy combination of soulless corporations—perhaps it is, in the matter of keeping up rates; but, since each line does its prettiest to hold the traveller to its own boats for as much of the distance as possible, competition is fierce; and it works out very well for the traveller.

He stops off at Hong Kong, or Shanghai, or the Japanese ports, as long as he pleases, then at each move takes the first vessel of the four which happens along. At Yokohama, the four lines give him the choice of going across direct to either Vancouver or Seattle, or to San Francisco by way of Honolulu, and a stop-over of any length in the Hawaiian Islands within his eleven months' limit. If he has bought his rail fare across the continent along with his steamer ticket, he may, after arriving at any of these three Pacific ports, choose his route over any combination of direct lines to any Atlantic port.

Just one big, painful disgorging at Manila, and a dozen

great carriers on sea and land strive with expensive blandishments for the privilege of transporting you. It's rather grand, after a considerable experience with bunks which invite you to go to bed with your clothes on.

In these disordered times, many travellers were seeing China by stopping at the ports, and perhaps venturing inland to near-by cities. The usual overland route from Shanghai to Peking, and on through Manchuria, Korea, and Japan, had not lived down the disrepute of the wrecking and looting of its famous Blue Express in the Chinese wilds, when a large number of English and American passengers were carried off into the mountains and held for ransom.

No decision as to going inland was necessary until I should reach Shanghai. There, at the beginning of the overland route, more definite as well as more recent information would be at hand.

* * *

The pleasantest thing about the steamer trip up the China coast in this middle of March was the beautiful open fireplace in the social hall of the *Empress of Asia*. In my years of travel I had never before experienced the luxury of a blazing coal fire on shipboard. I had never seen a fireplace aboard a vessel. In fact, I didn't know that fireplaces ever were on vessels. But perhaps this is needless exposure of my modest way of getting about.

Two days out of Hong Kong, and two more hours of careful steaming up the Yangtze River, brought us to the docks of Shanghai. Ocean liners were just beginning to go up to Shanghai; because of the shallow water and their own unwieldiness, they had always docked at Woo Sung, at the mouth of the Yangtze, and transported freight and passengers on lighters up the twenty miles or so to the big port. This was the *Asia's* second trip up; on her first, she had fouled another liner, and the *faux pas* had kept her three weeks in dock at Hong Kong, making repairs—right up to the morning of our departure on her. This is one of the reasons why we steamed up the Yangtze River carefully, at times to the point of downright hesitation.

Shanghai is a huge cosmopolitan seaport. As with Hong Kong, foreigners make the city what it is, and Chinese make up most of the population. Travellers will tell you that there is nothing of interest to be seen in Shanghai; that is a statement which does not hold strictly true for any place where human beings are beating their way through the jungles of life, especially in a cosmopolitan city like Shanghai.

You may Westernize an Oriental city, but its Orientals —never. Wander about in the Chinese sections of Shanghai; trolley cars clang their way through crowds untouched in dress and manner by anything from the West. Foreigners have made many of the streets wide, and the squares square, and plate glass and steel may show in the store fronts; but the vertical signs, the gay red streamers waving from lines stretched across overhead or hung above the shops, are the signs and decorations of China. Many of the goods displayed are imported, yet even these are limited to the comparatively few lines which appeal to the Oriental. On the whole, a slow conversion, considering the many decades of foreign control in Shanghai.

Here, too, is the same cheapness of human beings as in Hong Kong and Canton; and the same expensiveness of other human beings—Shanghai boasts the limit in her society night life. Contrasts which might disturb the tough consciences of aristocrats elsewhere are accepted in China without a batting of the social eye. Nothing to see in Shanghai? A great nation's commerce going up and down in her greatest river, all of it touching here for transshipment both ways—enough in this alone for a month of entertainment in the ways of the heathen Chinee.

Shanghai deserves little of a traveller's time only, because things Chinese can be seen better in places less cosmopolitan. He naturally wants his Orient without the Occidental veneering; and China itself begins at the city limits.

Inquiry revealed that any extended trip up the Yangtze River was out of the question. Foreigners going into the interior, especially of the tourist variety, were regarded as an incitement to lawlessness and a burden to the officials. But well-protected trains were running on the Shanghai-Peking line, regularly and untroubled. Not one had been held up since the raid on the Blue Express, many months before. The various war lords were showing no signs of activity beyond rather ominous preparations; whether or when they might break out—that was anybody's guess, but in all likelihood warning would be given in plenty of time for anyone to slip out of Peking, and get across to Japan.

With only the faintest prospect of trouble, and that peacefully slumbering in the lap of the future, the thing to do was to go at once while the going was favourable. I booked for the overland route to Yokohama, and took the night express up-river to Nanking.

Aboard the train was a little group of steamer-made

friends, bound for Peking. When people travelling my way are attractive, it is easy for me to discover that we are going to the same hotel; so in this case we fell in with each other for our time in Peking.

After a night in a comfortable stateroom sleeper we arrived in Nanking, and changed to a passenger ferry which in course of time got us across the Yangtze River. If this had not happened before breakfast, the delays might have been less noticeable. On the north bank of the river the Blue Express, the finest train in China, awaited us. Also a good breakfast in the dining car.

Whether the cars were painted to fit the name, or the name given to fit the paint, I do not know. Whichever happened first, the effect of the richly coloured train was striking against the snowless winter drab of the Chinese landscape. Its string of compartment cars are American-made, although slightly modified in their arrangements toward the style of European corridor trains. Not luxurious according to the American idea, but the train and its service left nothing to be desired in its treatment of us during the almost two days and a night from Nanking to Peking.

The crew was Chinese, from the ticket collectors—they go in pairs—down to the Chinese gun-men stationed in every vestibule. Perhaps I should have said "guards" —one should not judge hastily by appearances. The dining car served simple, inexpensive meals, adapted in their bills of fare to both Chinese and foreign tastes. But the train, suiting the large majority of its passengers, was distinctly for the Chinese. This was emphasized in the dining car. On all foreign vessels plying in the East, Orientals are given separate tables, even in the first-class saloons; in this and other dining cars in China *we* were the foreigners, and ate by sufferance with the Chinese.

I only wish that they had carried the changed relation to the point of segregating us as we segregate them. The table manners of all except the best of them make eating difficult and, at times, threaten the safe repose of one's dinner.

This road to Peking, although it runs most of the time across the direction of the streams, traverses an extraordinary amount of level country. In the middle of March, apparently a season between the cold of winter and any green thing to remind one of spring, the country was as dreary, drab, and dry as it is level. Remains of old ice were in a few of the low places, but in most cases the water seemed to have disappeared from under it. If this part of China has spring rains, they were not in evidence in this first month of spring.

China, or as much of it as I saw along the railroad all the way from Shanghai up to Manchuria, is an almost denuded country. Not only is it treeless, but without bushes or shrubbery; everything that will burn is gathered for fuel in the Chinese homes, and even at that the people have mostly to keep out the cold of winter by wearing several layers of cotton-padded clothing. The weeds and dead grass, even the stubble of last year's crops in the fields, are laboriously scraped together for the little warmth there is in them.

A winter of this searching for a bit of heat makes the country look absolutely bald. And this baldness brings out strikingly its most unique feature—the incredible number of graves scattered over the landscape.

Ancestor-worship has made of China one vast cemetery.

If it were a collection of cemeteries, farming in China would have less to contend with; but the graves are scattered promiscuously all over the farms. The placing of new graves is determined by a sort of soothsaying priest, whose one idea seems to be to hinder the pursuit of agriculture. There is no apparent grouping: the plough, the harrow, the spade, must forever be dodging graves—to say nothing of the aggregate area of good soil wasted in a starving country through this broadcasting of the dead.

The vast majority of these graves are little round mounds two or three feet high, with no visible markings. Periodically, the levelling-down effect of storms is repaired by heaping up the mounds anew; in several places men were doing this. A few have markers, and a few have small monuments, especially in some localities—custom in this respect seems to differ. Whether anybody knows who is buried in the millions of unmarked graves, I could not find out; but the single thought seems to be that not one of the mounds shall disappear. So China is covered with graves from all her long ages, superstitiously tended as an honour to the dead, which in some mysterious way redounds to the advantage of the living.

These graves were, and still are, the greatest single obstacle in the way of railroad construction in China. Of course, it is impossible to lay out a thousand feet of road-bed anywhere without encountering one or a score of mounds. This road over which we were passing had a running fight on its hands with outraged Chinese during its entire construction, but the road had to be built, and any palliative, such as moving human remains a thousand years buried, was out of the question. Undoubtedly this necessary overriding of their pet superstition figures large in the Chinese hatred of foreigners.

At nightfall we were entering the rugged country of the Blue Express robbers. More armed Chinese soldiers were taken aboard, and after dark, great searchlights at the rear of the train played off into the hills all night long. The display was spectacular, but less convincing than the steel cagings and East Indian soldiers on the vessels of South China. I wondered what all this would have to do with possible wrecking bands just beyond any one of the curves in the road. Far more satisfying was the knowledge that the Chinese Government had recently lured most of the Blue Express bandits from the mountains under promise of taking them into the army, and then had summarily executed the lot of them. It was cheering to think that that particular gang had acquired well-deserved little mounds on somebody's farm.

After another short day of gazing at bald-headed landscape bumped all over with the hillocks of the dead, we pulled in alongside the immense wall of the Tartar city —Peking.

CHAPTER XI

PEKING

W E WHO are used to a land of open front yards and undefended towns don't quite understand about people who still have to live behind walls. China sticks to walls as a modern necessity.

Peking consists of three walled cities one within another. A "lean-to" city two thirds as large is walled in against its southern side. The Legation Quarter is walled, and so are the different embassies within it. All temples and palaces are behind walls; walls line the streets of the residential quarters, and back of them people of consequence, both Chinese and foreign, live in compounds, walled off from each other.

Speaking of walls, enthusiastic travellers have called Peking all sorts of fantastic names, but nobody has yet thought of dubbing it "the City of Brotherly Love."

To form an idea of Peking's grand outlines, picture in some locality familiar to you an area roughly four miles square; in imagination surround this with a battlemented stone wall forty-five feet high, fifty feet thick at the base, and as wide on top as an average city street.

When you have this mapped out around your home town, add a suburb two and one half miles deep along one of the four-mile stretches, and wall it in with masonry thirty feet high and twenty feet thick. Then you will have the beginnings of Peking.

256

A large part of Peking's foreigners are in the Legation Quarter, a restricted district just inside the great south wall. The main railway terminal station is on the other side of the same wall, and the Water Gate connects the two. This is not one of the original nine gates of old Peking; it is a high archway cut through the wall to accommodate the Legation Quarter, giving foreigners quick and easy access to the railroad station without leaving the protected area.

On a clear, chilly March afternoon, we left the Blue Express—rather cheerfully, after the last four hours of the run up from Tien Tsin through flat, sandy country— and walked with the usual escort of porters through the Water Gate into the foreign quarter. Inside, not half a block away, was the Hôtel des Wagon Lits—Peking's finest, until another hotel was built a little finer but no better. From an American-built train, we entered almost at once a European hotel run on the American plan. A large, pleasant room with an up-to-date tiled bath, ample steam heat everywhere, meals well served while a white orchestra discoursed music delightfully free from jazz— all quite Occidental, even if the place was manned wholly by Chinese. A traveller, were he so disposed, could alight from the train and live indefinitely in this foreign area without seeing anything at all of Peking.

Anything at all except rikisha men; they lie in wait at the hotel door. But seeing rikisha men is not seeing Peking—they belong to all parts of the Orient. Only, in Peking, so bare of tourists in these risky days for China, rikisha men were perhaps more desperately in search of fares than in other parts of the Orient.

On that first late afternoon I set out for a stroll about

the Legation Quarter, intending to peer out through its gateways into the Tartar City and get my bearings. The Quarter has a wall of its own, not particularly formidable, yet higher than those around the different legations. A stroll about the Legation Quarter is a wandering between walls, all of them dwarfed to insignificance by the huge gray battlemented city wall, against which they lie as a sort of patchwork.

At the hotel door the rikisha men beset me, importuned me; followed me, implored me; but I was adamant. After two days on Chinese trains, I wanted to stretch my own legs instead of theirs. Not getting me as a fare, they followed me in a flock as volunteer guides. "Russia legation!" "There—British!" "That—America!" Sure enough, the Stars and Stripes, without prejudice the prettiest among all the flags. Each man contributed to the babel of information, hoping to impress me with his command of English, but all shouted in unison as we came to "America!" Clever chaps—I must have looked like an American.

Cheated out of my quiet stroll, irritated, I turned to order them to clear out. But something in the look of their faces made me think of a hard winter and a poor spring; also of a bunch of rabbits after a single kernel of corn. By all the signs, they were at the point where "fare" spelled "FOOD" in big letters.

I explained that I would not need a rikisha until to-morrow, and wanted to walk alone. "All right!" "Yes!" "Yes!" At once, all backed off a few feet, eager to show that they did not wish to annoy me; but each pointed to his number.

"Me, to-morrow—forty-eight!" "Remember six-three-

seven—I come hotel!" "Two-thirty-one—good!"—
thumping the upholstered seat. "One-fifty-six!" This
last from a young, strong-looking man. He at least
wouldn't have to pant, so I remembered number 156.
For two weeks he trotted me all over Peking—faithfully,
but with few English words. He didn't have as much as
the "You go in?" of my man in Macao.

But in the little group of us always travelling about together we had one rikisha man who talked for all the rest,
as well as considerable on his own account. He so loved
to display his English that he talked as he trotted, until
shut off by his own panting. There were times when I
rather liked to hear this man pant.

* * *

Peking, with no general means of transit faster than a
trotting man, is a city of magnificent distances. So everybody who can afford it hires a trotting man—by the trip,
day, week, or month.

Not long ago a trolley system was laid out on the
principal streets, but the project died in its early stages.
To-day, Peking has considerable of a street railway somewhere down under the dust.

For the first three days of the stay in Peking, our little
party of four had the services of a guide. The places of
interest are scattered all over the city; even if one were
able to get to them alone by the aid of a map, the total
lack of English among the attendants, and the absence of
readable signs, would make sightseeing in Peking a rather
futile business. A traveller cannot go about these Oriental cities as he does in Europe, making fairly accurate
guesses at what the various placards and notices are

trying to tell him. Chinese characters are not to be picked up in a day or a fortnight.

In a city so filled with celestial wonders as Peking, a three-days' gorge of temples and palaces, tourist-fashion, is profitable in itself, and gives a proper Chinese flavour to the remaining days of just browsing around. One assimilates the gorge in the leisurely hours of wandering about afterward in the Oriental atmosphere.

On that first crisp morning we began our conducted tour with a visit to the Temple of Heaven. Out through the Chien Men—the main gate in the south wall—into the Chinese City our little rikisha cavalcade went at a brisk trot. Held most of the time to the wide, straight thoroughfares, we were always glancing curiously into the numberless little side streets, where quaint Chinese shops and squalid Chinese quarters almost touch each other.

Here the talkative member of our trotting force unlimbered. Our official guide seemed to be conserving his voice for use at the temples; our trotter dispensed street information as we went along.

"Here, Lantern Street"—puff—"mos' wunneful lanterns, all kind"—puff, puff—"'mericans buy lanterns take home."

Business of trotting, fifteen seconds.

"Jade Street—jewellery—mos' wunneful, all kind"—huh, huh, huh—"'mericans buy jade, agate, take home."

Breath now in short pants.

"That street, 'broideries. Mos' wunneful 'broideries, all kind"—huh-he, huh-he, huh-he—"an' mandarin coats —otta see mandarin coats—mos' wunneful"—honk, honk —"'mericans buy 'broideries, mandarin coats, take . . ."

My rickisha man, Peking

Pailou, and ornate palace building, "Coal Hill," Peking

Funeral bier, Peking

Peking wedding—bride's chair

He didn't say where—his vocal works had shut down—
but we knew. It began to dawn on us that this man was
having a vision of the days when he would lead us to the
Chinese shops like so many lambs, and afterward gather
his commissions from the shopkeepers. But why shouldn't
he? Somebody would have to pluck us—he seemed as
honest as any. And look at his wunneful command of
English?

Visiting temples in China is not at all like visiting
churches in Europe. A temple is not a single great edifice. It is a collection of unlike structures, scattered
about in a more or less extensive walled compound. The
Temple of Heaven, the largest of these enclosures in
Peking, comprises more than five hundred acres.

I do not intend to describe this or any other temple.
In the case of Peking's temples, impressions seem more
to the point than descriptions. Visiting the Temple of
Heaven is like visiting a great, beautiful park, and finding
there the imposing relics of a religion more splendid in its
trappings than any known to our Occidental half of the
earth. Relics, because the fall of the Empire shut off most
of the State funds which kept these acres of woodwork
and tile and marble in repair; the short dozen years of
neglect are beginning to show—plainly, wherever delicate
woodwork is exposed to the weather.

In those three days we visited the great Temple of
Agriculture, second in extent only to the Temple of Heaven; the Lama Temple, the Temple of Confucius, and a
half-dozen others less impressive. Palaces, too—the
Sea Palaces of the Emperors, within the city, magnifi-
cently built around artificial lakes and hills; the Summer
Palace of the Emperors, more magnificence built against

natural hills eighteen miles outside the walls. And, of course, the centre gem in all this galaxy of splendours, the Forbidden City.

As one does the circuit of these show places of Peking, the conviction grows that the decay manifest in them is not wholly the effect of the Republic's few disruptive years. They seem to belong to a high tide of creative effort from which the Chinese have receded. The familiar signs of a glory departed are the same for both East and West. These temples, like the stately old churches of Italy and Spain, give the impression of functioning about fifty-fifty as sanctuaries of the present and monuments of a greater past.

In only one of all the prominent temples were there enough people to give anything like a human setting to the elaborate paraphernalia. The great Lama Temple of the Thibetans, in the northeast corner of Peking, is redolent of priests and acolytes in the last stages of filth and rags. It is more of a monastery than a temple of worship. The stoppage of Imperial funds, once generously bestowed for their political effect on Thibetans and Mongolians, has reduced these unfortunates almost to starvation. Beggars assail the visitor at every step of the way through the huge, dilapidated compound, priests in the various shrines urge him to pay twenty cents Mex for a "good luck" turn of a prayer wheel in his behalf. But one look at their frightful images would make the unluckiest man alive sit tight with whatever the ordinary gods have done to him.

The Lama religion is a distorted form of Buddhism imported from Thibet. A more hideous and repulsive lot of idols could not be imagined. Many of them are so obscene that they have to be draped.

These gods are not of the kind from whom good is sought; they are bad devils who must forever be propitiated, or evil will befall. The supplicating of evil spirits is the chief burden of most Oriental religions; Lamaism merely carries it to extremes in the number and devilishness of its devils. Where others pervert the nobility of Buddha's teaching to make it conform more or less to their older paganisms, the Lamas borrow the great name for a paganism unmitigated.

Near by, in striking contrast, is the Temple of Con-ˌfucius. Confucian temples have no idols, no incense, no garish trappings of any kind. They are places of retreat for the contemplation of Confucian philosophy. Great stone tablets set up in parts of the enclosure have carved upon them the essential teachings of Confucius. Confucianism stands out from among all the world's creeds in that it depends upon no superstitions, no miracles. It is a philosophy for the guidance of mankind. Confucius is a guide, not a god.

In these days of waning faith in a pagan-steeped Christianity, one who stands in the serenity of a Confucian temple and contemplates these things has to wonder what the simple teachings of Jesus Christ might do for the world, were they to be freed at last from the senseless mysticism of two thousand unchristian years.

* * *

The Summer Palace of the Emperors, the Sea Palaces, the Forbidden City—what, humanly speaking, is to be said about these gorgeous shells of an imperialism done for, if one refuses to describe mere things, and there are no humans about except a few watchmen?

These palaces in themselves make Peking, for me, the most enthralling city in the world. Cold, silent acres of barbaric splendour, waiting aimlessly for the years to go by; each year to chip off a few overhanging yellow tiles, crack flagstones here and there in the unattended courts, deepen by another shade the stain spots on exquisite marble-work; each year to dim the picture until it finally becomes a majestic ruin.

This magnificence at the beginning of its long decay made me think of Rome. I pictured fantastically her monuments in the early years of her decline: perhaps the Coliseum a bit weedy, but brick-stealing from its walls not yet begun; only a few unimportant nicks in the Arch of Constantine; stately mansions on the Palatine Hill "To Let," or turned into museums; the Vestal Virgins wondering where their next lunch is to come from; the Forum only ankle deep in the rubbish which in a thousand years will bury it.

An unreal picture, of course, but it may help one to think of these no less imposing monuments here in Peking as silently waiting for the ages to resolve them into interesting relics of antiquity. Fifteen hundred years hence, archæologists may be digging the glories of the Chinese Empire from under the refuse of fifty generations of uncomprehending Chinamen.

Or will China, after a few more years of her futile Republic, rehabilitate the Empire and fill this emptiness with the life that once belonged to it?

China may come back to her loose-jointed Empire, but

anything so anachronistic as the life that went on within these royal enclosures could never come back anywhere into the Twentieth Century. The great mandarin ruling class is reduced to opening its precious "gift chests," one after another as poverty encroaches, to the purses of rich foreigners. The two ruling passions of most Chinese statesmen, intrigue and "squeeze"—the Orient's better name for graft—may thrive off in the provinces among the contending war lords, but while China owes the world more money than she can pay, her professional bleeders will have to go easy in Peking. The foreign diplomats in the Legation Quarter are sitting close to China's treasury.

Gaudiness is no longer an emblem of power. Hundreds of wives and concubines of a pampered ruler, thousands of useless attendants, royal whims which cost millions, or send luckless men and women to execution— these are corruptions which, once put down, are down for good, even in China.

The kind of government which will suit China's creditors is not going to fit into this gorgeousness of a stone-dead régime. The future rulers who are to pay off China's foreign debts may be monarchs, but they will probably work at an oak-top desk and dictate only to stenographers. International borrowing makes the whole world kin, and rather solicitous kin at that.

I am glad to have seen in their freshness these wonderful structures which in ages to come may be exhibited as still more wonderful ruins. Will the people of that day learn from them as little about the frailty of human institutions as we have learned from Babylon, Egypt, Greece, and Rome?

Life in Peking lacks at first view the congestion of some other Chinese cities, mainly because at first view one sees only the wide, straight thoroughfares which cross the city in both directions. But off these thoroughfares, Peking is a network of little Chinese streets often hardly wide enough for two rikishas to pass, swarming with life and loaded with smells.

The twenty-five square miles within the walls of all Peking would give ample room for its population of less than two million, if it were not for the great areas taken up by temple and palace enclosures, imperial grounds and artificial lakes, the Forbidden City and the Legation Quarter. Many governmental and residential compounds of generous proportions cut down the area still more.

But the Chinese masses everywhere live congested for reasons of economy. A recent survey in Peking disclosed that the cost of living for an average coolie family of five, including rent, food, clothing, and such little heat as they get for cooking, is nine dollars Mex—four-fifty gold—per month. This is three of our cents per day for each individual.

Rikisha men—probably the best paid of all coolies—may net six dollars gold out of a monthly wage after paying rent for their rikishas. These live in comparative affluence. If they depend on street fares, as the vast majority of them do, they may make more, but are apt to make less, especially in such precarious times as these.

Wages here look like nothing at all to an American. The one big solace of foreign women living in the Orient is the cheapness of domestic help. An American army officer told me that his entire expenses for living in European style with an establishment of fifteen rooms

and nine servants, including considerable entertaining
of guests, was less than twentv-five hundred dollars gold
per year.

Nobody worries along with less than five servants.   The
lady of the house is supposed to do nothing whatever—
nothing even for her children, if it resembles work.   This
may not be an unmitigated blessing, but it is an alluring
prospect for one who has had to pay in America twenty
dollars a week for a half-done cook.

*   *   *

"Lanterns, 'broideries, all kind. Mandarin coats,
jade, mos' wunneful." We did shopping in the little
streets of the Chinese City, under the guidance of our
talkative speed boy. Things rare, strange, and beautiful—much of it ill adapted to Occidental settings. Suave,
smiling young Chinese merchants blandly asking twice as
much as they expect to get. A fascinating pastime—and
apt to be expensive.

When shopping in China, don't make the usual American mistake of disputing an Oriental's price. Name your
own quite as blandly, and never find fault with his goods.
Carefully look for faults, but keep your observations to
yourself. Remember that in his eyes you are a crude
Western barbarian—and in point of Oriental good manners, you probably are.

If I were to give only one bit of advice to Americans
travelling anywhere outside of the United States, it would
be this: Do your prettiest to be polite. More of us, then,
might get by without seeming absolutely rude.

Among all the goods on display, the most fascinating
were those which had found their way into the shops

from high-class Chinese families brought to dire straits by the coming of the Republic. Rare old silks, held perhaps for generations in the family "gift chests"; silks exquisitely embroidered in patterns designed for the making of rich vestments, but never cut from the original piece; mandarin coats——

Mandarin coats are the particular craze of American visitors in Peking. The embroidery on the newer ones shows signs of commercialism in the long stitch and coarser design; but the robes of the old days, made for the critical eyes of mandarins by China's most expert needlewomen, are works of art.

Most of the new coats, too, are rich with the needlework of the old in the borders, collars, and immense cuffs taken from mandarin coats which were too much worn to be put on sale. The exquisitely embroidered designs cut from the discarded body parts of these old coats captivate the ladies as doilies or pillow facings.

Of course, the supply of this old needlework cannot hold out much longer against the present demand. These are the golden days for buyers of mandarin coats. Before many years, we will be depending on the kind of work more hastily done for tourists, quite as we now buy Oriental rugs which are sad imitations of those once made to please discriminating Turkish or Persian grandees.

The streets of Peking are fascinating because so much of Chinese life is to be seen either in the street or openly facing it. Funerals—huge catafalques overdecorated in red, carried on the shoulders of as many as forty men, and preceded, surrounded, and followed by innumerable hired ragamuffins bearing all sorts of gaudy symbols and banners. Weddings—a close second to funerals in elaborate-ness and colour, with rather more noise-making contrivances which pass in China for music.

Drop into any one of the little theatres along the street, sit on a bench and watch the show. In fifteen minutes you will have seen about what you would see in fifteen hours of it: action incredibly slow, scenery of no interest, squeaky actors buried in costumes meaningless to the foreigner.

But the towel-throwers! The Chinese love to swab their faces with hot cloths. Through the aisles goes a man dispensing steamy face towels to all who want them. At the back of the room stands the towel-thrower with a fresh supply.

Up goes the empty hand of the dispenser; whiz! comes a big steaming wad over the heads of the audience, and biff! the catcher catches it. He then fires back a bunch of used towels unerringly at the supply man. This odd performance happens about once a minute.

I stayed an hour, hoping to see the pitcher throw wild, or the catcher miss, or somebody in the audience pop up and intercept the boiling missile with his head. No luck. A Big League battery could not have played a more faultless game.

Five minutes off the main thoroughfare, in the little winding, dirty streets, one might as well be in the Chinese interior. The people act as if they had never seen a white man. With my rikisha man, I had many excursions into this China—getting indifferent snapshots of odd places too dark, of tangled scenes which look promising but "take" poorly, and rubbing up against the population, both figuratively and literally.

Whenever my rikisha stopped, men, women, and children crowded about, gaping, staring. If I got out, the crowd doubled; when I changed a film, the street became a solid mass of stony-faced Chinamen.

I never saw anywhere else so many wooden expressions. They showed no lively interest in the camera or in me; only a dull wonder that spent itself in staring. They call the Chinese face inscrutable, but in most cases it seems to be the inscrutability of plain dullness.

I discovered that a bland smile on my part would crack expressions which looked as if they could resist the attentions of a club. My smiles trebled the crowds. The special fascination seemed to be somewhere about my face. Women particularly, when I caught their eyes, would forsake the modest habit of their kind and gaze at me with startling intensity.

At first I was flattered. My face is not commonly regarded as a spellbinder. But soon it dawned on me that these Chinese of the back streets were being struck dumb with astonishment at sight of my green-gray eyes. Evidently they had never before seen the like in a human being.

It is natural that dark peoples, seeing among themselves only rich, lustrous eyes, should have a peculiar interest in the various eye colours to be found among light-complexioned foreigners. The impressionable young white traveller in foreign lands need not always pride himself over the earnest glances of dusky maidens there. The chances are that they are merely searching him for washed-out eyes.

Filth which in Canton is banked along the little streets must here be carried out and dumped into stench-exuding sewer holes on the main thoroughfares. In this way,

Peking concentrates her smells without much subduing them. Dirt is a fixed habit in China.

Speaking of dirt, it is estimated that there are a million lepers loose in the population of China. The right number may be half or twice as many. In any case, one rubs elbows with lepers at all stages of disintegration in China's little streets.

Attentions to the person, from shaving to shoe repairing, are dispensed in the open streets by itinerant craftsmen. They advertise their trades by working various kinds of noise producers.

Lumber cutters demonstrate, in the midst of busy traffic, the incredible cheapness of labour in China. A Chinese sawmill consists of a log propped up at an angle, a coolie perched on top of it, another coolie below, and a cross-saw, which these two men pull back and forth through it. It must take them a week to cut an ordinary log into board thicknesses, but I was told that our portable sawmills, which reduce a big log to lumber in a minute, cannot compete with this hand labour. Power, machinery, oil, repairs—Chinamen are cheaper than any one of these.

And the street-sprinkling! One coolie draws the water hand over hand with rope and bucket from a shallow well, and empties it into a deep tub on a crude sort of wheelbarrow. Another trundles the shrieking barrow—oil is too expensive to waste on the wheel—to the street to be sprinkled. Here, two more men lug the tub along the middle of the roadway, stopping every dozen steps to throw the water about with a shallow dipper on the end of a bamboo stick.

The Chinese may have been sprinkling streets in this way

since the time of Confucius; they may be doing it for another thousand years. Meantime, Peking is one of the dustiest cities in the world—when it is not the muddiest.

From the top of the great south wall, one looks down upon the Legation Quarter; and if he thinks of the frightful Boxer uprising of 1900, when the Chinese so nearly succeeded in carrying out their dream of killing all the "foreign devils," he must wonder just how much safer the foreign devils are to-day in that same Legation Quarter.

It was from this wall that the starving foreigners of Peking, all huddled in the British Legation, were sniped and bombarded by the Chinese for many long weeks before rescuers got in from the coast. Now, not a Chinaman is allowed on the city wall where it touches the Quarter—between the two south gates, Chien Men and Hata Men. None are permitted to live in the Quarter—no armed Chinese may even come into it on any pretext. Every foreign embassy has its own armed nationals on guard, and housed in the Quarter. From the American Legation rises a great radio apparatus, capable of summoning help from warships at sea, or in Chinese ports. And the Water Gate opens directly upon the railway station.

Sizing up all these mimic defenses and means of escape, and the pretty rules which tell the Chinese where they shall not trespass, one has to admit that foreigners in Peking are quite as safe from a determined Chinese assault as if they were to bury their heads, ostrichlike, in the dust of Peking's streets. But help from the outside will never again be so slow at getting in to Peking as it was in that fearful summer of 1900.

Now, off to Chosen. Chosen, if anybody doesn't happen to know, is Korea.

CHAPTER XII

KOREA

IT IS a night and a day from Peking to Mukden, over the South Manchuria Railway. As on the Shanghai-Peking route, the train was run under guard—if desperate-looking armed Chinamen throughout the train may be called guards.

In China, most bandits are unpaid soldiers—and one of China's ways of getting soldiers is to hire dissatisfied bandits. The two occupations are so closely associated that at a certain stage of unpaidness a Chinese soldier must honestly doubt which he is. If a conscientious man, he solves the doubt by being both. As a bandit, he goes into some shop and helps himself to goods; then, in his official capacity, he quells the disturbance raised by the proprietor.

On a clear, cold morning we reached Shanhaikwan, where the Great Wall of China descends from the mountains and meets the sea.

Travellers speak of seeing the Great Wall of China. As a matter of fact, they never see it. What they see is a comprehensible bit of an incomprehensible thing. It is the *stretch* of it across a vast empire that stuns the imagination.

At Shanhaikwan its bulk comes up out of the sea like a huge, creeping thing; reaches off across the plain, lifts itself into the distant foothills; climbs again, dotted with citadels, over great shoulders of the mountain range until it gains the topmost ridge, then disappears. Disappears only because there the eye has to let go—and there the imagination takes hold, and struggles feebly with the thought that for fifteen hundred miles that immense bulk goes winding on over ranges and rivers and plains; obstructed by nothing, itself the Great Obstruction, the only thing of its kind on earth, the most gigantic single piece of work ever achieved by man.

A mere bit of it fetches one up against the limitation of words. Then why try to express the Great Wall of China?

Through an ancient break in the Wall, the train passes northward into Manchuria. The land of the Manchus gave us no thrills on that last-of-March day. A countryside may be picturesque under the frigid blanket of winter, or beautiful in the variegated greens of summer; but early spring is an off season for scenery in a farming district. It is then like a child in the disagreeable business of getting up—caught between the serenity of its bed and the vigour of its play.

Passing from Peking's province, Chihli, into Manchuria offers no more change in scene than crossing the invisible line between Ohio and Indiana. State lines in America serve mostly to plague the railroads with swiftly changing laws; they have to ring the bell in one state, and must not allow their passengers to play dominoes in the next. Provincial lines in China separate the political ambitions of war lords—in a haphazard way which doesn't mean much to the people, because they have to pay tribute to whichever happens along.

The war lords of China! In slipping through the Great Wall we passed from the shadowy rule of China's President

to the sphere of influence of Manchuria's war lord—a lively
gentleman who is said to find recreation in planning a de-
scent upon the shadow in Peking. Shanghai, Canton,
the west, the north—all burdened with useless "generals,"
sapping the country of men and money, paralyzing business, turning the desperate populace into soldiers and
bandits indiscriminately.

Poor old China! Never a united people, born and bred
without a national spirit, ignorant of patriotism, perhaps
more broken to-day than at any time in the last thousand
years. Is this the final disruption?

Those who understand China best say, No. China is
hardened to internal dissensions, to a continuous performance of looting and "squeeze," quite as her people
are inured to physical hazards of living incredible to a
foreigner.

So these peasants and villagers of Manchuria are like the
peasants and villagers in Chihli, or in any other part of
China: they live in poverty when tax collectors are sack-
ing the country in the name of peace, and they live in hell
when soldiers ravish the country in the name of war. But
somehow China lives on—and will live on, so say those
who know her best.

Futile China! In point of numbers, the Chinese could
whip the world; but they haven't the man stuff in them to
whip their own country into shape.

*   *   *

In Mukden, the capital and principal city of Manchuria, I saw the last of China and the first of Japan.
The imitatively Western streets of the Japanese quarter
might be mistaken for a white man's town given over to

the yellow races.   With half an eye one can see in Mukden that the Japanese are decidedly in Manchuria, even if he knows nothing about Dairen and other key situations already under Japan's control.

A night's run, in a Japanese train made up of imitation Pullman sleepers, brought us to the northwestern border of Korea.   Antung is the last Chinese city before crossing into the Hermit Kingdom.   In the custom house there, Japanese inspectors collected a Chinese export tax on all purchases made in China—a tax which, curiously, had to be paid in Japanese money.   They did it so courteously that it was almost painless—not even bothering me with a receipt.   I left the place wondering how they could remember to turn my thirteen yen and sixty sen over to China, and whether the war lord of Manchuria would get it, or the shadowy government in Peking, or—— Anyhow, I paid it to a smiling Japanese.

Korea is a peninsula about the size of Florida, and in shape remarkably like it.   As with some other little countries, its history is built around its capital, Keijo—or Seoul, as Europeans know it.   But the picture which one gets of Korea through a stay in Seoul will have a more faithful colouring if one makes daylight trips of the journey lengthwise through the country, from Antung on the northwest to Fusan on the southeast coast.

What one sees most outstanding in the long day from Antung to Seoul is a Western railroad, with the usual complement of prosaic yards and wires and buildings, meandering through an orientalism which it has not really penetrated.   Less than forty years ago this was the mysterious Hermit Kingdom, sealed against all other nations.   To-day, the country wears awkwardly the bor-

Sawing lumber, Peking

Peking street sprinkling. Throwing the water about with dipper

Koreans

Street scene, Seoul, Korea

rowed modernism of its Japanese conquerors, while the people themselves hold to the customs and ideas of hermit days. It's a clear case of submitting without accepting. The Korean costume for both men and women is of white cotton—or rather, once-white cotton—made up in bulky fashion, flowing airily when not held down by padded outer wear. Farmers driving their wooden-wheeled carts along the country roads were as much encumbered with this padded cotton stuff as the aimless onlookers about the stations. There was no more than the chill of early spring in the air, but the Koreans appear to be as careful as the Chinese about discarding the successive layers of clothing piled on during the winter.

A Korean gentleman looks ridiculously funny at first sight, grotesque at second, and thereafter, pathetically out of step with the new order of life which gradually is being forced upon his country. Above his swaddling Korean dress is a solemn face, given over to the few long hairs which consent to adorn the Oriental cheek and chin. On his head is a crownless skullcap, through which protrudes a braided tuft of hair, standing upright; and over this is his hat—an absurd little crown of black horsehair gauze, flat-topped and flat-brimmed. Through this draughty crown one faintly glimpses the upright twist of the gentleman's hair. The contrivance is held on its perch by two black ribbons tied in a bow underneath the chin. The effect is heightened by the gentleman's dignified bearing.

Of another age, too, are the farm villages: straw-roofed, mud-walled houses, with a considerable showing of flimsy stockades apparently designed to keep out nothing more formidable than domestic animals. Numberless cemeteries occupy sites on the hillsides—without detriment to agriculture, as in China. Some of the burial places are quite elaborate; others consist of no more than a few mounds shelved into the hillside.

*   *   *

The Seoul of to-day would hardly be recognized in descriptions of it written twenty years ago. The train arrives in an up-to-date railway station, red-caps and a Japanese hotel runner do their parts with pleasing dispatch, and passengers are whirled away in smart American cars, through paved and electrically lighted streets, to a well-appointed European hotel run by Japanese.

In all this the Korean is either absent or an onlooker. Yet, as one gazes out in the morning from a hotel window over this old city of two hundred and fifty thousand, the Oriental picturesqueness of most of it relieves to some extent the numerous bald spots of Japanese modernism.

But picturesqueness stands little show against progress. The ancient walls of Seoul are giving way to utilitarian demands for new roadways and more space. Trolley cars clang on the few streets wide enough to accommodate them, and run up to within a few hundred feet of the royal enclosure, the sacred heart of the old Hermit Kingdom.

The most pronounced and disturbing encroachment of the Japanese upon the ways of the Koreans, if one is to believe the tales of a short generation ago, is an insistence upon cleanliness. Of course, the ancient crust of Seoul's filth could not be washed away at a stroke. The new cleanliness is relative; the old pools of slime have become respectable mudholes, surface sewage flows less reluctantly, and not so much garbage is thrown into the little streams where women pound clothing back to comparative whiteness. One can walk now almost anywhere in Seoul without holding one's nose.

The hotel's folder describing Keijo, written in an ornate Japanese version of English, is more entertaining than it was intended to be. It is a folder worthy of a hotel which modestly alludes to itself as "A revelation in the refinement of luxury on this part of the globe."

Its assurance of "latest and most modern comfort" certainly gets the idea across that nothing can be more recent. Seoul, we learn, is "the most thickly populated city in the country." I had previously gathered that there were none thicker. Several short excursions are recommended; on two of them, the folder says, "a luncheon basket should be carried." The inference is that one has to eat it.

For the zoölogical garden this ambitious sheet claims an "assortment of animals from rodents to the elephant," then it spoils the Noah's Ark effect by adding, "besides, some splendid lions, tigers, leopards, and bears."

Yet I owe my liberty in Seoul to that folder and its good map. Guides don't understand about browsing around —they are always dragging one to see things. With a guide, I should have had to spend time in the zoo which I put in to better advantage on the streets of Seoul. One can see "from rodents to the elephant" in America.

For three days I wandered about Seoul, seeing common things mostly, now and then stumbling upon something unusual. One of the most striking of the old Korean objects in Seoul is the Big Bell, hung in a little enclosure near the centre of the city. In Korean times the deep boomings of this bell marked the order of daily events, and at midnight gave the signal for the closing of the city gates. But it rings no more. As the folder has it, "the practice has now fallen into destitude."

Seoul is not a city of temples. Buddhism, once introduced from China, was later "disestablished," and now only relics of its altars remain. In other parts of the world, peoples so decadent and ineffective are invariably in the grip of designing priesthoods; but the abysmal superstitions of the Koreans seem never to have been shaped into a religion. While Confucian philosophy has a following among the educated classes, the commun run are reputed to be as nearly without a religion as any people on earth—an admittedly sad state for any human beings. Christian missionaries look upon this as a rich field for their work. Plenty of raw material, surely, but its richness for the successful planting of high Christian ideals is not obvious. Christian superstitions, however, like weeds, will grow in any soil.

By all outward signs, the old Hermit Kingdom of Korea was due to fall into the clutches of some designing nation when Japan took her over. It was a gorgeous, degenerate Empire in which the chief source of individual wealth was "squeeze," and incredible poverty the chief characteristic. China is the world's present example of national ineffectiveness; Korea, in her own day, must have been a worse one.

Incompetent though they are, the spectacle of these people being slowly deprived of their own culture is pathetic enough, especially as the Westernized imitation which they are compelled to accept is nothing better than a raw experiment in the hands of their conquerors. Japan is busily dressing up Korea in clothes which she herself has not yet learned to wear gracefully.

Japan's invasion of the royal grounds in Seoul typifies her invasion of Korea. Facing the majestic old gateway in the royal wall were the Korean palaces; rebuilt, it is true, by one of the late Emperors after a fire, but splendidly done in the low, spreading style and rich colourings handed down through the Korean ages. They are as truly relics of the ancient Hermit Kingdom as if they were a thousand years old.

Directly in the foreground of these palaces, on the front lawn, so to speak, the Japanese are completing a huge, many-storied administration building, built of gray stone in the latest architectural style of Chicago.

Its utilitarian bulk almost bumps into the ancient gate in front of it, and makes a back yard of the exquisite low palaces behind it. To a Westerner, it is the West made ridiculous; what the feelings of the Koreans must be as they look at the thing can only be guessed at.

But old Korea was ripe for somebody's picking, and I suppose the picker might as well have been Japan. Decadent nations are never permitted to die naturally. As with wounded animals in their native habitat, some devouring enemy is always lying in wait to make their finish tragic.

* * *

Again a day's journey in Korea, this time from Seoul to Fusan, where the night boat waits to take us over to Japan. At this stage of the route across Korea, Japanese are more in evidence, both aboard the train and in the towns along the way, than in the country north of

Seoul. Their occupation of the new land is naturally more complete as one approaches Japan.

We had a bright Japanese princeling of six in our car, returning to his royal family after a visit to Seoul. As the train pulled out of the station, every Japanese head on the platform bent with one accord to the level of as many Japanese hips, and stayed there until we were out of view. They must have done it on signal.

Down through the south country, immense areas on the denuded, thin-soiled hills have been reforested by the Japanese—or, rather, by Koreans under persuasion of the Japanese. The Japanese point to this work as something done for the benefit of Koreans. There's a mistake here of two letters. It was done for the benefit of Korea. Korea is the new land of Japan; in it, Koreans are no more than a subservient people.

Japan has done no worse than other more civilized nations, including our own, in dispossessing weaker peoples from coveted lands. It is an accepted world habit, so universal that in some obscure way it must be for the world's good. But it is as absurd for Japan as for any of the rest of them to claim a shred of altruism in this business of dispossessing.

The night steamer at Fusan had "latest and most modern comfort" for the few first-class passengers who got aboard. It managed somehow to stow away an incredible number of second- and third-class, nearly all Japanese. Like the Japanese whom we had been seeing all the way down through Korea, this throng at the boat had the characteristics which distinguish even the common run of Japanese from Koreans and Chinese: cleanliness, good order, thrift. Sure signs, in this world of killing rivalries, of a people coming on. They have Korea, they are in Manchuria. And the Chinese bear the marks of a people slipping back. Rather an impressive sight, watching these clean, neatly dressed Japanese thriftily packing themselves into the hold.

CHAPTER XIII

JAPAN

THE month of April in Japan is Cherry Blossom time. Cherry blossoms fit in with the exquisite creations of the Japanese, and set them off to the best possible advantage. Dainty and dolled-up always, Japan bedecked with cherry blossoms attains perfection in her own particular style of beauty.

April commends itself further as being a holiday month among the Japanese. In Cherry Blossom time they visit the shrines and temples in great numbers, flock off into the country, crowd the trains and trolleys, and fill the parks. The Japanese people are to be seen at their best and worst in April.

I had come across to Shimonoseki, the landing port on Japan's western tip, with a keen American business agent whose success had been built on his practical understanding of the Japanese. Here was the same odd mixture of things Oriental and Western as in Korea.

"What do you think of it?" I asked him, waving at the Kansas construction about us.

"Well," he said, "it means, for one thing, that Japan is disrupting her own ancient culture quite as effectually as she is that of Korea. You'll see this sort of thing all the way to Tokyo."

"Becoming westernized?" I suggested.

"Oh, no! The Japanese can never be westernized.

284

That's impossible for an Oriental. They are—perhaps
this expresses it—becoming *imitatively* Western."

Charming Miyajima is five hours to the eastwara,
through mountainlike hills interspersed with valleys cultivated to their limits. Cultivated beyond their limits,
up the terraced hillsides, and on little shelves of level
ground clinging here and there above the terraces. In
Japan, every bit of soil has to give an account of itself in
terms of food.

There is more than the usual variety of scenes in this
part of the overland trip by rail: Japanese country life
spread out on one side; glimpses of the Inland Sea, dotted
with boats, on the other; a rugged shore line, and steep
green islands scattered along it. And everywhere, Japanese. Thrifty, busy Japanese.

Farming in Japan is done in miniature. Wheat, bar-
ley, and the like were being raised by the handful on neat
little patches of ground, which later in the season will be
planted to rice, a single blade at a time. Crops are tended as we tend flower beds. Labour is nothing; yield is
everything, on the little farms of Japan. Farms? We
would call them gardens. Pretty, colourful gardens.

Strange that an overpopulated nation's grinding struggle for food can be so picturesque!

The little Japanese prince—he was still with us, somewhere on the train—attracted crowds of men, women, and
children to the stations. In some of the smaller towns,
school children, massed to greet the prince, waved banners and shouted as the train went by. Perhaps they
called it singing. Whatever it was, I had the pleasure, if
not the honour, of special demonstrations by Japanese
all the way to Miyajima.

Miyajima is a summer resort on one of the beautiful islands in the Inland Sea.   It is not only a tourists' point of interest because of the fine views to be had from the heights; its many paths, winding off into the silent places, make it a retreat for those in need of rest.   Visitors to shrines, too, come here especially at this season to pay their devotions at Miyajima's famous temples.   To judge from the lines of shops displaying a remarkable sameness of shiny new tourist souvenirs, Miyajima is also a centre for the dispensing of useless articles.

I got from a young Japanese whom I met casually still another view of Miyajima.   After the first salutation, thinking that he might know a little English, I tried an easy sentence on him.   On such occasions I always strip my English down to fighting weight—that is, until every word left in it has a punch of its own.

"You—have—nice—place—here," I said, fanning the air appropriately.

"Yes," he replied, "it is an ideal rendezvous."

Before I could recover, he politely asked me, "From what place in America do you come?" I acknowledged Boston.

"Boston?   Ah, the home of Franklin."   I was about to say that that kind was made in Detroit, when I happened to think of Benjamin.   On the spur of the moment I was unable to recall any sure thing about Benjamin except that he was dead; and something told me that this would not be news to the young man.

Luckily, he let Franklin rest, and commented on Boston as a centre of music and culture, incidentally mentioning Washington and Jefferson.

These and many other educational facts about us he

had got wholly from Japanese schools. He had never been outside of Japan. He expressed the idea, although not in these words, that in trying to learn American ways the Japanese study our inspirational characters. The Japanese certainly teach America to their students more appreciatively than we teach Japan to ours.

* * *

After Miyajima and its calm, I had Kobe—and its confusion. Western Japan centres in three great cities —Kobe, Osaka, and Kyoto, quite as the newer Japan in the east centres in Yokohama and Tokyo—or did, until the earthquake wrecked that part of the country.

Kobe, practically unhurt by the great earthquake of September 1, 1923, would seem to be in a fair way to succeed ruined Yokohama as Japan's chief seaport, in spite of Yokohama's good harbour and more advantageous location. The only thing against Kobe's succession is the fact that never in history has an earthquake, however frightful, prevented a general return to the wreckage of an otherwise favoured city. The prospect of commercial advantage is enough to make some people sit over an acknowledged crack in the earth's crust and hope for luck.

After the severe destruction wrought in what was the heart of the Japanese Empire, most of the foreign agencies in Yokohama and Tokyo, as well as many Japanese commercial houses there, reëstablished themselves in Kobe. This town offered a good port, and a place to live outside the earthquake zone.

Of course, under the sudden influx, Kobe grew—or rather, swelled—and it was in this state of hectic prosperity that I found it in April, 1924. The foreign-built half of the city might have hung out a general sign of "Standing Room Only," so far as business and living space were concerned. "Foreign-built" in Japan does not mean built by foreigners; most of these Yankee-English-French-German structures are the imitative effort of Japanese.

"Imitation" is mapped on the face of Japan. In her whole modern scheme there does not appear to be an original invention as complex as a pen-wiper.

With my rikisha man always with me, whether awheel or afoot—I never did get over a desire to spell these fellows by walking part of the time—I wandered about in the little streets of the old Japanese city; down to the forty-eight-foot bronze Buddha at the far end of town, through gaudy theatre streets, and shopping streets almost as colourful, to drab little alleys lined with the open stalls of artisans busily making the confusion of flimsy stuff for sale in the shops; and into the exclusive section which is in every Japanese city, the Yoshiwara.

Japan runs her Houses of Joy and Sorrow as a municipal enterprise, and with Japanese efficiency. They seem to be all of a pattern. A wide entrance gives an enticing view of a court decorated with flowers, greens, and possibly a fountain, and prettily dressed little creatures peep out daintily—almost modestly!—at the passers-by.

It is a squint-eyed seductiveness, in more ways than one. For so many centuries specific diseases have been broadcast in Japan that the natives, it is said, have acquired a certain immunity. Not so the foreigners. Tales of white men wrecked for life in a careless hour, of tourists gone stone-blind before they get back as far as Vancouver —warnings enough against these playthings of native hordes.

The Japanese multitudes. Those of Kobe's native town are said to have doubled under the rush from the stricken area; but no foreigner could guess whether this or any other Oriental population had been doubled or halved. The number of humans in sight is to him always incredible.

In spite of the terrible disaster of only seven months before, the common run of Japanese seemed remarkably cheerful. They smile delightedly when they meet, and as they talk they break constantly into hearty laughter. It is difficult to believe that they can be simulating a mirth which bubbles forth so genuinely, yet the Japanese are accused of simulating every emotion known to man.

In their profuse bowings down to the level of the hips, usually thrice repeated, they impress a foreigner as having reduced politeness to an absurd formality. Two gentlemen meet; down they go to the horizontal, wagging the crowns of their heads at each other very like a pair of game cocks, and murmuring sweet nothings to the ground. One or the other now and then tips up an eye for a peek —but dodges back to position if the head opposite still shows top foremost. The game is, apparently, to see which can stay down the longer. They come up finally, only to go through the performance again, and perhaps a third time.

As a mode of expressing mutual regard, this act is so disconnected from any human impulse that an observer is apt to question the realness of their other courtesies. Even their constant smiling and laughter come under suspicion.

The westernizing of Japan has scarcely touched the customs and dress of its people. The *geta*, a flat wooden clog set up from the ground on two cross-pieces of wood, is the almost universal footgear for men, women, and children. Shoes are affected only by the few men who wear European dress. Women without exception stick to full Japanese costume.

The *geta* is precariously held on by two cords which are drawn back from between the great toe and its neighbour, through a slit in the moccasin-like cloth shoe. At the heel it flaps loosely. A more inefficient footgear cannot be imagined. In walking on two crosspieces set six inches apart, they lose entirely the prehensile effect of the toes. Every step is a double jolt, as one foot rocks forward on the little flat board, while the other jerks its clog along with its toes.

Walking, for the Japanese, is a tiresome necessity. The clatter on the street, with a hundred clogs usually within close hearing, sounds like a rainfall of overcooked biscuits.

In the dull-coloured, flowing robes of the men there appears a slight variation in cut, but the kimonos of the women, so far as an untrained masculine eye can discern, are all of the same pattern. Japanese women satisfy the feminine love of variety, partly through marked differences in quality and colour of the cloth, but mostly by skilful manipulations of the gorgeous *obi*—sash—the coiffeur, and the cosmetics which entirely make up a woman's complexion, if she pretends to have one. With these means, a high-class Japanese lady distinguishes herself from the common run quite as effectually as European women are able to do the trick with an unlimited range of styles.

One does not get halfway across Japan without acquiring at least two distinct impressions regarding Japanese women: one, that their costume, whether of richest silks or plain cotton, is mightily pleasing to the eye; the other, that nothing short of a fetching outfit could successfully disguise the more than occasional homeliness of the women's faces. So many dull, heavy expressions, even among the better dressed, do not fit in with all that one hears about the beauty of the Japanese women. Their commonest natural charm is in the plump cheeks of youth, but the plump cheeks of youth are a limited asset anywhere. There's a reason in Japan for a general dependence on make-up.

The same heavy expression lends a brutishness to the faces of many of the men. If the expression is not heavy, it is as likely as not to be cunning, or sinister.

After China and Korea, Japan's cleanliness, good order, and thrift are a relief to the senses; but the composite Japanese face develops in one a mental shiver as novel as it is hard to define.

* * *

Kyoto, two hours east of Kobe, is delightfully Japanese underneath a raw veneer of modernism. A successful imitation of a good trolley system on the main streets does not affect the old Japanese character of the narrow little ways leading off them; nor can the garish buildings erected to Japan's new god of commerce taint the Oriental atmosphere of Kyoto's famous temples and shrines. One merely has to get away from the clatter of machinery to find himself in the clatter of *getas*, and all that they stand for in the life of old Japan.

For centuries Kyoto was the Empire's capital. In 1868 the seat of government was removed to Tokyo, a day's rail ride farther east. Along with its imperial trappings Tokyo took Kyoto's name, merely reversing the syllables; but the spell of Japan's ancient culture was something which could not be moved away. The old handicrafts thrive here in Kyoto as one might think of them as thriving hundreds of years ago. Work in lacquer, damascene, cloisonné, is carried on in little shops with extravagant disregard for the hours and days of manual skill involved; producing articles more exquisitely useless than modern civilization can afford to bother itself with making.

The amusement streets of Kyoto at night are fairly banked with Japanese lanterns of all shapes and sizes, most of them advertising movies, theatres, and a multitude of little shops which display trinkets and toys quite as flimsy as the lanterns themselves. Outside of standard lines of goods, frailty characterizes Japanese merchandise. Ornaments, playthings, and many articles for household use seem destined for an early trip to the waste basket. A great number of their things are frankly made to be used only once. But the stuff is pretty, and incredibly cheap.

Moving pictures have invaded the Japanese amusement section, but aside from the films and the machinery to work them the settings are strictly Japanese in character. Playhouses have scarcely a touch of modernism beyond electric lighting, and in many of them, foreign patronage is regarded as of so little account that not even chairs are provided. Except the few which are advertised in the hotels, Kyoto's entertainments are for the Japanese.

Flimsy daintiness, a blaze of high colours, pretty costumes, and the everlasting patter of *getas*—these are every-

Daibutsu, in Kobe, Japan

Steamer, Lake Biwa, and boarding-school girls

"Their prettiness lent enchantment to an already well-favoured scene." Japanese young ladies at Temple of Ishiyama

where in the enchanting picture, as one walks through Kyoto's amusement streets at night. At every entrance are rows upon rows of *getas*—checked by the patrons within as we check hats. All enter in their *tabes*—the noiseless cloth foot-covering. Street footwear never defiles a Japanese interior.

One evening, in strolling along Theatre Street with a friend, we came across a playhouse which had at the top of its Japanese announcement the legend, "1 Yen." We paid the one yen each, and presented ourselves at the door. The only other concession to foreigners proved to be huge cloth slippers, such as are kept at all first-class Japanese shops for tying over the shoes of the uncivilized. Donning these, we went in.

The show was evidently rather cheap vaudeville. The entire audience was seated on the floor. From somewhere two chairs were hastily brought, and placed in the little balcony, in a space evidently reserved for those who might be rash enough to pay one yen to see the performance. We were its only occupants, and the only foreigners. For a time we were too obviously a part of the show.

A deadly dull show most of it was. A show of its class in America would have been rottenly suggestive, but this one had nothing of the kind. The raciest thing in it was a posing affair by girls in skirts reaching to the knees; this shocking exposure was mitigated by heavy stockings. In Japan, women are always covered from neck to feet by their kimonos. They wear no stockings, but even glimpses above their ankle-high *tabes* are rare.

There is this virtue about Japanese entertainments: they are either wholly free from sex suggestions, or they are nothing else but that.   You go to a respectable show place in Japan with a sense of ease on this score which you rarely have in America.   The Japanese are so absolutely frank with their immorality that they exhibit it by itself.   They are not forever trying to put it over on the decently inclined, after the habit of so many of our own amusement magnates.

In this little theatre there were acrobats, monologists, an elocutionist, and—heaven barely saved us—a singing man.

If there is anything more lacerating to the ear than Japanese singing, it is the Japanese speaking voice when used for entertainment.   Phonograph records done by famous Japanese actors give off a succession of discordant growls, roars, and bellowings.   The idea seems to be to let out as many cruel and unusual sounds as the vocal organs are capable of producing.   Exaggeration in describing them is impossible.

The star performer at our show was a young woman elocutionist.   Dressed in the usual kimono, she squatted behind a desk raised six inches above the floor, and read from a book.

She began with a series of warning shrieks which sounded like a midnight engagement of two unusually earnest cats.   She shifted from fast to slow, from shrill to low, with a suddenness that had my friend jumping. He had taken the sea voyage over from America to quiet his nerves.

For half an hour this talented young girl tore through the octaves in a welter of triumph, sorrow, and despair. If there are any bars in Japanese music, they failed to stop her.   In the tragic parts—most of it was tragic—she swayed back and forth and groaned and howled and wrung her head until the perspiration ran off the end of her nose. And she did all this without a perceptible change in her stony expression, while she rested her hands on the book before her, and sat on her feet.

It was wonderful. It showed us the terrible possibilities of the human voice.

On another evening we attended the prettiest of all Japanese entertainments, the annual Cherry Blossom Dance; a celebration carried on through the month of April in most of the larger cities. The spectacle begins at five in the afternoon and is repeated at intervals until late in the evening.

The short street leading to the Cherry Blossom theatre, as well as the theatre itself, outside and within, was a mass of gaudy illumination, done in as many shapes of lanterns as only the Japanese can contrive; but they do the trick so daintily that its extravagances of light and colour are passed by foreigners as "delightfully Japanese."

The affair is high class in every detail. In rikishas by the score, and in a continuous stream on foot, the well-dressed crowd arrived, checked its footwear at the door, and took its wraps in on its arm. The few barbarians shoe-shod like ourselves were furnished with the usual awkward slipovers.

"Let's check our shoes," suggested my nervous friend, "and go in in our stocking-feet. We're apt to skid in these baggy things." This sounded feasible enough—until I happened to think of something.

"How about holes in the hosiery?" I observed pointedly.

"H-m. I—I'm not dead sure," he ruminated. Neither was I. We donned the felt contrivances and shuffled along with the crowd.

From seats in the balcony—the select part of the house —we watched the slow, rhythmic movements of the thirty-two young women who carried through the exquisite scenes of the dance. Their kimonos, of the most gorgeous silks, varied in their colourings with each act to harmonize with the motive and the scenery. Down below us, a compact mass of Japanese squatting on the matted floor gazed in a dead silence.

The eight different settings of the wide, low stage were manipulated in full view of the audience, and with astonishing dexterity. There are no drop curtains, no stiff scenes to be lifted upward. Everything is of the usual Japanese daintiness.

With not a human being in sight, the scenery begins to change. Trees suddenly vanish off to the left, or off to the right; a mountain drops backward flat on the stage and is whisked away; other pieces fold upward out of sight, or sink straight down through the floor; filmy curtain effects dart about on invisible wires; but the weirdest thing of all is to see a curtain the full length of the stage suddenly collapse and go soooting down through a six-inch hole in the floor.

Sixteen other girls, brightly costumed, furnished the music. Japanese music, drawn from various odd-looking instruments, is simply a barbaric clanging and pounding, utterly devoid of musical values as we know them. Yet somehow this orchestra did not in the least mar the beauty of Kyoto's famous Cherry Blossom Dance.

Each young girl in it is an exquisite Japanese picture. The graceful motions of arms, head, and body are made in exact unison. There is no dancing as we know it—the dance is a constant posing, heightened in its effect by the pleasing manipulations of whatever the girls have in the right hand—a magnificent fan, perhaps, or a branch of cherry blossoms, or some other beautiful thing appropriate to the act being given.

For an hour one sits and looks off into a Japanese fairy-land. Compared to it, our most ambitious "folly" spectacles are strident, vulgar show pieces. Big, blatant, expensive. That's what we seem to like. Somebody remarked after the show, "What a hit this would make in America!" I doubt it. It is too fine. Fine's the word, taken literally.

* * *

How all this fineness, this daintiness, so in evidence everywhere among the people, ever came to a race like the Japanese is beyond the ability of any Occidental to comprehend. Lafcadio Hearn, having spent fourteen years in the country studying its people, says in his "Japan: An Attempt at Interpretation":

Long ago the best and dearest Japanese friend I ever had said to me, a little before his death: "When you find, in four or five years more, that you cannot understand the Japanese at all, then you will begin to know something about them." After having realized the truth of my friend's prediction—after having discovered that I cannot understand the Japanese at all—I feel better qualified to attempt this essay.

Japanese music, it seems to me, is more than an unchanged survival of Japan's barbaric days; it is a symbol of something unchanged in the nature of the Japanese themselves. It somehow fits the composite Japanese face. Listening to their music and looking into their faces, one can easily picture these people as of not many hundred years ago, when human life was at the mercy of

ferocious overlords, and cruelties too fearful to relate
were inflicted as common punishments.

Yet here are these signs of a delicate culture. Can it
be that the true Japanese character is no more than thus
exquisitely veneered?

* * *

The cleanly ways of the Japanese are proverbial. Most
of their personal habits we might regard as indicating an
instinctive cleanliness; others would be open to question.

The hobbling, crippling *geta* survives because the Japanese stick to the view, against all suggestions as to shoes,
that any footgear which touches the defilement of the
ground is not fit to tread upon the clean floors and mats
of interiors. *Getas* are slipped off or on at every entrance,
perhaps forty times a day, with an ease impossible in
case of shoes. The feet, too, must be kept up from the
ground; so they go jolting along on wooden blocks set
crosswise under the *getas*. These blocks on fair-weather
clogs may be only an inch high; in some styles they are
left off altogether. But a rainy-day pair lifts one at least
three inches off the ground. These have all the tricky
attributes of miniature stilts.

Few Japanese outside of rikisha men, labourers, and
farmers know the comfort of a yielding sole in contact
with the ground. Yet because of the *geta*, all floors in
Japanese interiors are clean and unworn. Their frail
matting, always looking fresh and new, would not last
through one rainy day under the treading of shoes.

The Japanese idea of personal cleanliness in travelling
seems to be to discard at once all refuse upon the floor of
the railway carriage or trolley car. And they are forever eating something—luncheon, confectionery, or fruit.

Many of them, especially women, deposit their *getas* on the floor and sit on their feet in the seats. Thus the floor takes the status of the street, and the seat becomes a Japanese interior.

This partly explains why every scrap of paper wrapping, lunch box, or fruit peeling goes straight to the floor. Refuse must not accumulate within the zone of cleanliness. The car attendant has to make half-hour sallies with shovel and broom to keep the place habitable. Fastidious Japanese men and women avoid contact with the seat by spreading down a cover of their own, but I have never seen one of them who did not throw refuse on the floor with the utmost unconcern. As a demonstration in cleanliness, it is rather puzzling to a foreigner.

In this Cherry Blossom time the Japanese were flocking to their temples. This led me to a mild pursuit of temples.

There is a striking similarity in the temple architecture of China and Japan. Low roofs turned up at the corners—said to be a survival from the days of the tent; massive, intricate adornments under the eaves, and all woodwork coloured very much alike in both countries; in both, too, a temple is a collection of buildings with ample space about them.

Here is the first marked difference: the Japanese do not surround their temples with forbidding walls. The temple areas are more in the nature of sequestered spots. If there are walls, they are apt to be rather inviting.

Japanese temples differ again from those of the Chinese in being better cared for, and more generally used. They seem, in contrast, like going concerns compared to relics. People are almost constantly before the shrines. They toss a few coppers into a grated and hoppered box as big as a coffin, murmur a few words to the gorgeous Buddha seated cross-legged in the huge bronze petals of a lotus blossom, and pass on to the next shrine.

Buddhist shrines in Japan, as well as in China, often held me fascinated by their astonishing likeness to shrines in the more ritualistic of our Christian churches. A central image, and often one on either side; garish trappings about; something to burn—joss sticks usually, sometimes little candles, or open oil receptacles with protruding wicks; objects to fumble in the hands while praying—instead of beads, two little blocks of wood, which the worshippers snap while praying before the images.

An impressive showing, this, of the essentially pagan origin of many symbols and forms used in certain Christian churches. The close resemblance does not flatter somebody's originality.

* * *

Off to Otsu, on Lake Biwa, for a boat ride on the lake, as well as to see the famous temples at Ishiyama.

The best that can truthfully be said for Lake Biwa is that it is a large body of water, surrounded by a very ordinary landscape. This was my first experience with a strictly Japanese lake boat. It was a close imitation of our little fresh-water steamers, except that it had no seats. Passengers left their *getas* at the head of the gang plank, and squatted on mats spread all over the decks. I sat on the rail. The rail had merit as a safety device, but as a seat for a two-hours' trip it impressed me with its narrowness.

The temples of Ishiyama, as beautiful as any in Kyoto, have the added picturesqueness of a location on a steep hillside. But their fame will last with me chiefly because of a large bevy of boarding-school young ladies who happened that day to be visiting the place.

Their prettiness lent enchantment to an already well-favoured scene. They were smilingly complaisant before the foreign man's camera, as if having their pictures taken were a mild sort of lark. After each taking, my un-Japanese bow and "Thank you!" always brought a return "Thank you!" and a chorus of merry laughter. Even the watchful dowager in charge now and then released a guarded smile.

I record this as a shining example of youthful Japanese spontaneity. Perhaps we "cannot understand the Japanese at all," yet here was a little play without words in terms of universal understanding.

The spontaneity of youth! Character stiffens with age into all sorts of conflicting shapes, but, thank Heaven, the lighter emotions of youth the world over bubble up out of the same delightful spring.

* * *

Nara, two hours south of Kyoto, was a seat of Japanese royalty before Kyoto's imperial days. I went there to spend a day or two in the quiet of the old place. I stayed nearly a week.

Nara's temple areas show the mellowness of age. Its oldest building has stood for twelve hundred years. In one of the temples is the largest bronze Buddha in Japan, exceeding in height by a few feet the famous Daibutsu at Kamakura. As unique as anything in Nara is the Avenue of Lanterns—three thousand ancient stone and bronze lanterns set up along a narrow way to the temples, accumulated there during centuries as family thank offerings to the gods. Musical priests, wearing a huge wastebasket effect down over their heads, gather coins from the devout.

Tame deer are all over the great park of Nara, and in the temple grounds. It is said that, many hundreds of years ago, one of the gods rode into Nara on the back of a deer; since then, deer have had the freedom of the town. Their familiarity when sniffing at one's pockets for food is amusing until the novelty wears off; then you wish they would search someone else.

And everywhere, cherry blossoms at their very best. One could dream away any number of spring days in old Nara.

A few miles out from Nara by train or trolley is Horyuji, the oldest temple in Japan. Only one building in the area dates back to the original founding of the temple, in A. D. 607, and that one has had its roof several times renewed. Yet the place is naturally a sort of Mecca for the Japanese. Pilgrims were there in crowds.

It was always a source of wonder to me that so many Japanese, in these months following a paralyzing disaster, could have the leisure and the money to be travelling about. Trains and interurban trolleys were so overloaded that they usually were running behind schedule.

Women were travelling in almost as great numbers as the men—which also seemed remarkable, considering their decidedly inferior status as human beings. Perhaps they go along to look after their lords.

In case of standing room only in the cars, the women stand. No man gives his seat, even to a woman with a baby on her back. If a woman wants a window open, she first asks the consent of the men near by, then opens it herself.

Never once in a public conveyance did I see the ordinary signs of comradeship between Japanese men and women. But clearly enough, the women do not expect it. They chatter among themselves; their men speak to them only when necessary.

Regretfully I left the picturesque Old Japan of Nara and Kyoto, to spend the last few days of these "wanderings" in the earthquake region, eastward a day's journey by the Tokyo express.

I allotted time to Tokyo with the mental reservation that, if it had nothing but its desolation to show me, Nikko the Beautiful would be waiting, only four hours back in the mountains. In less than two days I was in Nikko.

Why spend days looking at wreckage which has been so altered by fire and reconstruction that there is little of the earthquake's work to be seen? Tokyo and its environs were no more than half wrecked, but I had no desire to pick the other half out of the débris and try to make myself think that I was seeing Tokyo. And I do not care to end this tale of browsing around among peoples with details of an appalling disaster.

Square miles of new one-story frame structures, roofed mostly with galvanized iron, have replaced most of the destroyed Japanese parts of the city. Substantial brick buildings, along with a number of tall, steel-framed ones which escaped destruction in the westernized section of Tokyo, house modern business. Reconstruction was under way everywhere.

One curious effect of the earthquake was noticeable on

these high steel office buildings: the veneering walls of stone on the two or three lower stories were badly broken, while the upper several stories were comparatively free from damage. They explain this on the theory that the foundations, rigidly set into the earth, had to take up all of its shakings, while the upper stories had the shocks greatly softened by the elasticity of the building.

These structures are pointed to as the best of arguments in favour of floating foundations in regions subject to earthquakes—foundations which are an integral part of the building and do not go down to bedrock. An interesting idea, even to a layman.

Only one hotel of importance in Tokyo survived the earthquake—the Imperial. It is said that the Imperial Hotel was built with an eye to earthquakes. Judged by its multitude of flat arches and brick overhangings, inside and out, I would have said that it was built to fall down at the first shake; but present evidence is against me. It is the most amusing freak in the way of a modern building that I have ever seen. Some people go to Tokyo to look over the Imperial Hotel. Perhaps the earthquake passed it by in sheer astonishment.

Nikko gives one a fitting last impression of Japan. The most beautiful of all Japanese temples are there—more elaborate, more ornate than any others, glistening like new in their highly polished red lacquer. Avenues of the stately cryptomeria, a fir tree as majestic as any that grows; trees three hundred years old, immense straight trunks with shaggy tops, rising everywhere along the roadways and paths and in all the temple areas. Cherry blossoms in profusion, giving their evanescent touch of beauty to the grandeur of the old trees and still older temples. The glen pathways, deep in the silence of the great firs. The quiet of the temple areas, broken only by the clatter of *getas* on the feet of pilgrims coming to the shrines. Over all this, the fresh colourings of spring, full-blown in this last of April, vivifying the picture, and quickening the senses to an ecstatic appreciation of it.

Why should I say more about those three days in Nikko? A spot which yields a satisfying impression should not be rudely searched for details. I went from Nikko straight to the boat in Yokohama.

To the *Empress of Australia*, bound for Vancouver. She was tied up at the same pier at which she lay on September 1, 1923, when the hundreds of visitors wishing their friends aboard *"bon voyage"* were suddenly tossed into the air, and then into the sea, by the fearful upheavings of that pier. Curiously, its surface to-day is as wavy as a congealed ocean swell. Not even the section of it that dropped into the sea with its human freight has been raised.

I walked and rode by rikisha about Yokohama; a city obliterated, now mushroomed all over with shiny-topped wooden shacks. The foreign quarter on the bluff— hospitals, churches, great schools, and palatial homes— all down in a scattering of brick and stone, and not a mushroom about to indicate the beginnings of a come- back. The Japanese port may grow again, but the foreign quarter on the bluff—well, foreigners seem less complaisant about living over a fault in the earth's crust.

Fujiyama. For days it had hidden behind the clouds. Now, the ship's hawsers were being dropped from the pier and hauled aboard. Tugs, officiously puffing, waited to

push us about.   Slight tremors ran through the vessel;
our own engines were slowly turning.

I seemed to be leaving Japan without so much as a
glimpse of Japan's most imposing spectacle.   A clear day,
too, but where the mountain should have been was only
fog, impenetrable.

Not quite; as we squared off for the harbour's entrance
a dim, triangular outline showed through, and then the
heavenly curtain fell.   Fell part way, not to the tree line;
and the great white cone glistened in the sun—a seared,
cold, unearthly thing fixed high above the clouds.

I saw Fuji, not as a mountain attached to a familiar
world, but as a huge, mystic symbol invisibly hung over
a land which the West "cannot understand at all."

THE END